Your
Lab's
Life

Also Available

Your Golden Retriever's Life by Betsy Sikora Siino

VIRGINIA PARKER GUIDRY

Joanne Howl, D.V.M., Series Editor

Your
LAB'S
Life

Your Complete Guide to Raising
Your Pet from Puppy to Companion

 THREE RIVERS PRESS · NEW YORK

Published by Three Rivers Press, New York, New York.
Member of the Crown Publishing Group, a division of Random House, Inc.
www.randomhouse.com

Originally published by Prima Publishing, Roseville, California, in 2000.

DISCLAIMER: While the Publisher and the author have designed this book to provide up-to-date information in regard to the subject matter covered, readers should be aware that medical information is constantly evolving. The information presented herein is of a general nature and is not intended as a substitute for professional medical advice. Readers should consult with a qualified veterinarian for specific instructions on the treatment and care of their pet. The author and Prima Publishing shall have neither liability nor responsibility to any person or entity with respect to any loss, damage, or injury caused or alleged to be caused directly or indirectly by the information contained in this book.

YOUR PET'S LIFE is a registered trademark of Random House, Inc.
THREE RIVERS PRESS and the Tugboat design are registered trademarks of Random House, Inc.

Interior photos by Kent Lacin Media Services
Color insert photos copyright © Isabelle Français and Joan Balzarini
Chapter 6 illustrations by Pam Tanzey copyright © 2000 by Random House, Inc.
Dogs and their people: "Kylee" and Rafael Perez, "Jack" and Brenna Carr, Audrey Bowman of Central California Lab Rescue, and Jackie Gilson.

Printed in the United States of America

Library of Congress Cataloging-in-Publication Data
Guidry, Virginia Parker.
    Your lab's life : your complete guide to raising your pet from puppy to companion / Virginia Parker Guidry.
        Includes index.
        1. Labrador retriever.
SF429.L3 G85   2000
636.752'7—dc21   00-028561

ISBN 0-7615-2046-5

10 9 8 7 6 5 4

To Daniel,
the blond Lab–boy

Contents

Acknowledgments

While writing this book I've learned that without a doubt, Labrador Retriever enthusiasts are as fun, good-natured, and helpful as the breed. Thank you, Lab lovers! I couldn't have done it without you. Thanks to all members of the LabsR4U and Labrador-L electronic mailing lists who generously contributed opinions, ideas and stories, especially: Ellen Morris, Robin Briguglio, Dianne Mullikin, Karen Dowell, Laura Michaels, Steve Hamilton, Dranda Whaley, Dana Hines, Kirina Di Lynne Fann, Janet Sampson, Elizabeth Foti, Dayna Rousseau, Pat Chesley, Deirdre Hoedebecker, Delores Gleason, Leland Perry, Karla McCoy, Rosemary Dunn, Linda Power, Mary Lynn D'Aubin, and Peter Hines. Thank you Luanne Lindsey and the Labrador Retriever Club, Inc. A heartfelt appreciation to Dr. Autumn Davidson, and a round of applause to the Prima staff.

Introduction

Congratulations! You're about to embark (no pun intended) on a grand adventure. As a prospective or new Labrador Retriever owner, you've joined myriad others in choosing this breed as your dream dog. And with good reason. The Labrador *is* a dream dog: handsome, smart, talented, strong, active, and good-natured—really good-natured. This breed is what you might call a dog for all seasons. As a family pet, he plays nicely with children and will even share toys. As a friend, he sits quietly and listens. As a retriever, he dashes after game or waterfowl with the greatest of ease. As a showman, he prances proudly about the breed ring. As a working dog, he detects smuggled contraband with a sniff of the nose or assists the physically challenged. As a competitor, he excels and displays true sportsmanlike conduct.

That's why for six years in a row, the Labrador Retriever has been the most popular breed of dog registered in the United States by the American Kennel Club. It's as if everybody and their cousin—even the president of the United States, William Jefferson Clinton, who has a chocolate Lab, Buddy—have gone crazy over Labs.

A Look Back

The Labrador Retriever's popularity isn't new, though. The love affair with the Lab goes way back but not to Labrador, as the breed's name implies. Breed historians say that the Labrador Retriever's ancestors—called The St. John's dogs, St. John's Newfoundlands, or Lesser Newfoundlands—originated in Newfoundland. It's not clear how these dogs came to Newfoundland, but one theory is that they were brought by Portuguese sailors. These early dogs were blue-collar workers, earning their keep as fishermen's helpers, fetching ropes, hauling fishing nets, and retrieving the catch from the chilly waters of the North Atlantic. They were bred to be sturdy, versatile and good-natured, and had short, water-repellent coats, characteristics very similar to those of the modern Labrador Retriever.

By the early nineteenth century, ancestors of the breed had immigrated to England, perhaps aboard a fisherman's vessel. According to the American Kennel Club, early in the nineteenth century the second Earl of Malmesbury (1778–1841) saw one of the dogs in England and was quite taken with it. The smitten earl arranged to have more of these dogs imported, and from there interest in the breed grew. The earl's son, the third Earl of Malmesbury (1807–1889), imported and bred the dogs until his death.

Why dogs from Newfoundland are named Labrador Retrievers isn't known, but there are plenty of theories. Some breed historians speculate it's because of geographic confusion. *Labrador* can refer to the peninsula in northeastern North America that is surrounded by the Hudson Bay, the Atlantic Ocean, and the Gulf of St. Lawrence. Others say the name Labrador was an attempt to distinguish between early Newfoundland dog breeds. Whatever the reason, the name Labrador Retriever stuck.

Trade of the Newfoundland Labradors to England stopped in the early twentieth century when Newfoundland implemented a stiff dog tax and England set up strict quarantine laws, making it difficult and expensive for fanciers to acquire the dogs. So breed enthusiasts began working with what they had, crossing their dogs with other retrievers to develop the Labrador.

The result was the lovable Labrador of today. The Labrador was recognized as a separate breed by the Kennel Club (British) in 1903 and by the American Kennel Club in 1917. A dog named Brocklehirst Nell, a Scottish import, was the first Lab registered by the AKC; Boli of Blake was the first Lab to earn an American championship in 1933.

A Lab in Your Life

When the Earl of Malmesbury imported those first dogs from Newfoundland, he not only acquired working dogs but became dedicated to the breed and remained so throughout his life, passing that devotion to his son. This unique human-animal bond develops between caring owners and their dogs. The bond is not limited to dogs, but can be experienced with all companion species.

When you become a Lab owner, you'll have the opportunity to enjoy a special friendship with a dog who returns blessings to you a hundredfold. Although a Labrador can't speak, his actions will tell you he's a devoted companion. When you're feeling sick, a Lab will sit by your side. When you're lonely, a Lab will keep you company. If you're exuberant and happy, a Lab joins in the fun and knocks everything off the coffee table with one ecstatic swipe of his tail. If you've just quarreled with a loved one and feel bad about it, a Lab will nuzzle your hand and lick your face. If you're going to the beach or lake, a Lab will rejoice in a refreshing swim with you. If you're eating a sliced turkey and Swiss cheese sandwich, your Lab will beg to join you. (Labs *love* to eat, which is an ongoing threat to their waistline. More on that in chapter 3.)

The Labrador Retriever will share in all aspects of your life and, as many Lab owners say, could become the best friend you ever had.

> The Labrador Retriever will share in all aspects of your life and, as many Lab owners say, could become the best friend you ever had.

The Cost of Friendship

Along with the many benefits of Lab ownership comes a price. It's not entirely a price paid in dollars, although money is essential to care for your dog. It's a price paid with your life! Owning a Lab means you'll make some changes—adjustments, additions, and subtractions—to your lifestyle. And it means a continuing commitment to those changes and to your Lab.

What changes might you expect? Well, if you normally sleep until 11 A.M., your sleepy mornings are over. You must rise early to take Labbie for a walk and feed him breakfast. Periodic visits to the veterinarian and/or groomer are in order—you'll have to fit them into your work/school/family schedule. You'll also need to fit training classes into that schedule. In case of emergency, you'll have to drop everything and rush your Lab to the animal hospital. You can't take off on a Caribbean vacation without planning a kennel stay or booking dog-friendly accommodations. If you have small kids, you'll need to constantly—repeat, constantly—supervise dog-child interactions for the safety of both parties. Then of

Guardian Angels

Until seven years ago, Peter Hines was a cat lover, and only a cat lover. Hines was completely opposed to the idea of having a dog of any kind. "Then my daughter, as a surprise, brought home a black Lab puppy," says Hines. He wasn't thrilled—at all.

Then something happened. Over the next seven years, Hines found this Lab to be the most extraordinary friend he'd ever known: a beautiful, innocent, intelligent creature who only wanted to be his companion.

What happened? "Well, here's my theory," says Hines. "Forget any human interpretation of an angel. The Labrador is the embodiment of all the virtues we expect in what is considered an angel. They're faithful, devoted to your safety, constant companions, and ask nothing in return but love (and the willingness to clean up the yard after them), and treat every creature (dog or otherwise) with kindness.

"What other animal seeks out illicit drugs, finds lost people under avalanches and collapsed buildings, guides the blind through the city, and willingly risks his life to defend those to whom he is devoted? If there's such a thing as an angel on the face of this all too cruel world, it must be those gentle, intelligent friends we call Labrador Retrievers."

course there are the mundane (and sometimes smelly) tasks of kennel and yard cleanup, bed washing, and vacuuming daily to pick up shed hair and fleas.

Get the picture? Owning a Lab will have an impact on your life—at least it should. Are you prepared to accept the reality of having a Lab companion?

You might not have given dog ownership that much thought. That's common, and it's why so many companion animals are abandoned at shelters by their owners every year. People think owning a dog will be great. They see a cute pup, buy it, and take it home. After all, how much work can an adorable puppy be?

What frequently happens is puppy chews on Papa Bear's designer shoes, Mama Bear's expensive handbag, and Baby Bear's toys. Puppy poops on the floor, jumps up on guests, barks excessively, and begs at the dinner table. As puppy grows, he's no longer as cute. Vet care is expensive, and so is food to fill the growing pup's belly. The yard is no longer the child's domain but is taken over by puppy, who digs endlessly. The owners find all this unacceptable—although it's normal for pups who don't have the benefit of training by informed or experienced dog owners. "This isn't what we wanted. That dog has got to go!" is the cry, and off to the shelter goes puppy. The future is questionable. Puppy may get lucky and be adopted, or he may be euthanized.

Uncomfortable with this scenario? Unfortunately it's reality, a reality dedicated Lab enthusiasts, dog lovers, and shelter workers would like to see stopped. And it can stop if you think through the costs of owning a dog before acquiring one.

First, ask yourself why you want a dog. Is it an impulse decision because you saw a cute pup or an adult dog? (Not a good reason to get a dog.) Are you lonely and in need of a companion? Do you want a guard dog? What is your true motivation for owning a dog?

Why do you want a Lab? Do you cherish the breed? Did you see one you admired on TV or in a magazine ad? Why have you selected a Lab as your breed of choice?

What do you really know about the breed? Have you read books or magazine articles about Labs that sparked your interest? Have you talked with a Lab owner or breeder? Does what you think you know match true descriptions of the breed and is the Lab a breed with which you can live?

Can you afford a pet? Can you purchase supplies and food and pay for medical care?

Your careful consideration of these questions is essential before bringing home a Labrador Retriever. In fact, it's only fair. Why bring home a dog for which you're ill-prepared and don't plan to keep? Because that's what will happen if you don't plan ahead.

The Good Stuff

But if you're able to answer a heartfelt, I-really-mean-it-and-have-thought-about-it yes to the question, "Are you prepared to accept the reality of having a Lab companion?" then get ready for a wonderful experience—your grand adventure! The planning you put into preparing yourself, your family, and your home for a Labrador Retriever will be a labor of love.

I wrote this book to help you prepare for and enjoy your Labrador Retriever, whether you buy a ten-week-old pup from a breeder or adopt a three-year-old adult from a rescue organization. I'll show you who the Lab is, what it takes to be the best owner you can be, and the fun, joy, and other rewards awaiting you.

In chapter 1 we'll take an in-depth look at what makes a Lab a Lab, from the breed's personality, to how much exercise is best for your Lab, to where to acquire one. Getting your home ready for a puppy or dog is covered in chapter 2. The basics of good nutrition, or what to feed your Lab when, is discussed in chapter 3. Every Lab needs medical care, including routine exams and vaccinations, and chapters 4 and 5 provide general medical information and information on the Lab's unique health concerns. Basic training and lifetime schooling for Labs is covered in chapter 6 and grooming to keep your Lab looking her best in chapter 7. The many activities available for this energetic breed are detailed in chapter 8 along with a discussion on what to expect from family life with a new Lab member. Chapter 9 looks at what you can expect as your Lab ages and the difficult decision of euthanasia.

At the end of the book is a list of breed clubs, purebred registries, activity clubs, trainers, associations, and publications. These resources come from Lab enthusiasts who really want to help you enjoy, appreciate, and care for the breed.

So, You Want a Lab

In This Chapter

○ What Makes a Lab Special?
○ Keys to Your Lab's Happiness
○ In Search of the Perfect Lab

S o, you want a Labrador Retriever. Are you ready to learn all you can about the breed? Getting to know the Labrador Retriever is like taking a journey. First you've got some planning to do, then some packing and repacking, and you might change your plans, but eventually you'll take off for your destination. Let's start our journey into the world of the Labrador Retriever by taking a look at what makes a Labrador a Labrador. How is this breed distinct from other breeds?

What Makes a Lab Special?

Long ago, wolf ancestors to the domestic breeds of dogs we know today made contact with humans. No one knows exactly how these wolf-dogs became domesticated, but it's thought that our human ancestors saw potential in wolf-dogs and sought to capture and raise the young in captivity. From there the relationship between people and dogs began. In time, these wolf-dogs became domesticated, socialized, and bred for specific roles, including guarding, herding, hunting, and toting. This happened over thousands of years.

Eventually specific breeds developed. The Labrador Retriever emerged as an individual breed between the nineteenth and twentieth centuries. An individual breed is defined by what's called a breed standard, which specifies a breed's ideal physical characteristics, such as height, weight, body type, color, or coat.

> While a registration certificate identifies a dog and its progenitors as purebreds, it does not necessarily guarantee the health or quality of a dog.

The breed standard also spells out the breed's desired temperament and personality and lists faults. The breed standard assigned by a kennel or dog club may vary slightly from nation to nation and can change over time. The current American Kennel Club (AKC) official standard for the Labrador Retriever was approved in February 1994.

In a nutshell, the breed standard paints a picture of what the ideal Lab should look like, making it distinct from other breeds. Only those dogs that most closely meet the standard (nobody's perfect) receive championship status or are bred—at least that's how it's supposed to be.

The Breed Standard

General Appearance

The AKC breed standard describes the Labrador Retriever's general appearance as that of a strongly built, medium-size, short-coupled dog with a sound, athletic, well-balanced conformation that enables him to function as a retrieving gun dog. A Labrador Retriever should have the substance and soundness to hunt waterfowl or upland game for long hours under difficult conditions, the character and quality to win in the show ring, and the temperament to be a family companion.

The most distinguishing characteristics of the Labrador Retriever are a short, dense, weather-resistant coat; an "otter" tail; a clean-cut head with a broad back to the skull and a moderate stop; powerful jaws; and kind, friendly eyes, expressing character, intelligence, and good temperament.

Above all, a Labrador Retriever must be well balanced so that he can move in the show ring or work in the field with little effort. The typical Labrador possesses style and quality without over-refinement and substance without lumber or cloddiness. The Labrador is bred primarily as a working gun dog, and so his structure and soundness are very important.

Size

According to the AKC breed standard, the ideal size for a male Labrador Retriever is 22½ to 24½ inches at the wither, or point of the shoulder. Females are somewhat smaller, at 21½ to 23½ inches. Any variance greater than half an inch above or below these heights constitutes a disqualification in the show ring.

What's the American Kennel Club?

Founded in 1884, the American Kennel Club (AKC) is a non-profit organization dedicated to the protection and advancement of purebred dogs. Composed of over 500 dog clubs from across the nation, the AKC's objectives include maintaining a registry of purebred dogs, promoting responsible dog ownership, and sponsoring events, such as breed shows and field trials, that promote interest in and appreciation of the purebred dog.

To be eligible for AKC registration, a puppy must be the offspring of individually registered AKC parents, and the breeder must obtain the proper paperwork before the puppy's sale. Once registered, a dog is eligible to compete in AKC-sanctioned events and, if bred with another AKC registered dog, to have his/her offspring registered.

The AKC approves an official breed standard for each of the 147 breeds currently eligible for registration. The standard is written and maintained by each individual breed club. An attempt to describe the "perfect" dog of each breed, the breed standard is the model responsible breeders use in their efforts to produce better dogs. Judges of AKC-sponsored events and competitions use the breed standards as the basis of their evaluations.

Because of the AKC's emphasis on excellence and high standards, it is a common misconception that "AKC registered" or "AKC registrable" is synonymous with quality. However, while a registration certificate identifies a dog and its progenitors as purebreds, it does not necessarily guarantee the health or quality of a dog. Some breeders breed for show quality, but others breed for profit, with little concern for breed standards. Thus, a potential buyer should not view AKC registration as an indication of a dog's quality.

The ideal weights of male and female Labs in working condition are 65 to 80 pounds and 55 to 70 pounds, respectively. Labrador Retrievers should be shown in working condition: well muscled and without excess fat.

Head

The Lab's skull should be wide—well developed but not exaggerated. The skull and foreface should be on parallel planes and approximately equal in length. The dog's brow should be slightly pronounced so that the skull isn't absolutely in a straight line with the nose. The head should be clean-cut, without fleshy cheeks, and under the eyes the bony structure of the skull should be chiseled.

The ideal Lab's nose is wide, and the nostrils are well developed. The nose should be black on black or yellow dogs and brown on chocolates. Nose color fading to a lighter shade isn't a fault.

The teeth should be strong and regular, with a scissors bite—the lower teeth just behind but touching the inner side of the upper incisors. A level bite is acceptable but not desirable in the breed. Undershot, overshot, or misaligned teeth are serious faults.

The Lab's ears should hang moderately close to his head, set rather far back and somewhat low on the skull, slightly above eye level. His ears shouldn't be large and heavy but in proportion with the skull and should reach to the inside of the eye when pulled forward.

The Lab's kind, friendly eyes show good temperament, intelligence, and alertness. They should be of medium size, set well apart, and neither protruding nor deep set. Eye color should be brown in black and yellow Labradors and brown or hazel in chocolates.

Neck, Topline, and Chest

The Lab's neck should be of the proper length to allow the dog to retrieve game

Did You Know?

The wolf, from which dogs are descended, was the first animal to be domesticated.

easily. It should be muscular and free from throatiness. The neck should rise strongly from the shoulders with a moderate arch.

A Lab shouldn't be narrow chested, giving the appearance of hollowness between the front legs, or have a wide-spreading, bulldoglike front. Correct chest conformation will result in tapering between the front legs that allows unrestricted forelimb movement. Chest breadth that is either too wide or too narrow for efficient movement and stamina is incorrect. The underline is almost straight, with little or no tuckup in mature animals. The loins should be short, wide, and strong and extend to well-developed, powerful hindquarters. When viewed from the side, the Labrador Retriever shows a well-developed but not exaggerated forechest.

One of the breed's hallmarks is the tail. The tail should be very thick at the base, gradually tapering toward the tip, of medium length, and extending no longer than to the hock. The tail should be free from feathering and clothed thickly all around with the Labrador's short, dense coat, giving it the peculiar rounded appearance that's been described as the otter tail.

Forequarters and Hindquarters

The Lab's forequarters should be muscular, well coordinated, and balanced with the hindquarters. The Labrador's hindquarters are broad, muscular, and well developed from the hip to the hock, with well-turned stifles and strong, short hocks.

Coat

The Labrador Retriever's distinctive coat should be short, straight, and very dense. He should have a soft, weather-resistant undercoat that provides protection from water, cold, and all types of ground cover.

Color

The Labrador Retriever coat colors are black, yellow, and chocolate. A small white spot on the chest is permissible but not desirable. Blacks are all black; yellows may range in color from fox red to light cream, with variations in shading on the ears, back, and underparts of the dog. Chocolates can range in shade from light to dark chocolate.

Temperament

The Labrador Retriever's temperament is as much a hallmark of the breed as the otter tail. The ideal Lab has a kindly, outgoing, tractable nature and is eager to please and non-aggressive toward people or other animals. The Labrador's gentle ways, intelligence, and adaptability make it a wonderful people dog.

> The ideal Lab has a kindly, outgoing, tractable nature and is eager to please and non-aggressive toward people or other animals.

Mere Mortals

No Labrador is perfect, but what about Labradors who don't live up to the breed standard in every way? Such dogs aren't good show or breeding candidates but can still make fine companions. A pet Labrador is hardly a second-class citizen.

Just Your Type

You'll see that there are two distinct types of Labradors in the United States: the field Lab and the conformation Lab. The field Labrador is bred for his working ability and has a slim, light-framed

What Will It Be—
Puppy or Adult? Male or Female?

Do you want a puppy Lab or an adult Lab? Male or female? They're all so cute! But depending on your lifestyle, one might be a better choice than the other.

Let's face it. Pups are adorable, especially Lab pups. Have you ever seen such a face? But the flip side of the cuteness factor is puppies are a lot of work. It takes time to teach a puppy the ropes—house training, manners, socializing. If you're home a lot—maybe you work from a home office or you're a stay-at-home parent—a puppy could be a good bet. Of course, you've also got to be willing to put in time, and not just a few weeks. We're talking years. Labs remain puppyish until they're two and a half to three years old and require constant supervision and training to make it through childhood and adolescence. Are you prepared for that?

Why not consider adopting an older Lab? There are plenty available in shelters and rescue organizations. With an older, adult dog, you're past house training, crying, jumping (maybe), and chewing.

Don't rule out a puppy or an adult dog. Figure out which might best suit your lifestyle. Then decide.

When it comes to choosing a male or a female Lab, there are proponents of each sex. For the most part, male Labradors are larger and more powerfully built than females, with less delicate features. But male Labs aren't necessarily more aggressive or dominant, although they can be. Some people say females are somewhat easier to train than males and that males can be more willful than females. But either sex can be a wonderful companion.

physique. The conformation Labrador is bred with an emphasis on conformation and temperament, and tends to be larger and heavier than the field Lab. Fanciers of each type sometimes disagree, with field enthusiasts claiming that show Labs have lost retrieving and hunting abilities and conformation enthusiasts claiming that field dogs don't look like Labs anymore and lack a good disposition.

Some people say that field Labs are more active, with a lot of drive, and that conformation-type Labs tend to be more laid-back. Not everyone agrees, but it's safe to say that if you want to do field work with a Lab, you should buy your dog from a field line and vice versa. The breeder of each type of Lab breeds her dogs with particular strengths and purposes in mind and can share her wisdom and experience about a particular activity with you.

Getting to Know You— Personality and Temperament

The Lab's temperament, or his natural disposition, is a main attraction to the breed. A Lab is a dog who can be trusted in any situation. Consider Mimi, a black female Lab owned by Dianne Mullikin of Rycroft Labradors. "I love to take her out in public with me because she brings a lot of joy to everyone she meets," says Mullikin. "At one particular meeting, I was having lunch at an outdoor café, and a group of children came over to see her. One boy, a 10-year-old with autism, fell in love with Mimi's thick, black otter tail. He held her tail and gently caressed it. I continued with my lunch while the children petted Mimi. Then I glanced down at Mimi, who was sitting next to me with a strange look on her face. I looked back at the boy, who was now standing on her tail. Mimi is such an accepting dog, and she was giving me this look like, 'Mom, can you please get him off my tail?' I don't know too many dogs who would have put up with that."

Robin Briguglio, a longtime Lab enthusiast, exhibitor, and breeder, says Labs' outgoing, sunny personality makes them good candidates for public relations work. "They are the perfect meeter and greeter of the home, as they have strong tendencies toward public relations work." Additionally, says Briguglio, most every Labrador is safe with children and "user friendly" by all people. In fact, says Briguglio, "They are safe at birthday parties and are quite willing to wear party hats, and carefully lick the hands and faces of small children."

As such good-natured party lovers, Labs aren't known as good guard dogs. They'll bark if something out of the ordinary goes on at home, but don't expect a full-scale attack. The Lab's easy going nature is fairly consistent throughout the breed though there are dogs that are less good natured due to poor breeding, abuse or neglect.

The individual Lab's personality varies. One Lab may be active; another, a couch potato. Some Labs like pizza; others prefer garbage. Some Labs like to dig up flowers; others like to bark. But regardless of her individual preferences, a Lab is always delighted to see you.

Life Expectancy

Labrador Retrievers are fairly healthy dogs, so expect your dog to live on average 10 to 14 years. The length of a Lab's lifetime may vary, depending on her genetic makeup, the health care and nutrition she gets, and whether she maintains the proper weight.

Keys to Your Lab's Happiness

Do you wonder what a Labrador Retriever really needs to be happy? No, it's not a new Mercedes or Rolex watch. It's something so simple, you can probably guess what it is.

"It's the Family, Silly"

To be happy, a Lab needs to be a member of your family. Labrador Retrievers are extremely people oriented. It's why they're such excellent companions and working dogs. They love to please and need to feel they're part of the action. Labs want to be included in family life: sleeping in the kitchen, going to baseball practice with Mom and the kids, answering the door, playing with the kids, visiting Grandma, taking out the trash. (Don't you wish! More likely, getting into the trash.) A Lab who isn't included in family life—left in the backyard to live in a doghouse with an occasion pat—is miserable. Labs can't stand being ignored and will do whatever it takes to get attention.

Lab enthusiast Mullikin used to volunteer for a Lab rescue organization. She tells the story of a Lab rescued from a family who left the dog chained in the backyard for her entire life. "The family would feed her by standing just out of reach of the dog and sliding her food and water dishes to her. All she could do was jump up and down, up and down. The owners thought it was funny. When the dog was let off the chain, it would jump up and down and then try to bite at your face. Eventually she was placed with a professional trainer and rehabilitated, but without the training she had no future."

Action, Please!

The Labrador Retriever is a happy, boisterous breed that needs action. Of course, some individual Labs are more active than others. But for the most part, forget planning a sedentary lifestyle with your Lab. If that natural desire for activity isn't

Did You Know?

The word for "dog" in the Australian aboriginal language Mbabaran happens to be "dog."

satisfied, a Lab will think of ways to keep herself busy—not all of them good. A bored, antsy Lab may chew, dig, or bark. The dog doesn't mean to be naughty; she just needs something to do. Plenty of daily play and exercise is mandatory. Many enthusiasts recommend several 30-minute sessions a day (see chapter 8 for activities Labs love).

In fact, Mullikin believes that all Labs should have some type of job; it gives the dog something to do, something to work at. Says Mullikin, "Even if it is as simple as bringing in the newspaper, believe me, they'll learn to anticipate just when the carrier will be there and look forward to bringing in the paper. Labs have a real willingness to please. That's what makes them a great retriever. Everything they do is to please you."

> Labs have a real willingness to please. That's what makes them a great retriever. Everything they do is to please you.

Labs are bred to be water dogs, and most adore water sports. If you live by the ocean, a lake, or a pond, your Lab will be in heaven. Karen Dowell, author of the award-winning book *Cooking with Dogs* and the owner of two Labs, Mac and Maynard, says, "We currently live in what has to be one of the most ideal settings for a Lab: on eight acres far from the main road and right on the water. So our boys can burn off energy by swimming, running, and exploring."

School's In

What better way to curb an active Lab's energy and teach her a few manners than obedience training? All civilized Labs should know the five basic obedience commands: heel, sit, down, stay, and come. A Lab that obeys these commands is a trustworthy, livable companion. Labs grow into large, powerful dogs, so you have to make sure you can control yours. Advanced and ongoing training is a good idea, too, because it gives the Lab an activity to let off steam and challenges her mentally (see chapter 6, "Basic Training for Labradors"). "We took Mac, our yellow Lab, to puppy kindergarten and then supplemented that training with what we learned from books," says Dowell. "Maynard, our black, was home schooled. They're not von Trapp dogs—they don't run downstairs at the sound of a whistle and line up by the door—but they have good manners and rarely get into trouble. They know right from wrong."

Training should begin when a Lab is very young because they can be mischievous if they aren't taught the ropes from an early age. "I recommend puppy kindergarten at 12 to 16 weeks and regular training sessions until at least age two," says Laura Michaels, a longtime Lab enthusiast, breeder, exhibitor, and owner of Woodhaven Labs kennel. "After that, the dog usually will settle in and might just need a refresher course every once in a while."

The Lab's keen wit makes training fairly simple. "They are very intelligent," says Briguglio, "and if that gift is not equated with an outlet for it, they can easily become bored and unhappy with life. Which can lead to destruction. Training is wonderful for them. They have a natural desire to learn and usually train quite quickly. They are easy to housebreak especially if crate training is used. But working together with your Labrador in obedience classes or one-on-one is a fulfilling experience for both owner and dog. The more involved they are with their owners, the better dog you will have. They are the gift that keeps on giving. The more time you give them in training and play, the better adjusted and happier your environment will be."

Don't Forget TLC

Of course, a Labrador needs your tender, loving care. That includes routine vet visits (even if the clinic does smell a little funny and the floors are slippery); good food, but not too much; fresh water; grooming; a comfy bed for naps and nighttime; something, anything, to hold in his mouth and retrieve; and last but not least, your heartfelt devotion.

Surefire Ways to Make Your Lab Miserable

Everybody has those "buttons." You know, the ones that get pushed and make you irritable, unhappy, or miserable. Well, Labs have buttons, too. And if you're going to properly care for your Lab, you've got to know what they are.

Keep to Yourself—Not!

The bottom line on Labs is they're people-oriented dogs. They need people, and they live to please. Even if their people aren't necessarily worthy of this devotion, the desire to please is inherent in the Lab's nature. Being part of a family is enough to make the Lab's cup runneth over.

A Lab who is expected to keep to himself is one unhappy camper. "Labradors aren't happy if they're left home alone because they're such people- and family-oriented dogs," says Briguglio. "They get lonely when they're separated from their people. This is the surest way to make their life unpleasant and consequently your own. Leaving a Lab alone, leaving it tied outdoors away from the activity of the family, will make her lonely and get her into trouble."

Labs can be trusted alone for short periods, which is a necessity for most dog owners, who must work, run errands, visit the dentist, or stop at the Dairy Queen. But for those who work extremely long hours and are rarely home, the Lab (or any dog, for that matter) isn't a good idea. "Labs can be left alone for a good part of the day," says Mullikin, "but if they become bored you can come home to a very messy house. That is where crate training comes in handy. I do not like to leave a dog in a crate for more than six hours at a time, so if possible, coming home for lunch is a good idea."

Although Labs can tolerate being home alone all day, they're not really happy about it. Most of the problems you hear about from owners occur when Labs are left home alone for extended periods. "This is when bored Labs chew, knock over garbage cans, learn how to break into cabinets to get food, and destroy large pieces of furniture," says Dowell. "Boredom can lead to recreational barking, which may not go over well with the neighbors. Some Labs develop separation anxiety that causes them to lick or chew their paws or tail."

Dowell and her husband both work at their home in Maine, which means they spend plenty of time with their dogs. When they both worked in a traditional office environment away from home, they took turns going home for lunch and walking the dogs. "If we had to work late, we'd go pick up the dog and bring him into the office after hours," says Dowell. "We really don't think it's

Did You Know?

The United States and France have the highest rates of dog ownership in the world (for countries in which such statistics are available), with almost one dog for every three families. Germany and Switzerland have the lowest rates, with just one dog for every ten families.

fair to leave a Lab alone for more than a few hours at a time, except on rare occasions."

Don't ask a Lab to keep to himself. It's mean if you do.

School's Out?

You've just read about the benefits of training your Lab. But do you realize how miserable a Lab is if you don't train her? If a Lab isn't pleasingly civilized with people of all ages, she's destined to be locked away behind closed doors or tied out in the backyard away from the family fun. The result? A miserable dog who's being deprived of what she really wants: to be part of the family. But she can't be since the family can't tolerate her behavior. It's a vicious circle.

Prevent misery. Train your Lab.

Sit Still!

Just as satisfying the Lab's propensity to be active makes for a happy Labbie, denying this breed the activity it craves is practically criminal. And if you do neglect to keep a Lab busy, you may think you have a criminal on your hands. The Lab thrives on mental and physical activity. If you can't provide the space, exercise, and attention a Lab needs, he'll turn toward whatever activity he can—usually a destructive one from the owner's viewpoint—to keep himself occupied. A Lab doesn't want to make you mad by decorating the kitchen and laundry room with garbage, but he does need something to do.

A Lab is probably best suited to a home with a yard in which he can romp, supervised (unsupervised isn't recommended unless you'd like your yard relandscaped!). "It would be great if every Lab owner had 50 fenced-in acres," says Lab enthusiast

Steve Hamilton, "and the dogs could go for wild runs every day. I think every Lab would love that, but that's not realistic for most people."

Apartment or condo life can work for a Lab, but only if an owner is dedicated and can take the dog out every day for fun and exercise. "When we lived in the Bay Area," says Dowell, "in a small, rental house with a small, unfenced yard, it was hard to find a place for Mac to run off leash, and I never did feel he was getting enough exercise. He spent most of his day sleeping be-

> **D**enying this breed the activity it craves is practically criminal.

tween the couch and the coffee table until we got home. We also had a large Lab in a relatively small San Francisco apartment. As long as you can walk the dog regularly and convince him not to bark at every honking car, it's not a bad life for a Lab."

Don't expect a Lab to sit still and do nothing. It's not going to happen.

Go Ahead, Eat All You Want

It's been said that the Labrador who doesn't eat is a sick dog. Labs are very good eaters. In fact, they've earned a reputation as easy keepers, which means that if Labs are left at the dinner table, they'll eat themselves off the scale. Some experts say that in addition to a hearty appetite, the breed may have a genetic tendency toward putting on weight. A Lab can become obese if owners aren't careful. Overweight Labs are miserable. They don't feel well, and they aren't as healthy as they should be.

Whatever you do, don't overfeed a Lab. He'll eat and eat and eat and doesn't know when to say no. As his owner, you must just say no for him.

In Search of the Perfect Lab

So, you're sure you want a Lab and are prepared to count the costs of dog ownership. How do you find one that's a good fit for you and your family?

It's not that difficult if you have the right information You'll find that below: sources for Labs, along with thoughts on each source.

What's the bottom line on finding the Lab of your dreams? It's like buying anything else. Do your homework. Shop around. Ask questions. Simply, be an informed buyer.

Reputable Breeder

The Lab lover's number-one source for locating the pup of his or her dreams should be a reputable breeder. A reputable breeder is someone who knows, understands, and loves the breed. This person breeds with a specific purpose and plan—to improve the line, eliminate faults, create champions—not just to produce more pups.

Anyone can say he or she is a reputable breeder, but actions are proof-positive. For example, reputable breeders are very particular about to whom they sell pups. If you're dealing with a reputable breeder, chances are you'll have to pass her inspection before you take a pup home. Expect to be grilled!

You can also tell a breeder is someone with integrity if she requires that pet-quality animals (dogs that don't meet show standards but are perfectly wonderful as pets) be spayed or neutered and requires a contract. Contracts vary from breeder to breeder but usually spell out the rights of seller and buyer, health information, and altering and buy-back/return policy. Another sign of a reputable breeder is that she shows a genuine love of and

What to Ask a Breeder

○ What are common health problems found in Labs?

○ Are your dogs routinely screened for heritable diseases?

○ What health certifications can you show me for parents and grand-parents?

○ What are the most positive and negative characteristic of the breed?

○ What kind of temperament should I expect from a Lab?

○ How long have you been breeding dogs?

○ Can you name five other Lab breeders you'd recommend?

○ What do you expect of potential puppy owners?

○ What type of guarantee do you provide?

○ Will you take back this puppy at any age, for any reason?

○ Do you require limited registration and/or spay/neuter contracts on pet-quality puppies?

knowledge about the breed and is actively involved in the breed fancy. You should also find the kennel or home environment sparkling clean and well maintained.

A reputable breeder is willing to answer questions, even about genetic faults affecting the Lab. She's willing to provide the names of other people who have purchased pups from her and will allow you to meet the puppy's parents if they're on the premises. If they're not, she should show you pictures.

Labrador Rescue Groups

Labrador rescue groups are another great way to find a Lab. There are many throughout the United States. Like animal shelters and humane societies, Lab rescue groups are nonprofit agencies, dependent

To the Rescue!

"I just found a Lab wandering along the street. He looks kind of sick and hungry. Can you take him?" Right now, somewhere in the United States and beyond, there's an individual who just received a phone call with this request. Specific circumstances vary, but the bottom line is the same: A Lab needs help and a home.

Who's answering these calls and lending a hand? Labrador Retriever rescue volunteers, that's who. Across the country, there's a dedicated network of Lab enthusiasts—individuals and nonprofit organizations—who are putting their love for the breed into action. They are literally rescuing Labs from a variety of sad situations, taking them in and finding good homes.

Why is it necessary to rescue Labs? Unfortunately, Labs are routinely relinquished to shelters, dropped on street corners, left at vet clinics, abused, neglected, and mistreated. They need rescuing. And those who love the breed are determined to save as many as they can.

What's the profile of the average Lab who finds itself in foster care? According to Luanne Lindsey, national coordinator for the Labrador Retriever Club, Inc., rescue program, it's a dream puppy who grows up a little and does what a pup does naturally: chews, barks, and digs. The family who acquired the Lab isn't prepared for the reality of dog ownership or the reality of a barking-chewing-digging bundle of energy. The Lab is a breed that demands time, energy, training, and plenty of room to move. Owners are unable or unwilling to meet those demands, so the once adorable Lab pup is now relegated to the backyard—where isolation and continued lack of training and socialization wreak havoc. "Then they really get to be monsters," says Lindsey.

Owners see getting rid of the now one-and-a-half- to two-and-a-half-year-old Lab as the only solution to the nightmare. "People turn them in to the pound because they don't want to fool with them anymore. It's nearly all

on donations to care for animals. Most don't have funds to operate a shelter and rely on foster-care volunteers to house and care for puppies and dogs until they're matched with a good home.

behavior related," says Lindsey. "People are too busy. They get the dogs for the kids, and kids don't raise dogs. Parents do."

Besides behavior problems, which are usually completely correctable with a little training, owners give up Labs when they move, get divorced, or the dog has medical problems they don't have the funds or interest to treat.

The sad fact is, the number of Labs that end up in rescue is enormous. Exact numbers aren't available, but according to Lindsey, the LRC rescue program keeps a referral list of approximately 90 U.S. Lab rescue organizations and individuals. Most rescue anywhere from 100 to 400 Labs a year.

"We're putting too many human qualities on Labs," says Lindsey. "We have to remember they're still dogs." What people don't realize is what Labs are really like as pups. "As puppies, they aren't couch potatoes. They can eat your cable TV, take out the siding on your house, and do all kinds of things."

Lindsey and dedicated volunteers keep working to help homeless Labs and educate the public—because many sad beginnings have very happy endings. Consider Buddy, a Lab owned by Dranda Whaley. When this poor fellow was found lying in a field, he had a shattered front leg and had been peppered with buckshot. The rescue workers didn't have the funds to pay for his care, but thanks to a group of dedicated on-line enthusiasts, money was raised to get Buddy on the road to recovery. Dranda later adopted him—and his plight inspired the startup of LabMed, a nonprofit, web-based organization dedicated to funding medical care for rescue Labs.

Rescue work is difficult at times, and many rescue workers suffer burnout. But it's equally rewarding to help the breed and work alongside others who love the breed. Says Lindsey, "They're doing it because they want to help the breed, and to me, they're the saviors of the breed."

If you'd like to adopt a rescue Lab, see the Resources section at the end of the book for names and numbers.

Lab rescue volunteers are an extremely devoted bunch—they often pay for the dogs out of their own pocket—and they know a lot about the individuals pups and dogs they foster.

The people-oriented personality of the Labrador makes it a good candidate for adoption, whether he's a pup or an adult. Rescue Labs adjust very well to new homes and bond quickly with loving families. If you have children, be sure to let the adoption counselor know so you can adopt a Lab who's kid friendly. Although most Labs love children, an abused one may not.

Animal Shelters

Humane societies are a good place to find pups and dogs, but sometimes it can be difficult to find a Lab. Breed rescue organizations frequently monitor incoming dogs at shelters and pick up purebreds for placement through individual breed rescues. But at times shelters do have purebreds available for adoption, with all types of backgrounds and temperaments.

The great part about adopting a Lab from a shelter is you'll be giving the dog a chance at life. But keep in mind that you might not know as much about a shelter Lab as you would a rescue Lab. This is because breed rescue dogs live with families in a home environment. Volunteers are able to observe the dog very closely—how it interacts with kids, cats, and other dogs. Dogs in animal shelters live in kennels and aren't observed as closely. They can't be, with the number of incoming and outgoing animals.

> The great part about adopting a Lab from a shelter is you'll be giving the dog a chance at life.

Most shelters are extremely careful to adopt only healthy animals, but be aware that there's a chance you'll take home a sick dog. Take your shelter-adopted Lab to the vet for a checkup as soon as possible.

Newspaper Ads

No matter what the town, no matter what the newspaper, you'll always find a classified ad reading, "Labs. AKC registered. $400." Or something very similar. But are newspaper ads a good source for finding the Lab of your dreams?

According to most Lab enthusiasts and reputable breeders, no. In most cases, these ads are advertisements from "backyard breeders." There are reputable breeders who do advertise in this manner, but it's not common. What's a backyard breeder, and why should you avoid one? A backyard breeder is basically a person who owns a Lab and decides it would be a great idea to breed his dog to the neighbor's Lab. The result will be a fabulous litter of pups, and they'll both make money! These Labs could be registered, but that doesn't really mean anything. Any dog can be registered by a breed registry, but it doesn't mean the dog is of sound mind and temperament. The problem with backyard breeding is there's little consideration for conformation, health, or temperament.

Reputable breeders don't advertise in local newspapers—they don't have to. They usually sell pups by word of mouth, and pups are often requested well before they're born.

The best advice about buying a Lab through newspaper ads is, "Let the buyer beware." If you're set on buying a newspaper-ad Lab, be prepared to ask a lot of questions. Investigate the background of the advertiser and ask questions about the pup's medical history. Ask if the

Did You Know?

The Labrador Retriever has been the top dog registered with the American Kennel Club every year since 1991.

parents have health clearances for the hereditary diseases Labs are prone to (see chapter 5, Common Health Concerns).

What about ads for Labs in Lab or all-breed publications? Serious, reputable breeders are more likely to advertise pups in well-respected magazines, but there's no guarantee. In fact, many magazines have disclaimers, advising potential buyers to investigate puppy advertisers. Approach sellers in magazines the same way you approach newspaper advertisers—skeptically—and be sure to investigate the source.

Pet Stores

There's never a shortage of puppies at pet stores. But are pet stores a good place to acquire a Lab? No, say most reputable breeders, rescue volunteers, and humane society workers. In fact, the American Humane Society is absolutely opposed to anyone purchasing pups at pet stores.

Why? Because reputable breeders don't sell wholesale pups to pet stores, but puppy mills do. Puppy mills are large breeding operations that breed many kinds of dogs in volume with little regard for their health, temperament, or conformation. Although puppy mills aren't illegal, many dog lovers consider them immoral. Puppy mill pups are frequently ill, unsocialized, and poor examples of a breed.

Another problem with pet stores is that buyers often purchase on impulse. They walk into a pet store, see an adorable puppy, and buy it with little thought. Impulse buying and pups aren't a good combination. Too often, the owner regrets the purchase later and ends up dumping the dog at the shelter.

If you absolutely must buy from a pet store, there are laws to protect you from the nearly in-

What If?

It can and does happen. You've acquired a Lab, maybe even done a tad of research about the breed beforehand, but after living with the dog for a month or two, you realize maybe it's not the dog you thought you wanted.

Don't panic. And don't immediately see getting rid of the Lab as a solution to the problem.

"If a person acquires a dog and realizes he's not the dog they wanted, they should at least try to exhaust all options to keep the dog, whether it's training or neutering. Try to work out the problem," suggests Dianne Mullikin of Rycroft Labradors.

Know that this can happen no matter what breed you bring home. It's rare for anyone to initially have the "perfect" canine companion. Rather, good companions are partly created, which means they're the result of your efforts. If you put some time, energy, and effort into a puppy or dog, chances are you'll have a suitable companion.

It's true you might not have exactly what you wanted. But who has everything they want, all the time? For example, maybe you've found the Lab's boisterous antics, like jumping up to greet you, annoying. Labs are just that way. You won't change who the dog is. You just need to teach your Lab how to control her exuberance. Seek guidance from a professional trainer. Make a list of unwanted behaviors or dislikes about the dog and take the list to someone who can help you work through them.

The answer for solving the problem is your willingness to work on it, not getting rid of the Lab.

evitable. Called puppy lemon laws, modeled after lemon laws that were enacted to give car buyers a way to get a refund, these laws give owners recourse if a pet store animal proves to be ill or unsound (which is often the case). These laws vary from state to state but usually cover illness or disease that exists at or before the time of sale. Buyers have a limited time to have the animal checked by a veterinarian, usually seven to 15 days after sale.

State warranties for congenital or hereditary conditions vary from 10 days to one year. State statutes also require sellers to disclose to buyers the history of the animal, including its medical history, who its parents were, and where the animal was bred.

On a positive and progressive note—and perhaps to get away from a well-earned negative image in the industry—several U.S. pet superstores, such as PetSmart and Petco, have teamed up with local shelters to offer pets for adoption. Instead of selling puppy mill pups, these stores offer healthy dogs and cats, puppies and kittens, for adoption.

Giveaways

What if your coworker tells you he has a puppy—and it's a Lab!— he wants to give away? Should you immediately say, "I'll take it"?

The American Humane Association recommends potential owners be very wary of "hand-me-down" pets. There's usually a reason someone wants to rid themselves of a dog, and it's usually not a good reason. The dog may be sick, ill-tempered, or chew incessantly. Be careful not to have someone else's problem pawned off on you.

Of course, there's a chance, however slight, that this dog might be a good companion who's had a loving home, training, and vet care. In situations like this, proceed with extreme caution. It's risky, but some people are lucky gamblers.

Internet

Countless animal-related organizations, agencies, breeders, individuals, and shelters have made the leap into selling puppies and dogs through cyberspace. If you shop the Internet for Labs, use the same caution you would with newspaper advertisers. Check references, ask questions, and stick with well-known Lab clubs.

Pick of the Litter

"There he is! That's him. I just know it—I feel it!" you exclaim on viewing the breeder's litter of eight-week-old Labrador puppies. "That's the one I want." So you take your Lab puppy home, it grows up to be the greatest dog of all time, and you live happily ever after.

Ha! If you think it'll be that easy to choose the right pup for you from a litter, think again. It's often a difficult decision, there are no hard-and-fast rules, and you don't have a crystal ball (wouldn't that be nice?). Every Lab puppy is different, and there isn't one perfect pup in each litter. They all have potential; they just need the right owners to bring out the best in them. Besides, every breeder, behaviorist, veterinarian, or Lab lover will tell you something different about how to choose a pup. In many cases, breeders don't even allow you to choose your own puppy. They make the choice for you, based on what they know about their pups and what they learn about you.

But if you ask yourself the following questions, you can learn enough about what you want in a Lab to share it with a knowledgeable breeder or adoption counselor, who can help you pick.

○ What do you want to do with your Lab? Do you primarily want a companion, or are you planning to compete in field trials or conformation shows? Do you want to try obedience or agility?

❍ What type of lifestyle do you have? Are you home a lot, or do you travel frequently? Are you active, or do you enjoy sipping tea in the shade? How and where does a Lab fit in your life?

❍ What is your temperament? Are you strong willed or laid-back?

Armed with the answers to these questions, visit several Lab breeders or adoption counselors. Share the information with the breeder, and ask for her help in choosing an appropriate pup. After all, the breeder knows best when it comes to her pups. If you're fairly laid-back, for example, and wish only for a companion, a sharp breeder will know if she has an equally laid-back dog to match your needs. No sense in selling you a fireball with competitive aspirations. You'll be frustrated with a dog who won't sit still, and the dog will be frustrated with an owner who doesn't offer enough challenges.

Testing, Testing

Dog breeders and behaviorists may use what are called puppy or temperament tests to predict what a puppy will act like when it grows up. Technically, temperament testing assesses puppies for motor ability, sensory and emotional states, sociability, problem-solving ability, how they interact with other dogs, and how they interact with people. Puppies are tested at specific ages for their responses to stimuli or situations; they're then assessed as having temperaments such as outgoing, aggressive, passive or timid, dominant or dependent.

Unfortunately, there is no consensus among dog breeders, trainers, behaviorists, or veterinarians on what temperament testing is or should be, whether or not it's accurate and useful, or who should test the pups, breeders or prospective buyers. There's no standard test, and there isn't even a standard name. Besides puppy or temperament testing, these tests are also called puppy evaluation testing or puppy aptitude testing. These confusing terms—used by breeders and other canine professionals—can be difficult for prospective puppy buyers to decipher.

Generally, puppy tests try to determine:

❍ Levels of dominance;

❍ How accepting of training the pup is;

❍ If the pup will retrieve;

❍ Whether the pup is outgoing or introverted; and

❍ Whether the pup is people oriented or unsociable.

To Your Health!

Fortunately, determining if a Lab puppy is healthy is much easier than trying to predict his temperament and personality. When you visit a breeder, look for these signs of good health in a puppy:

❍ Proper weight, not too chubby or thin

❍ Clean, odor-free, and kept in clean surroundings

❍ Clear eyes and nose

❍ Clean, odor-free ears

❍ Full hair coat, with no balding patches

❍ Friendly, happy, playful

Not all medical conditions can be spotted with a visual exam. Be aware that

Did You Know?

The Saluki, a hunting dog raised by ancient Egyptians, is the oldest known breed.

heritable diseases such as hip dysplasia, elbow dysplasia, eye problems, epilepsy, or heart disorders can affect the breed (see chapter 5, "Common Health Concerns"). Routine screening for these conditions is the best assurance (there are no guarantees) of acquiring a completely healthy Lab pup.

Welcome Home!

In This Chapter

○ Pre-Lab Decisions
○ Batten Down the Hatches!
○ Make Yourself at Home!

If you're a parent or know people who are parents, you've experienced the intense planning and preparation needed for the new bundle of baby. There's baby furniture to buy—a crib, dresser, cutesy nightlight, rocking chair—and don't forget the changing table and diaper pail. Baby's room must be decorated with teddy bear curtains and comforter; adorable clothing, bottles, and baby-friendly toys must be purchased; diapers and wipes stockpiled; and so on. Then there's the labor and delivery classes (men just love those), infant care classes, baby book purchases, baby announcements, and a baby shower complete with the game of guessing the pregnant Mom's waist measurement.

The idea behind the planning and preparation for the upcoming bundle of joy/work is to make life easier for all involved: mom, dad, and baby. It's a difficult transition from no baby to baby, but it can be less stressful if you're prepared.

Not surprisingly, the same is true for your new Labrador Retriever. The more prepared you are before you bring Labbie home, the happier you all will be. You need to decide where puppy or dog will eat, sleep, and play. You need a veterinarian, and you must prepare your home and yard for a mischievous newcomer. So, here's how to do just that.

Pre-Lab Decisions

If you put together a checklist of all the decisions a family must make before bringing home a Lab, what would it include? Have you given it any thought? If not, you should. Because it's the best way to begin planning and preparing for the big day, the day you bring home your new Lab friend.

Decision No. 1
Can you afford a dog?

Let's face it. It takes money to own and care for a pet. And the purchase or adoption price of a Lab puppy or adult is a drop in the bucket compared to the ongoing costs of owning a pet. You must also consider veterinary fees, equipment and supplies, training costs, food, grooming, and boarding. If you don't have enough money in your budget for all of these necessities, you won't be able to care properly for your Lab.

Before you even think about bringing home a Lab, review your household budget. Be honest with yourself. Do you have a good handle on how much you make and spend? Do you pay bills on time and put a little away each month for emergencies? Or are you barely able to pay the minimum payments on your high-balance credit cards? If you're struggling to keep your head above financial water, then it's best to delay acquiring a Lab until you're on stable ground. Although you may really want a Lab, pet care isn't cheap. It's unfair to the dog if you don't have enough funds to provide proper care. For example, feeding a dog can cost $115 to $400 a year, according to the Humane Society of the United States, and training classes can cost $50 to $120 for eight sessions.

Take a good look at your budget. Then make a realistic evaluation of whether or not you can afford a dog. If you find you really don't have the funds right now, don't despair. Work toward lowering your debt and create a Lab savings fund. Perhaps you can bring home that Lab in six months or a year, which really isn't that long to wait for a dream come true!

Decision No. 2
Do you have time to spend with your Lab?

Experienced Lab owners can attest: Labs are extremely social creatures and require a lot of time and attention, especially pups. Do you have time in your life to give to your new puppy or dog? If you're a workaholic who's rarely home, give up the idea of getting a Lab. Consider a few goldfish. A Lab needs your constant and sometimes undivided attention, whether

Did You Know?

According to the American Animal Hospital Association, over half of all dog and cat owners give their pets human names.

it's for training, play, affection, or care. If you can't give that, Lab enthusiasts practically guarantee misery for both you and the Lab. As we've seen, a Lab who isn't trained and isn't included in family activities (who's parked in the backyard instead) will soon be a barking, chewing, jumping, digging mess. And a mess you'll be, too, frustrated by behaviors you find annoying.

> If you're a workaholic who's rarely home, give up the idea of getting a Lab.

You can prevent such difficulties, and it's quite simple. Take inventory of your life. Can you squeeze in, and do you really wish to, Labbie time? Are you willing to haul your sleepy self out of bed to serve kibble and take your dog for a walk? (You don't have to comb your hair. Labs don't care what you look like as long as you're providing some action.) If you work, can you drive home at lunch to take out your dog? How about training classes every Saturday morning or tossing a ball every evening after work? You get the picture. It's all about time. Be honest. Do you have time, or can you make time, for a Lab in your life?

Decision No. 3
How are you going to train your Lab?

Yes, you read that right. "How," not "if." Training is a must for all companion dogs, but Lab enthusiasts are especially adamant about training for this breed. Labs are big, bright dogs, and they want to learn. In fact, says Dana Hines, a Lab lover who owns two Labradors, the Lab thrives on learning. If a Lab is denied the opportunity to learn, she'll expend her energy in other ways, usually destructive. Early, consistent training and socialization will go a long way toward pointing a Lab in a positive, not negative, direction (the Lab that just ate the couch versus the companion who sits quietly alongside while you chat with the neighbor).

With that in mind, you must decide how best to train the Lab before you bring her home. Which means doing your home-work—learning about training techniques, interviewing trainers, and signing up for classes.

Decision No. 4
What veterinarian/clinic will you use?

Regular veterinary care by a skilled practitioner is essential for your Lab's health, and it's something you must take into account before acquiring a pet. With pups, there are frequent checkups, dewormings, and immunizations. Adult dogs need regular check-ups once or twice a year, immunization boosters, or treatment for various ailments. Golden-year Labs require more frequent checks and boosters and may suffer from a chronic or geriatric condition such as arthritis. Regardless of age, the Lab needs regular veteri-nary care. Who will provide that for your dog?

Decision No. 5
Who is responsible for walking, feeding, and cleaning up after the Lab?

If you want to start a family feud, neglect your Labbie chores! So before bringing home your Lab, discuss with your family who is going to do what and when (no worry if it's just you and Labbie). Your Lab is depending on you or another family member to make sure he eats, stretches his legs, gets nature breaks, has clean bedding for nap time, is brushed, and the like. After all, your dog can't really care for himself, although he may try. Work out a

What Do You Mean, It's My Turn?

Divvying Up Dog-Care Responsibilities

Parents often buy a dog "for the kids" and end up taking on all the responsibilities of caring for the pet themselves. Even couples have been known to purchase a puppy with the understanding they'll share dog-care duties, only to find one spouse doing the majority of the work once the pup arrives. When family members shirk their responsibilities, it not only can cause resentment, it can also prove detrimental to the puppy's care. To avoid these problems, call a family meeting before bringing your new dog home and divide all dog-care duties among family members. Keep in mind that, although children should be given some responsibilities related to puppy care, other jobs, such as obedience training an adolescent or adult Lab, must be taken on by an adult in the household. Also, clearly spell out during the meeting the boundaries you expect the dog to follow, so all family members will be consistent in their dealings with your new pet.

Questions you should answer include:

❍ Who will feed the dog?

❍ Who will walk the dog?

❍ Who will clean up after the dog?

❍ Who will groom the dog?

❍ Who will train the dog?

❍ Who will obedience-train the dog?

❍ Who will play with the dog to ensure he gets to release his energy and doesn't become bored?

❍ What kinds of games are acceptable to play with the new dog (such as fetch)? What kinds of games should be avoided (such as rough-housing and tug-of-war)?

❍ Who will take the dog to the vet for his regular check-ups and shots, as well as if he becomes sick?

❍ Where will the dog sleep at night?

❍ Where will the dog stay during the day when people are home? Will he have free run of the house or will he be confined to certain rooms?

❍ Where will the dog stay during the day when no one is at home?

❍ Will the dog be allowed on the furniture?

❍ How will the dog be contained in the yard?

❍ What kind of treats will the dog be given? Will the dog be given people food occasionally or never?

❍ How will the dog be corrected when he makes a mistake?

schedule, write it out, and put it on the refrigerator so it's clear to all family members who's responsible for what. Then appoint one person to oversee Lab chores and remind others to do their job.

Parents, perhaps you've chosen a Lab primarily as a dog for the kids. What you must realize is that *you*, not the children, are ultimately responsible for the Lab's care. It's true that caring for an animal is a good learning experience for kids. But it's parents who teach responsibility, not pets. Young children can join in the tasks with a parent, such as filling up the food and water dishes, but they should never be held accountable. Older children can do chores independently, with parental supervision.

Make sure your chore list is complete before you bring home a Lab. It will save you some hassle and ensure that your Lab gets what he needs every day.

Decision No. 6
If you work all day, can you come home at lunch to take the Lab for a walk and nature break?

How would you like to hold it all day? Probably you wouldn't, so don't expect your Lab to, either. If you work all day (and most of us do), plan on taking your lunch hour at home with your Lab. The sociable and boisterous Lab will adore the time you take to come home for a short visit. A trip outside to relieve herself and run about will do wonders for a Lab owned by a family who's gone during the day. Labs prefer not to be alone at all but can tolerate it for short periods. Plan on including your dog in family activities in the evening.

Did You Know?

The average cost per year for owning and maintaining a dog in the United States is $1220.

Might it be extremely difficult for you to make it home on your lunch hour? How about taking turns with another family member? If you absolutely can't, reconsider getting a Lab. Although you might enjoy solitude, Labs don't. A lonely Lab is likely to express himself in destructive behaviors.

Decision No. 7
Is there plenty of room for the Lab to exercise?

Do you have a fenced yard or access to a safe area in which your Lab can run, swim, and kick out the kinks? Labs love action, especially swimming, and you've got to give them room to move. They're an energetic breed, says Hines, and if they aren't given the opportunity to let it all out, they can become hyper. You don't need a two-acre fenced yard, but some space is essential. Before you bring a Lab into your life, make sure you can accommodate her need for plenty of physical activity.

Decision No. 8
Are you prepared to share your home
and lap with a big dog?

Are you willing to dedicate part of your home and yard to a good-sized dog who wants to be a part of your every activity? The Lab needs its own special area for food and water bowls and a crate or bed. But don't expect the Lab to stay there because he really wants to follow you around, assisting you with chores, begging for snacks, inviting play, and offering friendship.

Are you willing to share? Or does the idea seem annoying to you? Think carefully.

Decision No. 9
Can you live with the breeder's contract, and are you prepared to honor it?

Reputable breeders usually provide buyers with a contract. Although these contracts vary from breeder to breeder, they usually spell out items such as spay/neuter requirements, return policy, health certifications, and the guarantee. Be sure to read carefully any contract you sign, and be willing to abide by it. For example, some breeders require that if for some reason you give up the Lab, you must contact the breeder first. He will usually take back the dog rather than risk him going to a bad home. Others require that pet-quality Labs be spayed or neutered because the breeder has decided those individuals aren't of breeding quality.

Although it's essential to read any contract you sign, don't misunderstand why reputable breeders ask you to do it. The intent is to protect the Lab, not to stick buyers with unreasonable demands. If you're working with an experienced, trustworthy breeder, rest assured that his number-one concern is what's best for the Lab pup or adult.

Decision No. 10
Where are you going to put the Lab's crate?

Lab owners wholeheartedly endorse crate training (see chapter 6, "Basic Training for Labradors," for in-depth information on this). Since the Lab is a breed that can be very destructive if bored or left to itself, confining it when you're away or busy will prevent disaster, or at least prevent the garbage from being spread throughout the house. Crate training is especially helpful for pups, who are the most apt to wreak havoc in a household. With that in mind, before you bring home your Lab you should be familiar with the basics of crate training and have a specially designated spot for the crate.

Batten Down the Hatches!

Hang on to your hat. A Lab is coming to town. And you, your home, and yard better be ready. Because from the Lab's point of view, especially a puppy's, your house and yard look like a big toy chest! Everything looks like fun. If left unsupervised, a Lab puppy or adult will do its best to determine what's the most fun. But it probably won't seem fun to you when your Lab chews on your antique furniture, kitchen cabinets, wood sun deck, or expensive Italian shoes.

So before you bring home a Lab, your job is to Lab-proof your home and yard. Just as parents of toddlers must carefully put away breakables, secure dangerous items, and block off areas in the home and yard to protect the youngster, so must you go through your home and yard with a fine-tooth comb.

> It's important to know that Labs are naturally "mouthy." Everything goes in the mouth.

It's important to know that Labs are naturally "mouthy." Everything goes in the mouth. So if you don't want your Lab to pick up items and carry them around, advises Lab enthusiast Dianne Mullikan, nail them down or put them out of reach!

Kennel owner Laura Michaels seconds that. "Don't leave anything lying around that can be chewed. If you do, it will be chewed up. Labs are mouthy. Everything goes in their mouth. This is instinctive and cannot be changed. You cannot scold a Lab when he has something in his mouth. Scold yourself for leaving it out where the dog can get it."

Let 'Em Rip!

If you talk with Lab enthusiasts for any length of time, you'll soon hear of a Lab behavior called "butt tucking." According to longtime Lab enthusiast Robin Briguglio, butt tucking usually occurs in dogs less than one year of age. "All of a sudden, out of nowhere," she says, "they begin to run these charged-up laps around the room or your whole first floor. They run with their butts tucked in close behind them, and they run and scramble really fast, like they're being chased by imaginary friends who are playing tag with them."

Each episode doesn't last long; maybe a few minutes. "They have a grand time," says Briguglio, "but it's a time when you'll want to pull yourself up onto the couch, keep your legs and arms out of the way, and let 'em rip."

What causes Labs to race about with their rears tucked? "I think it's a way of releasing physical energy that's suddenly surging," says Briguglio. "It's usually preempted by something slight, like a sight or a sound, and then off they go!"

Preparing the House

The Lab's mouthy nature can get her in a lot of trouble around the house. Not only might you have something of value chewed up or carried away, but the Lab may chew on or ingest something dangerous or toxic. You can minimize the chance of harm by supervising your Lab carefully when she's in the house and confining her in a crate when you can't oversee her activities.

Get down on your knees—not to pray, but prayer may help!—and take a look at your home from Labbie eye level. It may seem silly, but if you can take a look at the world from the Lab's perspective, you might be able to see what "toys" are within reach. The best approach is a systematic, room-by-room investigation. Use common sense. If something seems dangerous, it probably is.

Kitchen. Mmmm. What an enticing room to the Lab! Not only does it smell good (from cooking and garbage), but there's a lot of family activity in this room. Your Lab will undoubtedly want to join in. Look at your kitchen carefully to determine potential dangers. Then take steps to make it a safer place. Are there breakable items on counters that could be easily knocked off by a naughty Lab jumping up to take a look? How about dangling electrical cords that could be chewed? Are cleaning supplies within reach? If so, put them away in cabinets with child-proof latches. How about the garbage pail? Labs love garbage, so make sure it has a lid or is stored where the Lab won't be tempted.

Bathroom. This is another room that's filled with potential dangers. Keep all medications locked away in child-proof cabinets to prevent accidental poisoning. Keep the toilet lid down to discourage the Lab from drinking from the bowl and possibly ingesting toilet bowl cleaner. Puppies seem especially fond of licking those flush-activated cleaners that hook under the rim. Keep the bathroom trash can out of reach. Toilet bowl brushes and plungers make dangerous meals for Labs with bored mouths.

Living room/family room. These rooms are like a treasure chest, filled with furniture, electrical cords, houseplants, and books and magazines waiting to be nibbled. Eating any of this stuff is dangerous. Then there are lamps and beautiful glassware carefully arranged on end tables—which will be knocked off with one sweep of the Lab's tail. Do your best to eliminate such dangers, and supervise your dog carefully.

Bedroom. Don't leave your clothing, shoes, socks, purse, or wallet lying around here! You're practically asking your Lab to chew it or relocate it. Don't leave out toiletries, makeup, brushes, or

Common Household Hazards

- Coins
- Household cleaners, laundry detergents, bleach, furniture polish
- Medication
- Suntan lotion
- Poisons (such as ant poison)
- Mouse traps
- Trash (poultry bones, spoiled food)
- Pins, needles, buttons, other sewing accessories
- Chocolate
- Hair products
- Houseplants
- Fishhooks
- Panty hose, ribbons or string that can get lodged in the throat or intestine
- Plastic
- Rubber bands, paper clips, twist ties, thumb tacks
- Shoe polish
- Alcohol
- Cigarettes and other tobacco products
- Matches and lighters
- Antifreeze, motor oil, brake fluid
- Windshield-washer fluid
- Paint and paint remover
- Nails, screws, saws, etc.

hair clips. Store them in dresser drawers. If you enjoy reading before you doze off, take care to put away your books in the morning. Be especially careful in children's rooms, which are usually filled with all kinds of fun toys. Have your child put away toys or keep the door shut—shutting the door is probably the most realistic preventive measure. It's easy for a Lab to choke on or ingest a small toy.

Garage. The family garage is frequently the storehouse for antifreeze, snail bait, paint, insecticides, and gasoline. If possible, store all these potentially deadly items in locked cabinets or on tall shelves. Probably the best advice is to prohibit the Lab from entering the garage. There are far too many risks if he's allowed in there, and accidents take only a second. Antifreeze, for example, is deadly. Just a few licks, and that's it. Its deadliness is compounded by the fact that it apparently tastes good to pets.

Preparing the Yard

Having a yard is a great asset for Lab owners. Once you make sure it's safe, a yard is the perfect place to let your activity-oriented Lab have some fun. Lab enthusiasts suggest fencing the yard, at least part of it, so the Lab has a designated area to dig, play, and otherwise have fun. "If they have an area of the yard they can call their own," says Lab fan Robin Briguglio, "you and he will be much happier."

Although a yard is definitely a great play area for the Lab, it's also chockful of potential dangers. Before you send your new friend out to play, you've got to make sure the area is safe. Just like in the house, the Lab sees everything as fair game. That includes decking, sheds, grills, patio furniture, a child's plastic sandbox, lawn equipment, decorative plants, and the garden. Either remove such items from the yard or fence off a separate Lab play area. Briguglio suggests making the yard interesting and fun by creating a playground of tunnels from PVC piping, a kiddie pool with a few inches of water, and sturdy toys. "Being sporting dogs," says Briguglio, "and loving the water, makes it important to provide the things they were bred to do such as swim, run, and play games."

Lawn and garden chemicals are big dangers and many mulches are toxic, so it's best not to use them in the Lab's play area. Decorative plants can be poisonous if ingested, too, so remove them.

Common Poisonous Plants

This list contains some, but not all, of the common plants that can harm your dog. Consult a plant book or a nursery or the National Animal Poison Control Center (800-548-2423) if you have any doubts about a plant in your home or yard.

Alfalfa

Amaryllis

Asparagus (Sperengeri) fern

Azalea

Beach tree

Belladonna

Bird of paradise

Black locust tree

Caladium

Castor bean

Chinaberry

Coriaria

Crown of thorns

Daffodil

Daphne

Datura

Dieffenbachia

Elephant's ear

Euonymus

Foxglove

Henbane

Honeysuckle

Hydrangea

Iris

Ivy (especially English, heart, needlepoint, and ripple)

Jack-in-the-pulpit

Jerusalem cherry

Jessamine

Jimsonweed

Larkspur

Lily-of-the-valley

Mistletoe berries

Monkshood

Moonseed

Morning glory

Mums (spider and pot)

Nightshades

Oak trees (acorns)

Oleander

Periwinkle

Philodendron

Plant bulbs (most)

Potato (green parts and eyes)

Poinsettia

Precatory bean (rosary pea)

Rhododendron

Rhubarb (leaves, upper stem)

Skunk cabbage

Tobacco

Tomato vines

Tulip

Umbrella plant

Water hemlock

Wisteria

Yew tree (Japanese, English, Western, American)

Supply and Demand

A certain amount of stuff is necessary to keep your Lab in the lifestyle to which she's accustomed. We're talking pet supplies, including food, dishes, collar and leash, a crate, playthings, and brushes. As long as you've got the funds and you like to shop, stocking your cupboards should be fun.

Crate and bedding. Since so many Lab enthusiasts recommend crate training, let's put it at the top of your shopping list. If you don't buy one, you may be sorry. Lab enthusiast Kirina Di Lynne Fann learned the merits of crate training her Lab, Jake, the hard way. "Labs are very big on chewing," she says. "Jake ate rocks, wood, electrical cords, linoleum, baseboards, just about everything. Since he knew how to open the closet doors, he would get in there and eat my shoes. Now that he's older, he won't chew on anything that isn't his. But the first year he ate all the plants in our backyard and chewed up the landscape material. A lot of people use crate training. If I'd known about that, Jake would have been in one from the start."

Ask the breeder what's the best-size crate for your Lab. Generally the crate should be large enough to house an adult Lab comfortably, which means big enough to stand up, turn around, and lie down in without much room left over. There are two types of crate: enclosed plastic and wire. Preferences vary among enthusiasts, and both types have advantages. The hard plastic crate is great if you live in a cold climate because it's warm and snugly. On the other hand, it can be extremely hot in warm climates. Open-wire crates aren't as snugly but can be covered with a blanket in chilly weather. Some Lab enthusiasts like the open-wire crate because even when the Lab is inside the crate, say, in the kitchen, he can still see what's going on in the house and feel part of the family action. Whatever type of crate you choose, it should be well made, with a sturdy door and latch.

You'll need washable or disposable bedding for the crate floor, too. You can buy something at a pet supply store, but it's not really necessary. An old sheet is fine. You may be tempted to line the crate with something fuzzy or fluffy, but don't. Labs, especially pups, love to pull or nibble on loose threads or fuzz. Any bedding with a bored puppy can be hazardous. If the puppy chews—no bedding!

Some Lab enthusiasts recommend a dog bed or large pillow for sleeping. This is probably best reserved for an adult Lab who's trustworthy—he's not going to get up from his bed at 3 A.M. and chew up your shoes.

Meals and treats. One of the Lab's favorite activities is eating, so you'd better make sure you've got plenty of food on hand before you bring home your new canine friend. It's a good idea to ask the breeder or rescue volunteer what the Lab has been eating and continue with that diet, at least for a while. Switching foods quickly can cause digestive upset and diarrhea—something you probably don't want to deal with the first week you have your Lab. (For more information on what food to buy, see chapter 3, "Food for Thought.")

You may also want to have a few treats on hand. Mind you, the Lab does have a tendency to get chubby, so treats

Did You Know?

Researchers are almost positive that dogs dream. If you look at a sleeping dog, sometimes you'll notice its eyes move beneath its eyelid. Because this is what humans do when they dream, researchers believe it is an indication of dreams in dogs, too. No word yet on what they dream about.

should be fed sparingly. Buy snacks made of wholesome, quality ingredients, with no sugar or additives. Fresh vegetables are good snacks, too.

Feeding dishes. Your Lab needs her own dishes, one for food and one for water. Choose bowls big enough for a full-grown Lab; the breeder can recommend a good size. Many Lab enthusiasts prefer stainless steel dishes because they're easy to clean and don't break. Others like ceramic, glass, or plastic feeding dishes. Ask the breeder what the pup or adult is used to and buy that. Some dogs can be particular about their feeding dishes, refusing to eat out of certain types.

Collars/leads. You'll need to "dress" your Lab with a well-fitting collar and sturdy leash. The sky is the limit here, with an endless number of styles and types of leashes, collars, and harnesses on the market: leather, nylon, prints. The best advice is to ask the breeder to recommend her favorite collar and lead and give it a try. An adjustable nylon collar with a quick-release buckle is great for pups because you can adjust it as puppy grows. A training collar may be in order, but wait to buy that until you begin training classes. Trainers usually have a specific collar in mind for students. You must also buy an identification tag to attach to the Lab's collar. Include your dog's name, and your telephone number.

Toys. Toys, toys, and more toys! Lab enthusiasts stress the need to buy your new puppy or adult Lab plenty of sturdy, fun toys. Stay away from thin latex toys and stuffed toys and buy tough, durable rubber chews. Nylabones and Kongs are a few favorites. Ask your vet before giving your dog beef bones, and never give her chicken, pork or lamb bones. Remember, the

High-Tech Identification Protection

Identification tags are your dog's first line of defense if she ever gets lost. Many a dog has been quickly reunited with her family because she was wearing a tag with the owner's phone number. However, what if your dog's collar comes off or is removed? How will your Lab find her way back home? Two other forms of identification can supplement the ID tag: tattooing and microchip implants.

With tattooing, a series of numbers or letters, or a combination of numbers and letters, is imprinted onto your pet's body, and the code is then recorded in a database. If someone finds your Lab, they can call the toll-free number to a tattoo registry, which maintains a database record with your name and phone number, corresponding to your dog's tattoo ID code. The toll-free number usually is provided on a tag that attaches to your dog's collar. Advantages to the tattoo is that it is a permanent and visible means of identification. One disadvantage is that, if your dog loses her collar, whoever finds your pet may not know who to call. If your dog won't let a stranger near her, the person who finds her may not be able to get close enough to read the tattoo. Also, horror stories exist of stolen dogs who have had a tattooed ear removed to keep them from being identified. To prevent this, it is safer to tattoo your dog's inner thigh.

Like tattoos, microchips contain a unique code, which can be read by a hand-held scanner that is passed over the skin of the animal where the chip was inserted. The code corresponds to information in a database, such as the owner's name and phone number. An advantage to microchips is that they, too, are permanent. The microchip itself is composed of non-toxic components sealed in biocompatible glass. The chip, about the size of the lead tip of a pencil or a grain of rice, is fitted into a hypodermic needle and injected under the skin of a dog between her shoulder blades. A disadvantage is that not all scanners read all microchips. Humane societies usually have only enough money to invest in one scanner, at best, and if that scanner can't read the chip in your dog, it's useless. Again, if your dog is uncomfortable with being handled by strangers, she may be hard to scan.

Tattoos and microchips are gaining popularity as permanent means of identifying your pet. However, the standard ID tag that dangles from the collar of your pup remains an invaluable tool for helping to return your lost pet to you.

Lab is an avid chewer. She must have chew toys, but they've got to be sturdy!

Grooming stuff. Labs are a low-maintenance breed when it comes to grooming, but you'll need to brush your Lab's coat periodically, trim her nails, brush her teeth, clean her ears, and give her a bath. A rubber curry is probably the tool of choice for brushing. Since the Lab's short coat doesn't matt, your main concern is removing dead hair. Labs do shed, usually in the spring and fall. Some enthusiasts like using a shedding blade, which is a metal, saw-toothed "brush" with handles. It's great for removing large amounts of dead coat. A soft wire slicker is handy for brushing the Lab, too.

You'll also need large-size toenail clippers and styptic powder, cotton balls and ear cleaner, good-quality shampoo, a doggie tooth-brush and toothpaste, your choice of flea control products (more on that in chapter 5, "Common Health Concerns"), and spray-on coat conditioner.

Cleanup tools. Don't forget the delicate matter of cleaning up and disposing of the Lab's waste. You'll need a large-size poop scoop and a place to dispose of fecal matter. If you've got a yard, consider installing an in-ground, mini–septic tank made espe-cially for animal waste. For waste pickup at the park or on walks in the neighborhood, carry along plastic bags. You can purchase bags made especially for this or recy-cle plastic grocery bags.

First-aid kit. Be prepared! Lab enthusiasts recom-mend you have a first-aid kit on hand for your dog. Hopefully you'll never have to use it. But you never know. The following is a list of suggested items: add or subtract as needed. Ask your vet for suggestions.

Store the kit in an easy-to-find location and check it frequently to make sure liquids haven't spilled or dried up. Replace medications and materials after they're used.

- ○ Activated charcoal tablets
- ○ Adhesive tape
- ○ Antibacterial ointment (skin and eyes)
- ○ Book on first aid (<u>Dog Owner's Home Veterinary Handbook</u>, by Delbert Carlson, DVM, and James Giffin, MD is a good one)
- ○ Diarrhea medicine
- ○ Dosing syringe
- ○ Muzzle that fits your dog
- ○ Petroleum jelly
- ○ Rectal thermometer
- ○ Rubber gloves
- ○ Rubbing alcohol
- ○ Scissors
- ○ Sterile gauze bandages and dressing pads
- ○ Three percent hydrogen peroxide
- ○ Towel
- ○ Tweezers

Buying Budget

You no doubt realize there are many purchases to be made before you bring home a Lab. And those purchases add up if bought all at once. You might be shocked at the total! If you're like most working people, you've got to budget money carefully. Buying everything you need for your Lab all at once may be out of the question. Try making your purchases a year or six months ahead. If you're waiting for a puppy from a good breeder, you may have to wait that long. Check pet supply stores frequently and buy supplies on sale (except food). Or put away money every month toward supply purchases so they don't pinch your budget.

Don't be fooled into thinking you have to buy the most expensive products or that you have to buy them all! Shop carefully for quality products you really need. There have never been so many pet foods, services, and products to choose from. In fact, the U.S. pet industry is a billion-dollar business. It's easy to get caught up in the fun of buying and blow your budget or buy items you really don't need. So take your time. Make your purchases carefully.

> The U.S. pet industry is a billion-dollar business.

But once you've bought the essential supplies, if you still have cash burning a hole in your pocket, there are plenty of fun ways to spend your hard-earned money. You can buy Lab-motif mouse pads, stationery, collector plates, T-shirts, tote bags, coffee mugs, photo frames, clocks, key chains, flags, welcome mats, books, magazines, switch plate covers, and even wallpaper. All of this may seem irresistible, especially if you're a new Lab owner suffering from Lab fever. But first things first. Budget and buy essentials. If you have a little left over, buy a bit of Lab fluff.

Make Yourself at Home!

Have you ever experienced the feeling of being a welcome guest at someone's home? Warm, genuine hospitality is truly delightful—and it's rare. It makes you feel important, appreciated, even loved. So before you bring home your Lab, make it your aim to extend your warmest wishes to your new friend. In other words, make a point to help the Lab feel at home. True, you don't know each other well yet, but you will.

How Much Is This Going to Cost Me?

The basic supplies for your new dog can come with a hefty price tag depending on size and quality, and often it's a price you'll be paying more than once. Remember to factor in these costs when making the decision to get a dog. Prices likely will vary depending on where you live, but the following should give you a good idea of what to expect.

Item	Low Price	High Price
Crate	$20.00	$200.00
Food and Water Bowls	3.00	60.00
Collar	4.00	40.00
Leash	4.00	50.00
ID Tag	3.00	15.00
Pet Stain/Odor Remover	4.00	10.00
Brush	4.00	20.00
Toys	1.00	40.00
Food (8 lb. bag)	4.00	9.00
Bed	10.00	200.00
TOTAL	$57.00	$644.00

Puppy's First Night

Puppyhood has a number of firsts: the puppy's first look at the world through opened eyes, first bark, first tumble with littermates. And, of course, her first night away from mom.

A first night home with a new owner can be a little stressful for puppy and owner. Some puppies miss their mom and littermates.

First-time puppy buyers might also feel anxious. Dana Hines did. "I brought Shelby home on a very snowy December night," she says. "She was a very shy puppy. I recall my father asking me if there was something wrong with her because she didn't move around much and didn't have much to say. At this point, I was a little nervous that it wasn't going to work out with my parents and the puppy. But I had faith, and she was worth it. I remember sleeping on the kitchen floor next to her for the first several nights so she wouldn't be scared."

Reduce the stress of bringing home puppy by purchasing all supplies beforehand. Don't wait until the day you plan to pick up the pup from the breeder to stop by the pet supply store.

Plan puppy's eating and sleeping arrangements. Where will she eat and drink? Where will you put the crate? Think through these arrangements carefully and make a plan before bringing puppy home.

Ask the breeder for a list of dos and don'ts, and get the list prior to puppy's first night. Many breeders provide buyers with such a list, which may include suggested food, a vet referral, toys, and so on. The responsible breeder wants to make sure puppy's first and subsequent nights away from its first home are happy and safe.

Puppy may be a little homesick at first and may whimper and cry at night. This isn't unusual, but it can be upsetting. Try comforting her by placing her crate next to your bed. That way puppy can smell you and hear you and feel less alone. You might even try wrapping an old-fashioned alarm clock (the kind that ticks) in a towel and placing it in the crate. It can be soothing because the sound simulates the mother's heartbeat.

Ask the breeder what environment the puppy is used to sleeping in and try to re-create it. For example, use a similar blanket. And tire puppy out before bedtime so she's sleepy and ready for rest.

Making an Adult Lab Feel Comfy

It's unlikely that an adult Lab is missing her mom when she comes to live with you, but the move from one home (or foster care) to another can be stressful. The Lab doesn't know you, and you don't know her. But your job

The responsible breeder wants to make sure puppy's first and subsequent nights away from its first home are happy and safe.

here won't be terribly difficult. The Lab's naturally shiny disposition enables her to make these transitions gracefully and easily.

"Older Labradors bond beautifully with new owners," says Briguglio. "I have heard from many people who come to me with concerns about bonding. Within a few weeks, I have always gotten that call that says, 'Wow, this was the best thing we could have ever done. We love our dog, he is great and he loves us, too.' That is music to my ears!"

You can encourage bonding and help an adult Lab feel welcome by:

○ Learning as much as you can about the dog's likes and dislikes before you bring her home;
○ Trying to follow the routine the dog is used to;
○ Giving the Lab bunches of TLC. Stroke the dog, talk to her, and praise her;
○ Giving treats!

○ Spending extra time with the Lab. If you work, take some time off;

○ Playing ball or taking walks with your Lab;

○ Feeding the same food, out of the same type dishes;

○ Introducing new family members, other pets, and activities slowly; and

○ Being consistent with obedience commands.

Food for Thought

In This Chapter

❍ Why Good Nutrition Matters
❍ How Often and How Much Do I Feed My Lab?
❍ Is It Okay to Share My Food?
❍ What's All the Fuss About Supplements?

Labs love to eat. They bring to the dinner table the same unbridled exuberance they show for life. And as a new Lab owner, it will take you about two seconds to figure that out. Fill up the food bowl, and the food's gone in moments.

Although Labs are very willing eaters, they don't know much about canine nutrition. Perhaps you don't, either, which is why this chapter is so important! Proper nutrition—a balanced proportion of vitamins, minerals, fats, protein, and carbohydrates—enables your Lab to be his very best. It gives him sparkling eyes, a shiny coat, a sharp mind, a bounce in his step, and a strong, wagging tail that cleans coffee tables in a single swipe.

So, since Labs can't read (no disrespect intended!), your job as a new Lab owner is to read and study as much as you can about canine nutrition. That way you'll be able to serve up Lab vittles that are nutritious as well as delicious.

Why Good Nutrition Matters

You've heard it again and again—good nutrition is essential. But why? Several reasons, beginning with the most obvious and simple: Labs are important members of our family. Like children, they need to be cared for with love and kindness. We need to be sure they get the right food for their activity level, which will ensure good health and a good attitude.

Put more scientifically, good nutrition matters because food is the fuel required to nourish the body. The body needs a special balance of nutrients, which are found in foods, to create energy and good health. If that balance is upset either from lack of food or the wrong foods, health problems can arise. Dogs need some 45 to 50 different nutrients. A deficiency in or excess of any one of them can lead to illness. Each nutrient must be present in appropriate ratios to the others for the dog's best health.

You might compare the nutrients found in food to LEGOs, the brightly colored building blocks loved by kids of all ages—nutrients are the body's building blocks. The body uses nutrients to build good health: strong bones, an effective immune system, and a healthy hair coat. When the body lacks nutrients, it can't build or work effectively.

One such nutrient required by your Lab is *protein*. Proteins, which are composed of small chemicals called amino acids found in meats, eggs, fish, and soybeans, supply your Lab with the nutrients needed to grow, repair tissue, and maintain health. They also form antibodies to fight infection. The Lab's body produces some amino acids, but others must be obtained from food sources. Meat, eggs, and dairy products are considered complete proteins—they supply all the amino acids your Lab needs in his diet. Grain and vegetables are incomplete proteins, but they provide carbohydrates and fiber. If you wish to create a vegetarian diet (based only on grains and veggies) it is possible to mix these sources in such a way to provide a complete and balanced protein source. But it's best to get guidance from a veterinary nutritionist before trying this.

A Lab suffering a protein deficiency has a decreased appetite, poor growth, weight loss, a rough or dull hair coat, and lower reproductive performance.

It's almost become a bad word in today's health-conscious world, but *fats* are important, too, and provide the Lab with the most concentrated source of energy. Per unit of weight, fats contain two and one-fourth as

> A diet that's too low in fat may result in a dry, coarse hair coat, and dry, flaky skin.

much energy as an equivalent weight of protein or carbohydrates. Fats carry fat-soluble vitamins—D, E, A, and K—and supply linoleic acid, a fatty acid essential for skin and hair. Fat also helps the body to keep warm, move nutrients, and send nerve impulses.

A diet that's too low in fat may result in a dry, coarse hair coat, and dry, flaky skin.

The energetic Lab needs a fresh, ongoing supply of *carbohydrates*. The body uses carbohydrates for quick energy, sparing protein for body growth and repair. Cellulose, an indigestible carbohydrate, provides bulk for proper digestion. Corn, rice, wheat, and oats are common sources of carbohydrates.

Vitamins and *minerals* are essential for normal body functions, bone development, and certain chemical reactions. Vitamins aid in resistance to disease, and are an essential part of the structure of enzymes—molecules that bring about important chemical changes in the body such as the breakdown of raw food into usable energy. Vitamins also help convert mineral elements into structural components of bones and teeth. They play a part in red blood cell formation, reproduction, and maintaining a good appetite and healthy skin.

Vitamins are classified as fat soluble or water soluble. The fat-soluble vitamins—A, D, E, and K—are stored in the body, which means oversupplementing can be toxic.

Water-soluble vitamins include the B complex and C vitamins. They aren't stored in any appreciable amount in the body; those not metabolized are excreted in the urine. Water-soluble vitamins must be replaced daily either from the diet or by production in the dog's own body.

Minerals are essential for bone and tissue development and proper body function. The total mineral content in a dog food is called its ash content. Ash contains calcium, phosphorus, sodium chloride, potassium, and other minerals that are essential nutrients. Feeding too many minerals, or minerals that aren't properly balanced, can cause many problems in the dog.

The healthy Lab must be properly hydrated, too. Water is essential to proper cell and organ function. Without it, the body can't eliminate waste products, keep a constant temperature, circulate blood, or transport nutri-ents. Life may continue for weeks in the absence of food, but be-cause the body has a limited capacity to store water, a dog can only live for days without water. Water constitutes up to 84 per-cent of the weight of newborn pups and 50 to 60 percent of the weight of adult dogs.

Specifically, what will good nutrition do for your Lab? Proof is in the pudding, goes the saying. Growing pups will develop nor-mally, your Lab will feel good and act happy, and she'll have:

❍ A thick, shiny coat that doesn't shed excessively;
❍ Strong teeth and healthy gums;
❍ Plenty of energy (so much, you'll wish you could capture it and sell it!);
❍ A strong immune system, able to resist disease. But in case of illness or injury, the Lab will recover and/or heal quickly;
❍ Good muscle tone;
❍ Sparkling eyes;
❍ Firm stools with little odor; and
❍ A long, healthy life.

The Yummiest and Best Food

You're no doubt convinced of the benefits of good nutrition. That's the easy part of Lab Feeding 101. The difficult part of this course is figuring out what to feed your Lab so she receives the nutrients she needs. Which food is best?

Pet food companies have made feeding a dog fairly simple for owners today. You have hundreds of commercially prepared diets from which to choose. Feeding your Lab is as simple as opening a bag, can, or box.

Unfortunately, no one commercially prepared food is best. What's best for your Lab depends on him, since each Lab is an individual. Labbie A might thrive on Tasty Nibbles, but Labbie B might not. Deb Hamele of Dunn's Marsh Labradors says, "I don't believe there's just one good food on the market. I have seven dogs and three different foods in the house; some [dogs] do well on one food, and others do well on another."

As if that isn't confusing enough, every person you ask about dog foods—breeders, vets, pet food company representatives, pet store clerks, Lab owners—will have a different opinion on what diet is best. With so many dog food diets on the market, choosing one for your Lab is a head-spinning experience at the very least.

But the way to tell if a food is best is how your Lab responds to the diet. Again, a shiny coat, high energy level, good nature, and healthy teeth are signs that the dog is receiving the nutrients she needs from a diet.

Types of Pet Foods

To find this optimum diet that makes your Lab glow with good health, you've got to do some shopping. What you'll notice right away is there are three main types of pet food: dry, canned, and soft-moist. These food types vary in moisture content, texture, cost, palatability, and nutritional content.

Generally most dry dog food diets contain 18 to 27 percent protein, 7 to 15 percent fat, and 35 to 50 percent carbohydrate.

> Canned diets seem tastiest to dogs, but they're also the most expensive to feed per serving.

Dry kibble is the most economical way to feed a dog, and it's easy and convenient for owners. Dry diets have the added benefit of helping reduce plaque and tartar on the dog's teeth.

Soft-moist diets contain approximately 16 to 25 percent protein, 5 to 10 percent fat, 25 to 35 percent carbohydrate, and 30 percent water. Soft-moist diets are favored over dry by many dogs but are more expensive to feed.

Canned dog foods usually contain 8 to 15 percent protein and 2 to 15 percent fat; the moisture content is approximately 75 percent. Canned diets seem tastiest to dogs, but they're also the most expensive to feed per serving.

Pet Food Categories

A pet food shopping spree can take you across town and back—literally. In addition to the several types of diets (dry, canned, and moist), pet foods are further distinguished within the pet industry by where you buy them and a few other factors.

Superpremium pet foods are generally sold in pet specialty stores and veterinary clinics. The prices are the highest, but the diets are usually energy dense or have more calories per pound of food which means you can feed less food each day to meet your Lab's nutritional needs.

Premium foods are traditionally sold at grocery stores but are also available at pet supply stores. Premium diets are moderately priced.

Grocery store brands are pet foods sold under the individual store's name instead of as a national brand. Grocery store brands are designed to offer the same quality as nationally advertised brands at a lower price. They may or may not succeed in this mission.

Did You Know?

Houston topped the 1998 list of cities with the highest number of postal workers bitten by dogs, with Chicago a close second.

Nonpremium brands are usually found stocked at feed stores and sold inexpensively.

Generic pet foods were extremely popular in the 1980s, along with a host of generic products of all kinds. These generic foods were low priced compared to brand-name products and were purported to be nutritionally equivalent to national brands. Generic pet foods have declined in popularity, in part because of nutritional inadequacies and the increase of quality store brands.

Each category of pet foods has its proponents among veterinarians, breeders, and owners. Some Lab fanciers believe in feeding only superpremium foods; others think premium and grocery store brands are sufficient. The primary difference in the foods is density per volume. A serving of premium food is likely to have more nutrients absorbed and digested than a serving of nonpremium. The dog eats less but gets a higher percentage of nutrients.

A good way to evaluate a pet's diet is to examine the animal's feces. No, it's not a pleasant task, but it does tell all—or nearly so! The feces give clues about what's going on in the pet's digestive system. Healthy pets leave well-formed, firm droppings with little odor. Feces consistency indicates how well an animal absorbs nutrients from the food, showing the balance of fiber and water and the all-around quality of the diet. Firm feces usually mean the animal is getting a quality diet formulated so that his system can absorb as much nutrients as possible. Loose, ill-formed, fatty-looking stools often indicate inadequate food.

High-quality pet food is usually digested more quickly than that of poorer quality. The more quickly the food is digested, the less odor to the feces. Feces that are an unusual color, green or magenta, for example, can reflect coloring additives in the diet.

Feeding Stages

Within each pet food category, you'll find diets formulated for a specific life stage or nutritional need. There are puppy diets, with higher levels of nutrients to meet the young dog's rapid growth and development. Some foods are formulated to have higher levels of protein and calories for working dogs. Others are lower in calories and fat to help less active or older dogs maintain normal body weight. Diets vary among manufacturers, but you can generally find foods formulated for the specific nutritional needs of:

❍ Pregnant and/or lactating bitches;
❍ Puppies;
❍ Mature dogs;
❍ Working dogs (canine competitors, hunting dogs, sled dogs, herding dogs, and so on);
❍ Seniors; and
❍ Various medical conditions (usually available only by prescription).

Cost Differences

If you're a savvy shopper, you're sure to notice the price differences in pet food. From high end to low end, there's a price to please everyone. Price differences are usually based on the type and amount of ingredients in the diet. Higher-end foods use more expensive ingredients. For example, you might find lamb or turkey in a superpremium diet rather than less expensive chicken or beef.

Be aware that price isn't everything when it comes to dog food. In fact, a low price can be deceiving. The lower-end diet may be less expensive but also contain less nutrients per volume than a higher-quality diet. That means you have to feed your dog more to obtain the same nutrients. You may pay less initially, but you'll end up buying more food per year.

Complete and Balanced

When it comes to choosing a commercial diet for your Lab, remember these three words: "complete and balanced." This means your Lab will receive all the nutrients she needs to thrive at a particular life stage. Additional supplements aren't necessary. A food purporting to be nutritionally complete and balanced on the package must by law meet specific standards set by the National Research Council or pass performance tests designed by the Association of American Feed Control Officials (AAFCO). If the label states the food has met AAFCO standards by feeding trials, the manufacturer has followed the dogs' health when fed the food and proven that it meets their needs. Formulating standards are theoretical and the manufacturer may change ingredients due to costs or other considerations.

Be sure that the label on the food states that the product is complete and balanced for the life stage of the pet you're feeding. If you want to feed your adult Lab a complete and balanced diet, be sure the label states that the diet is complete and balanced for an adult dog.

Palatability

A commercially prepared diet may be nutritionally jam-packed, but it's no good if the Lab won't eat it. Palatability is essential. It's unusual for Labs to be picky eaters, but dogs do have eating preferences.

Research shows that when given a choice, dogs typically prefer high-fat foods. Dogs can detect subtle differences in the

What's on the Label?

The wide variety of cans, bags, and boxes of pet food shelved in shops throughout the nation has at least one thing in common: labeling. True, the colors, pictures, and words used on individual foods vary, as do the diets within. But all labels must by law contain specific information.

Pet food labels give basic information about the diet's ingredient content, nutrient guaranteed analysis, feeding instructions, net weight, the name and address of the manufacturer or distributor, and additional facts about the product. No, pet food labels don't tell everything about a product. But they do give a savvy consumer a good way to begin comparing foods.

Pet food labels contain several elements:

The product name must be placed on the principal display panel, that part of the label most likely to be seen by consumers.

Certain nutrient guarantees—guaranteed analysis—are required on all pet food labels: crude protein (minimum percentage), crude fat (minimum percentage), crude fiber (maximum percentage), and moisture (maximum percentage).

The package must include an ingredient listing of all the ingredients used to make the food; they must be listed on the label in descending order of predominance by weight.

Additives must be noted. That includes nutritional additives such as vitamins and minerals, antioxidants such as BHA or BHT, chemical preservatives, flavoring agents, and coloring.

The net weight must be placed on the principal display panel.

Manufacturer information, the name and address of the manufacturer, packer, or distributor, must be included on the label.

The label must state in the nutritional adequacy statement whether or not the product provides complete and balanced nutrition and if it is appropriate for all life stages or one particular life stage.

The amount of food required, or feeding directions, must be printed on the label.

The caloric statement, which is the calorie content of the product, must appear away from the guaranteed analysis and be under the heading "calorie content."

Last but not least many pet food packages include a toll-free consumer information number. This isn't mandatory, but it's a good resource for owners wanting to learn more about the product they're feeding a pet.

quality of ingredients used in foods. The way the diet feels in the dog's mouth—texture, density, size, shape—all affect whether or not the dog will eat it.

The bottom line? The Lab has to like eating what he's eating!

Feeding Directions

Commercially prepared diets are labeled with feeding directions of average portions for different weights and ages of dogs. Recommendations vary among diets. Read the label on the diet you buy. But remember, it's only a starting point. Actual feeding amounts will depend on your Lab's age, activity level, size, environment, and body metabolism. (For specific information on how much to feed your Lab, see page 75 in this chapter.)

Keeping It Fresh

How do you keep dog food fresh once it's purchased? Canned, unopened foods have a long shelf life and are easily stored. Simply place the cans in a pantry or kitchen cupboard where you store all other canned goods. Once you open a can, it must be covered and refrigerated until you use it again.

Store dry food in a cool, dark area. If you live in a hot, humid climate, keep the food in an air-conditioned room if possible. To prevent insects and bugs from sharing your Lab's meals, once you open the bag, put it in a large, plastic garbage can with a tight-fitting lid. Keep the food in its original bag to keep it freshest. Wash and dry the can after each bag is finished.

It may be tempting to load up on dog food, especially if your brand is on sale, but don't overbuy. Purchase only as much as your Lab can eat within a week or so. The longer the food sits, the more chance of spoilage or bug infestation. This is especially true for natural pet foods that don't contain chemical preservatives.

Au Naturel

A growing number of owners are choosing more natural ways to care for their pets, including what they feed them. Concerned that commercially prepared pet foods aren't as healthy as they should be, owners are buying "natural" diets; feeding raw diets of meat, vegetables, and grains; cooking for their dogs at home; or ordering premade meals from natural-oriented companies. And holistic-oriented veterinarians—currently there are 800 members of the American Holistic Veterinary Medical Association—routinely advocate fresh, raw diets or natural commercial diets as the best means of offering nutrients.

Why all the fuss about commercially prepared pet food? According to holistic advocates, the best way to prevent disease and maintain good health is proper nutrition. The cornerstone of holistic medicine is prevention and early detection of disease. Good nutrition is essential for preventing illness. Commercially prepared foods may not always provide good nutrition due to the high level of processing; use of questionable ingredients (by-products, for example, which are allowed by the government but can include diseased chicken, beef, or pork); use of inferior ingredients such as low-quality grains; and addition of artificial colors, preservatives, flavors, sugar, or corn syrup. Fresh, organic foods, say holistic advocates, are the best way to provide the body (dog or

> A growing number of owners are choosing more natural ways to care for their pets, including what they feed them.

The Importance of Water

Water is important to every living creature, and your Lab is no exception.

Water makes up around 65 percent of your adult dog's body and even more of your puppy's constitution. Dogs need water to help their cells function properly and to aid in proper digestion. Basically, dogs need water to live. Without water, a dog will die within only a few days.

The water in your dog's body needs to be replenished on a regular basis, since it is routinely lost through respiration, digestion, and urination. On hot days or when exercising heavily, your dog needs even more water to keep his body running smoothly.

To keep your Lab at optimum health, provide him with constant access to plenty of cool, fresh water.

person) with sufficient nutrition. Commercially prepared foods, although they're thoroughly researched and tested, are anything but fresh and are rarely organic.

The holistic perspective on feeding pets isn't without its critics. In fact, many holistic vets are considered flakes or "out there" by their allopathic colleagues. But there's nothing flaky about the positive results holistic advocates see after feeding their animals fresh diets.

Get to the Kitchen!

If you're interested in feeding your Lab a fresh-food diet, start by consulting a holistic-oriented veterinarian (contact the AHVMA for a referral in your area; see the resources section in appendix A for contact information), or a veterinary nutritionist. He or she is knowledgeable on all things holistic and is qualified to help you plan a menu. Since balance is essential to good health, it's best not to try making meals on your own—at least not at first.

There are several good sources for learning more about feeding natural diets (see appendix A for additional holistic resources). For a comprehensive look at natural health for pets and specific fresh-diet recipes, check out *Dr. Pitcairn's Complete Guide to Natural Health for Dogs and Cats*, by Richard H. Pitcairn, D.V.M., Ph.D., and Susan Hubble Pitcairn.

Don't expect your conventional veterinarian to get on board with this idea. Most are opposed to owners cooking for their dogs due to concerns about nutrient balance and safe handling of raw meats. Both are realistic concerns. But if you're working with a holistic practitioner or veterinary nutritionist, there's no need to worry. You can learn to prepare a balanced diet and handle foods safely.

Following a consultation with a holistic vet or nutritionist, get to the kitchen! If you really want to feed your dog a fresh-food diet, you'll have to prepare it. That means you'll be buying, mixing, fixing, chopping, freezing, and serving—a lot. It's definitely much more work than opening a bag, can, or box. But to those with a dedicated holistic mind-set, it's worth the extra work.

If you rarely cook for yourself now or disdain the idea of more cooking, perhaps a fresh-food diet isn't the best idea for you. Consider a pre-made fresh diet or commercial natural diet instead.

Fresh Diets

Recipes, amounts, and techniques vary, but fresh diets for dogs often include lean and fatty raw meats, dairy products,

Did You Know?

Veterinarians estimate that between 30 percent and 50 percent of today's dog population is overweight.

grains such as rice or oats (these should be cooked), legumes, vegetables, and supplements.

Fresh-diet enthusiasts recommend preparing raw diets with the finest-quality ingredients available: organic. Organic foods have the least amount of chemical residue and the highest nutritional value because they're grown or raised naturally, with every effort made not to use materials (such as chemical fertilizers or growth hormones) believed to be harmful to people, pets, and the environment.

Although organic foods were difficult to find and buy 25 years ago, they're readily available today. To find organic foods in your area, look in the yellow pages for natural or health food stores. Or locate a farm co-op or individual with a naturally cultivated backyard garden. Pick up a copy of the *National Organic Directory,* published by the nonprofit Community Alliance with Family Farmers.

Hand in hand with fresh diets are supplements. Bonemeal, nutritional yeast, kelp, vegetable oil, and vitamins are usually recommended to fortify the diet. It's essential to have a vet's guidance on which supplements are necessary for your individual Lab, though. Supplements can be a tricky business, and you'll need expert help.

Fresh diets aren't common among Lab enthusiasts. Most Lab owners feed commercially prepared premium kibble diets. But fresh diets do have a dedicated following in the Lab world, such as Janet Sampson, owner of Sampson's Labradors. "After careful consideration," she says, "it seems plausible to me that a carefully designed raw-foods diet can be just as good as premium commercial dog food. I have 10 chocolates, and for the last two years I have been fighting ear and eye infections, dry skin, hot spots, no coat, discolored coats, tartar buildup, bad breath, bad weight gain or too fat." No matter what she fed her dogs or what medications she gave them, the Labs were still suffering from a variety of these ailments.

"So, I took the plunge into a raw diet," says Sampson. "It took about one month to really figure it out. The problems have almost completely disappeared. Eyes are clear and happy, tartar is gone off teeth, no bad breath. Coats are coming in dark and full—hard to do in south Florida. It is more work, but really doesn't cost much more. I am very happy, and the dogs love it!"

Premade Fresh Diets

If you'd like to try feeding a fresh-food diet to your Lab but are turned off by all the fixing and mixing, consider ordering premade foods. Holistic-oriented individuals and companies will do all the prep for you and, for a price, ship to you a frozen batch of fresh food (usually meat and supplements). All you need to do is thaw the meal before feeding and add veggies and grains as recommended by your holistic vet.

Commercial Natural Diets

Keeping step with consumer interest in natural foods, pet food companies have developed diets for those who wish to buy natural but keep it simple.

How is "natural" defined? Good question. There are no regulations in the pet industry on how the term can be used, so it can mean a variety of things. For those with a holistic mind-set, a natural diet generally means:

○ The diet is made with minimal processing and low heat;

○ The diet has a high bioavailability—it's made with whole foods and contains chelated and esterized vitamins and minerals;

○ Ingredients are high quality, such as human-grade meats, grains, organic veggies, and dairy products;

○ No artificial anything! Including colors, preservatives, or flavors. No growth hormones or antibiotics;

○ The diet is preserved naturally, with vitamins E and C. No ethoxiquin, a preservative; and

○ The diet is protein based, with turkey, beef, chicken, lamb, or rabbit.

Natural diets vary in quality, so you must check them carefully. Read the label, and if in doubt, call the company. Be wary of diets with highly processed ingredients or by-products because it's difficult to determine precisely what's in them. You can purchase natural diets at health food stores, some pet supply stores, by mail order, or through the Internet. Because these diets use few preservatives, they typically have a short shelf life. Throw the food away if it looks or smells odd.

Vegetarian Delight

For vegetarian owners who wish to share their philosophy with the family Lab, the best advice is to consult a holistic veterinarian. Dogs like eating meat, but they're considered omnivores: animals that can meet their nutritional needs from a wide variety of sources. Wild coyotes and wolves, for example, eat grasses, berries, and other vegetable matter. That means dogs can subsist on a vegetarian diet or a diet low in meat. But dogs are individuals. Some can thrive on a meatless diet; some can't. It's essential that you work with a holistic veterinarian, who can help plan a vegetarian menu and chart your dog's health. Be aware that most holistic vets don't recommend a vegan diet for dogs, one that excludes all animal foods such as meat products or eggs.

Dogs like eating meat, but they're considered omnivores: animals that can meet their nutritional needs from a wide variety of sources.

How Often and How Much Do I Feed My Lab?

If your Lab could answer the above question, he would say, "All day, and as much as I want!" Labs are walking stomachs. If they're not hungry, something's wrong. But how much food, how often, is good for a Lab? That's another matter.

Unfortunately, the ever hungry Lab tends to gain weight easily. That, coupled with his hearty appetite, can make it difficult to keep his weight on target. So it's essential that owners be careful to feed a Lab only what he needs. Overfeeding can quickly lead to obesity.

That leads us back to the question of how much and how often you should feed your Lab. There's no exact answer. Feeding amounts and schedules depend on the individual Lab—his size, age, and activity level—what diet you're feeding, and how cold it is outside (dogs who spend a lot of time outdoors in cold temperatures require more food).

Feed and Observe

You can begin to pinpoint how much food your Lab needs each day by following the feeding instructions spelled out on the dog food package. Use the bag, can, or box as a starting point. Remember

Food Allergies

It's not common, but some dogs develop food allergies. Digestive upset, itchy skin, or hair loss can be signs that something in the animal's diet is triggering an allergic reaction. What exactly is an allergic reaction? It's an exaggerated response of the immune system to something that's usually harmless; wheat, for example. What the pet is allergic to is called an allergen.

The way the body responds to that allergen is called a hypersensitivity reaction. There are two kinds of hypersensitivity reactions. The immediate type occurs within minutes of exposure and often produces hives, itching, and sometimes, trouble breathing or collapse; anaphylactic shock is an example of this. The delayed reaction produces itching hours or days afterward.

The most common food allergens are wheat, milk, soy, chicken, eggs, beef, fish, and corn. Dyes and preservatives may also trigger allergies.

Treating allergies usually begins with a diet trial supervised by a veterinarian. But not just any diet—preferably foods to which the Lab hasn't been exposed. Changing from one pet food to another doesn't work because many foods contain similar ingredients. Dietary restriction is the only way to truly determine what food(s) the Lab is allergic to. Once the offending agent is pinpointed, an appropriate diet can be started.

that these instructions are general and apply to all breeds of a certain weight. Your Lab is an individual, and every dog is different. Usually it's necessary to decrease the amount suggested on a package because of the Lab's tendency to put on weight easily.

After you've read the instructions, the best thing to do is observe the Lab's body condition:

❍ Too thin. An overly thin Lab will have visible or easily felt ribs. The hipbones may be visible. The waist and belly are obviously tucked up when viewed from the side. Increase food.

❍ Just right. The ribs should have just a little fat over them; you can feel them easily with slight pressure. The Lab should have a waist when viewed from above and a tucked-up belly when viewed from the side. Continue feeding as is.

❍ Too heavy. If you can't easily feel the Lab's ribs and you can easily see fat covering the dog's ribs, she's too heavy. The waist is absent or barely visible when viewed from above. The belly may hang down. Decrease food.

How Often?

How frequently you feed your Lab depends on how old the dog is and personal preference. Pups must be fed several times a day. The average adult Lab can be fed once or twice a day: morning, evening, or both. Many breeders and veterinarians recommend feeding multiple meals—dividing the dog's daily ration into portions—to help reduce the chance of bloat (see chapter 5). Some owners like the idea of feeding twice a day; others find it inconvenient and opt to feed once a day.

Free feeding, or leaving out a full bowl of food all day, is not recommended for Labs. Some breeds won't overeat and even need to be encouraged to eat. The Lab isn't one of them! If food is available, your Lab will consume it. That's a promise!

The Routine

Dogs are creatures of habit and seem to enjoy eating at the same time every day. Feeding pups at the same time, at the same place, every day helps establish eating habits and makes housebreaking

Did You Know?

Dogs and cats in the United States consume almost $7 billion worth of pet food a year.

easier. Youngsters usually need to urinate or defecate after eating, so if you feed at the same time every day, you can predict when nature calls.

Feeding Puppies

Lab pups have special feeding requirements. A puppy's stomach isn't large enough to hold enough food in one feeding to provide her daily nutritional needs. When puppy graduates from mother's milk to solid food at three to four weeks of age, she'll require three to four meals a day. When puppy reaches about four to five months old, twice-a-day feedings may be sufficient. She can graduate to once-a-day meals at eight to nine months of age. Although free feeding is recommended for pups of some breeds, it isn't recommended for Labs. Meals several times a day are best so Lab pups don't gain too much weight, too fast. Lab pups shouldn't be pudgy or fat. Research has shown that Labs have a lower incidence of genetically caused bone disorders if they aren't obese during puppyhood and grow at a slower rate. Svelte puppies will still reach their destined height, weight, and size, but they'll be healthier adults than the adorable pudgy puppy.

> Research has shown that Labs have a lower incidence of genetically caused bone disorders if they aren't obese during puppyhood and grow at a slower rate.

A pup's nutritional requirements for growth and development are greater than those of an adult dog. If you opt to feed your Lab pup a commercially prepared diet, feed one that's formulated especially for pups to ensure your Lab gets the nutrients he needs. Some veterinarians recommend that Lab pups eat puppy food formulated for large breeds to keep their growth slow. A Lab pup that eats a complete and balanced puppy diet doesn't need additional supplements. In fact, adding supplements can cause nutritional imbalance.

Dry food can be moistened with warm water to encourage pups to eat. Milk can be used, too, but only in extremely small amounts. Milk causes digestive upset in some puppies and dogs. A tablespoon or so of canned food can be added to increase interest as well. But remember, pups shouldn't be allowed to get fat. The ideal puppy is lean—neither bony or round.

These are just general guidelines for feeding your Lab pup. Consult with your veterinarian for specific advice on feeding your puppy.

Feeding the Adult Lab

The adult Lab is usually mature at the age of one year or older (physically, not mentally! Labs are still very puppyish at one year). Feeding is fairly straightforward if you use commercially prepared kibble. Buy a complete and balanced diet made for the adult dog—it's called a *maintenance* diet in the pet food industry—and feed it to your dog once or twice a day. Add a tablespoon of canned food for taste if you want. Adjust the amount according to the Lab's activity level. That's all there is to it.

Healthy adult dogs who aren't pregnant, nursing, or hard-working have somewhat low nutritional requirements. The average family Lab, for example, doesn't need the same amount of food or type of diet as a Lab who works in the field.

Owners can reduce the adult Lab's chance of bloat by feeding small meals twice a day, by moistening a kibble diet with warm water, and by having a rest period after meals. This allows the kibble to expand and become more chewy before it's eaten. It also helps reduce that chance that the Lab will vomit after eating, as many do because they eat so rapidly.

Feeding Hardworking Labs

The highly active Labrador—a Lab who competes or works in the field, agility trials, fly-ball competition, or search and rescue—uses a lot of energy that must be supplied by a nutritious diet. (See chapter 8, Family Life.) The hardworking dog can require two to three time more kilocalories per pound of body weight than what's required for normal activity. The highly active Labrador needs a high-energy diet to maintain good body condition and stamina.

Many veterinarians recommend commercially prepared "performance" diets for highly active Labradors (not "weekend warriors" but dogs who are consistently active). These higher-fat, higher-protein diets supply the working dog with needed calories. Because performance diets are higher in protein than maintenance diets, there's a misconception that the active dog just needs extra protein, but all nutrients are required by an active dog in greater amounts. Research shows that high-protein diets don't cause kidney damage—although some breeders and owners mistakenly fear that they do.

Multiple, small meals are best for highly active Labs to keep up their blood sugar level. Snacks throughout the day may be necessary, too, and appropriate hydration is a must. But active dogs shouldn't be fed or watered immediately before or after a work session. Feeding meals too close to working can impair performance or cause digestive discomfort.

Meals for the Golden Years

Older Labs, who have reached the last 25 percent of their expected life span, are usually less active than younger adult dogs and pups. That means their energy requirements are reduced and they can gain weight easily if fed too much or fed a high-calorie diet. Some veterinarians recommend "senior" diets, foods high in nutrients but with reduced calories, to keep senior Labs at a healthy weight.

The Fight Against Obesity

The Lab's pure delight in eating has a dark side. Too much food, too much of the wrong kind of food, and lack of activity, along with the Lab's genetic tendency to put on pounds, can lead to obesity. Obesity is the excess accumulation of body fat: an animal weighing 20 percent or more than its ideal weight is considered obese. The risk of obesity increases with age, meaning that as your Lab grows older, it can be more difficult to keep her weight on target.

So what's so terrible about a little extra weight? It's unhealthy! Your overweight Lab may not live as long, and he may be susceptible to:

❍ Impaired heart;
❍ Trouble breathing;
❍ Heat stress;
❍ Stress on the skeletal system;
❍ Increased surgical risk;
❍ Increased risk of ligament, joint, and muscle damage; and
❍ Increased risk of diabetes.

Did You Know?

Greyhounds have the best eyesight of any breed of dog.

What causes obesity? Several factors contribute, including diet, genetics, and hormonal disorders.

Diet is the most common cause of obesity in dogs. The Lab eats more than he should, consuming more calories than he can use. Too much food, treats, and table scraps! Combine that with lack of activity, and *voilà!* Excess weight.

Some breeds have a genetic tendency to gain weight, and the Labrador Retriever is one of them. Although the Lab has this tendency, that doesn't mean he will or has to become heavy. A diligent owner who feeds carefully and keeps the Lab active can prevent obesity.

> Some breeds have a genetic tendency to gain weight, and the Labrador Retriever is one of them.

Hormone imbalances such as thyroid or pituitary gland dysfunction can lead to obesity.

Prevent your Lab from being obese! Here's how:

○ Feed only what the Lab needs.

○ Don't free feed. Serve the meal, and if it's not eaten in 15 minutes (it will be), pick it up.

○ Refrain from feeding fatty table scraps and high-calorie treats.

○ Guard garbage cans and additional food sources.

○ Keep your Lab active! Play, walk to the park, get involved in a canine sport.

○ Make sure everyone in the family agrees on being careful about feeding Labbie.

○ Consult with a veterinarian before starting your dog on a weight-loss program.

Toxic Treats

Treating your dog to a special tidbit here and there is okay; however, certain foods should never be given to your pet because of their potential to make him sick.

Avoid salty, calorie-laden snacks, such as potato chips. Excessive salt can dehydrate your pet, and extra fat calories can only translate into extra pounds.

Sugary treats, such as candy and cookies, are bad for your dog. At the least, they will fill up your Lab with empty calories and leave him less interested in his own food, which can result in poor nutrition. At the worst, they can cause diarrhea or vomiting in your pet.

Chocolate is especially dangerous for dogs; it can even be deadly. Different types of chocolate pose varying risks. While one small milk-chocolate candy bar probably will not be lethal to a Lab, it could easily kill a Toy dog, and it will make your Lab ill. Never leave any chocolate out where your dog can get it, including the middle of your dining room table. Susan James of Reading, Pennsylvania, came home one day to find a box of chocolate wrappers strewn across her table and a very sick dog lying on the floor. Luckily Penny the dog survived, but it was days before all the chocolate was flushed from her system.

Meats high in fat, like ham, are difficult for dogs to digest. Also, meats doused in rich sauces, rich gravy, or spices can wreak havoc on your dog's digestive system.

Bones are another danger for your dog. Never feed your dog bones left over from your meals, especially poultry, fish, and pork bones. Pieces of bone can break off and cause constipation, intestinal punctures, or blockage of your dog's digestive tract.

Finally, don't give your dog any beverage other than water. Soda contains sugar and unhealthy additives, and alcohol can be harmful or even fatal if consumed in large quantities.

Is It Okay to Share My Food?

You're eating a turkey and Swiss cheese sandwich, and your Lab stares at you from across the room like she hasn't eaten for days. She starts to drool and wags her tail a bit. Should you share?

The answer to that depends on who you ask. Some Lab enthusiasts say no, no table scraps, no people food for Labs. Others think it's okay to allow tidbits here and there.

Before you decide to share meals with your Lab, remember that the Lab's natural tendency to get heavy, combined with her hearty appetite, can lead to excess weight gain very quickly. Although another breed may indulge in table treats without a change in weight, the Lab is sure to pack on the pounds. Also, table scraps are usually high in fat, which can cause digestive upset.

The best idea is to avoid giving scraps. If you do share, limit it to small bites every now and then and only to a Lab who isn't overweight. A little bit is fine, but don't overdo it. Little bits add up!

Healthy Treats

Everyone needs a treat, you say. Especially your beloved Lab friend. If your Lab isn't overweight, you can offer healthy treats now and then. But remember, only now and then—and only if your Lab isn't struggling to button his jeans. Some favorites among experienced Lab enthusiasts include:

○ Hard biscuits (store-bought or homemade);
○ Carrots (yes, Labs love veggies!);
○ Apple slices;
○ Rice cakes; and
○ Cereal (especially high fiber, unsugared varieties).

Avoid giving your Lab sugary treats, candies, cake, or anything that contains chocolate. Although chocolate is considered the perfect food by some people, it contains a chemical, theobromine, that's potentially toxic to dogs. In very high doses, it can kill a dog, but lower doses can, at the very least cause digestive upset.

What's All the Fuss About Supplements?

More is better, right? That's the perspective of many pet owners. Feed a healthy diet, then add a little more vitamins, minerals, a little of this and that, and it's going to make the dog extra healthy. Especially if the dog is old or very young. Owners commonly want to add raw eggs, wheat germ oil, vitamins and minerals, milk, table scraps, or meat to their pet's diet.

Although these owners are well-meaning, thinking that more is better will get them and their pets into trouble. When it comes to adding to or supplementing your Lab's diet, more isn't better. In fact, more can be downright unhealthy!

If you feed your normal, healthy Lab a commercially prepared complete and balanced diet, no additional supplements

> When it comes to adding to or supplementing your Lab's diet, more isn't better. In fact, more can be downright unhealthy!

are necessary. That's how the manufacturer planned it. The diet contains the appropriate level of nutrients for the animal at a particular life stage. For example, if you're feeding your three-month-old Lab a diet formulated for pups, you don't need to add anything to his diet. (If you're cooking for your dog and feeding a fresh-food diet, supplements are necessary as directed by a holistic veterinarian.)

What can happen if you supplement your Lab's complete and balanced diet? If you add extra vitamins, for example, toxicity could result because the dog gets too much vitamin A. If you add too much wheat germ oil, your Lab could overdose on vitamins D and E. Eggs are a great source of protein, but too many raw eggs can cause a biotin deficiency. Biotin is necessary for a healthy coat and proper functioning of the nervous system. Raw egg whites contain an enzyme that destroys biotin.

Sometimes supplements are necessary—but only under veterinary supervision. For example, lactating bitches may require added nutrients, especially if they're nursing a large litter. Or a sled dog racing the Iditarod needs her diet supplemented with meats and fats so that she can consume the 10,000 to 15,000 calories a day needed to keep warm and maintain body weight while running 100 miles a day.

If you're feeding your Lab a commercially prepared diet that's complete and balanced and your Lab looks great, forget about supplements.

Medical Care Every Lab Needs

In This Chapter

○ Going to the Veterinarian
○ Preventive Medicine
○ Spaying and Neutering
○ Sick Calls and Emergencies

You are crucial to your Lab's good health. The loving attention, scrumptious diet, invigorating exercise, and fine-tooth grooming you provide are invaluable. Then there's veterinary care, which every Lab needs. Do you know what's required?

Going to the Veterinarian

Although you may not have given the idea much thought, regular veterinary visits are essential for your Lab's good health. Both you and the veterinarian are an integral part of your pet's health care team. Whether by preventing diseases through offering nutrition tips, or identifying and treating injuries as they arrive, the veterinarian is really your Lab's second-best friend. You're first, of course!

Your Lab will be healthiest when you take an active role in managing and overseeing her health, and that means partnering with a skilled veterinarian. As a caring owner you're responsible for the overall well-being and health of your Lab, from puppy-hood through her golden years.

The Right One

You can begin this oh-so-important partnership by choosing a qualified veterinarian whom you respect. Veterinarians are people, too, and they vary in personality, approach to treatment, and medical perspective. It's the veterinarian's job to diagnose your Lab's illnesses or provide preventive care, and it's your job to follow doctor's orders. But you must choose an individual you can work with. Suppose the vet recommends a treatment regime for your Lab's skin problems. You don't like or agree with the plan, so you ignore it. Who wins in this situation? Certainly not the dog. You must be willing to play your role on your Lab's health care team in order to win the game.

Veterinarians are people, too, and they vary in personality, approach to treatment, and medical perspective.

The usual academic degree for a U.S.-trained veterinarian is DVM or VMD, which both stand for doctor of veterinary medicine. Veterinarians usually operate a small- or large-animal practice. Small-animal veterinarians offer care for dogs, cats, birds, rabbits, and the like. Large-animal vets care for horses, cows, pigs, and goats. In spite of your Lab's good size, you'll want a vet

Oh, So Special

What's a veterinary specialist? That term can be confusing to owners. A glance under the heading "Veterinarian" in the yellow pages reveals a wide variety of listings under the vets' names: general medicine, specializing in surgery, cancer treatments, cardiology, vaccinations, dentistry, internal medicine. But a veterinary specialist isn't a practitioner who limits her practice to dogs or is interested in a particular area of medicine, such as dentistry. A veterinary specialist is a veterinarian who is board certified by a specialty board approved by the American Veterinary Medical Association (AVMA).

To earn the title of veterinary specialist, the veterinarian must complete a veterinary school program approved by the AVMA, usually extend her education by completing a one-year internship, and then finish a two- or three-year residency program in a particular discipline. He or she must be licensed to practice veterinary medicine in at least one state.

Once the educational requirements are finished, the vet then has to pass a battery of rigorous examinations in his or her field. Only then can he receive official certification by a specialty board, such as the American College of Veterinary Behaviorists or the American College of Zoological Medicine. Certification requirements vary but are governed by the American Board of Veterinary Specialists (ABVS).

The Board has specific guidelines on how specialists may list names or practices. Veterinarians may not imply or infer that they're specialists when they aren't. The terms an owner should look for when seeking out a true specialist are board certified (board eligible or board qualified aren't the same and are considered misleading by the ABVS), diplomate, ACVIM (American College of Veterinary Internal Medicine), and ABVP. The board-certified veterinary specialist's name and title are usually listed like this: Mary Veterinarian, D.V.M., Diplomate American Board of Veterinary Practitioners, Board Certified in Surgery.

If your Lab requires the services of a veterinary specialist, your general practitioner will usually give you a referral. If you want to contact a specialist on your own, contact your local or state veterinary association for a name or call the American Veterinary Medical Association at (800) 248-2862 for a listing of board-certified vets in your area. If you live near a school of veterinary medicine, contact the college. Many specialists work at veterinary colleges.

who works with small animals. This person will be your Lab's general practitioner.

Small-animal veterinarians may limit their practice to a certain species, a dog-only or cat-only practice, for example. Some vets have taken an interest in exotic pets, offering medical care to rabbits, birds, ferrets, and reptiles. Vets are also trained in medical specialties—currently 20 are recognized by the American Veterinary Medical Association (AVMA). Specialty disciplines include behavior, emergency care, dermatology, ophthalmology, and surgery. Although you won't want to start out with a specialist, you can find one for your Lab's specific health problem.

Veterinarians with a holistic approach to medicine can, in addition to their veterinary training, be certified in three alternative modalities approved by the AVMA: acupuncture, chiropractic, and homeopathy; certified veterinary acupuncturists are the most numerous. Licensed vets can get certification and accreditation for acupuncture through the International Veterinary Acupuncture Society and through a few state accreditation boards and veterinary courses. Chiropractic certification is available to licensed vets through the American Veterinary Chiropractic Association. Vets can get homeopathy certification through the Academy of Veterinary Homeopathy. Certification doesn't guarantee expertise in alternative therapies, but to the pet owner in search of a holistic veterinarian, it does indicate a vet's strong interest in the field.

How can you find the vet of your Lab's dreams?

○ Start by asking the Lab's breeder for a referral. Many times breeders have a favorite vet who treats all their dogs and pups. Word of mouth is always the best reference.

○ Ask a Lab rescue volunteer.

○ Ask a trusted dog-owning friend for a name.

○ Contact the local or closest Labrador Retriever club and ask for a referral.

○ Ask your Lab's trainer to recommend a vet.

○ Look in the yellow pages of your local telephone book.

○ Search the Internet. It's best to stick with national, well-recognized Lab clubs for a reference. Some have vet listings, or you can contact members who can recommend a vet in your area.

Once you've gotten a few names, visit the office. Look for a clean, well-lit, up-to-date, friendly environment. Chat with the staff and let them know you're searching for a vet. Don't be afraid to ask waiting clients what they think of the vet and staff. Ask for a tour (this might be difficult at busy times) and a listing of fees and services offered, such as grooming or emergency services. Does the vet sell pet supply products? Other considerations include location, convenient hours, and a helpful staff. Give the clinic a good look-see, make mental notes of what you like or dislike, and visit another clinic. Then make a decision.

Since *busy* is everyone's key word today, you may not have time to visit several clinics. It's the best way to research, but it does take time. If you really trust your Lab's breeder, chances are her veterinarian is a good starting point.

Since most breeder and adoption contracts stipulate that new owners must have the dog checked by a veterinarian of their choosing within a few days of purchase or adoption, you'll need to find the right vet before you pick up your Lab. That way you can have your new pet examined promptly.

Did You Know?

Shelters in the United States take in nearly 11 million cats and dogs each year. Nearly 75 percent of those animals have to be euthanized.

Questions to Ask Your Vet

Ask questions such as those listed below to evaluate whether a veterinarian is right for you and your dog.

○ What are your clinic's hours and where are you located?

○ How many vets work at the clinic? Can I request to see the same vet each time I visit or will I see whomever is available?

○ What type of equipment do you have on-hand at the clinic? If you do not have certain equipment, where would you send my dog to receive treatment? What is that facility's reputation?

○ Do you have a lab on-site or do you send out for test results? How quickly are results available?

○ Do you offer any add-on services, such as boarding or grooming?

○ What are the average fees for check-ups, spaying/neutering, vaccinations, etc.? Do you offer a wellness program or a multi-pet discount?

○ Do you treat any other Labs in your practice? (While much canine medicine applies to all breeds, certain diseases and health concerns apply specifically to Labs. You'll want to make sure your veterinarian is knowledgeable in such areas as Lab nutrition and genetic problems that run in the breed.)

First Impressions

The first visit with a veterinarian is an important one. It's the beginning or the end of a relationship. If you're pleased with the practitioner, it will be the beginning of a partnership aimed at supporting your Lab's good health. If you aren't pleased, it's all over. Either way, you've got to be prepared beforehand.

Whether your new Lab is a puppy or an adult, you must have the dog examined within a few days of purchase or adoption to determine his health status. To make the most of this first visit, it's wise to bring along the following:

❍ All health records, including vaccine history, deworming schedule, genetic tests/certification, surgeries, treatments. Be sure to obtain these from the breeder, owner, or rescue group;

❍ Breeder or adoption contracts;

❍ Medications your Lab is currently taking;

❍ A list of what your Lab has been eating, including specific ingredients in the diet;

❍ A stool sample, if requested by the clinic staff; and

❍ A list of questions or concerns you may have.

Getting the Lab to the clinic is often problematic for owners. If the Lab is a puppy, she may not be accustomed to car rides, and some adult dogs aren't either. To make the journey as safe as possible, fit your Lab with a collar and leash and put him in a crate in the car. It's better for the dog to be confined during the ride, especially if it's a first ride. You certainly don't want to risk the dog jumping about the car, distracting you and causing you to have a wreck. Later on you may want to teach your Lab to sit in the backseat with a safety restraint. But for this first, important visit, plan on using a crate.

What to Expect

What can you expect at this first visit with a veterinarian? For you, it's an opportunity to meet the vet up close and personal and learn more about proper health care for your Lab. It's a time to ask questions and chat with the vet to determine if this is the person you want caring for your dog. For your Lab, it's a time to determine her health status.

When you arrive at the clinic, the veterinary staff should or will ask you to fill out forms stating basic information to start a file: your name, address, and telephone number; your Lab's name, age, breeder, health history, and so on. Be sure to inform the staff that this is a first visit with a new dog, recommended by the breeder or rescue agency. After you've finished with paperwork, you and your dog may have to wait a few minutes. If so, be sure to keep your Lab on the leash, or if it's a small pup, in the crate or on your lap. That way your dog won't come in contact with other pets, who may be ill or quarrelsome.

Next, you and your Lab will be ushered into an examining room to await a consultation with the vet. A veterinary assistant may come in to ask a few questions or take the Lab's pulse, respiratory rate, and temperature.

When the veterinarian arrives, he'll greet you and your Lab, then get down to the serious business of investigating your Lab's health status. Most likely, the first exam will include:

○ A review of your Lab's health and vaccination and certification history;
○ Specific questions/discussion about your Lab's health history, diet, and lifestyle;
○ A careful check of the Lab from head to toe for signs of illness or infectious diseases, such as cloudy eyes, a runny nose, infected ears, irritated skin, or hair loss. This will include a look in your Lab's eyes, ears, and mouth and listening to her heart and lungs with a stethoscope. The vet may manipulate her legs and knees for soundness and feel her abdomen for lumps that could indicate a hernia or tumor. A distended belly can be a sign of internal parasites;
○ A check for congenital defects;
○ Planning a spay or neuter;
○ Planning a vaccination schedule;
○ An examination of the Lab's stool sample under a microscope for internal parasites and deworming if necessary;

❍ Heartworm testing/preventive;

❍ Discussion of behavior and training issues; and

❍ Grooming suggestions/toenail trim.

Although your Lab's appearance doesn't tell all, the veterinarian can learn a lot about your pet's health during this comprehensive physical exam. It's like checking a watermelon for ripeness. A watermelon that's ripe, juicy, and ready to eat feels and looks right. A Lab who's healthy feels and looks right, too. A veterinarian is trained to see and notice subtle signs of good or bad health.

But some illnesses can't be detected by a physical exam or may not be noticeable in the Lab. Many heritable diseases, such as hip dysplasia and elbow dysplasia, can't be found by a quick look-see. The vet may recommend tests to screen for these conditions. He may also advise testing for heartworms; it's essential before placing a dog on heartworm preventive medication. The vet may also recommend testing such as chest x rays or electrocardiogram if he hears a heart murmur, or blood tests to rule out liver or kidney problems if your dog is an older adult.

Once the vet completes the exam, it's your turn to ask questions. Perhaps you're unsure of how often to vaccinate or how to keep fleas at bay. Now is the time to ask the vet and make the most of your visit, especially if you're a new puppy owner. Remember, you must be able to communicate with this important member of your Lab's health care team. Ask away!

Go, Team!

Veterinarians generally agree that owners are crucial in managing the health of their pets. Your Lab will be the healthiest when you take an active role in overseeing her health. You and the veterinarian are both an integral part of your pet's health care team, In fact, your vet is counting on you!

The ideal situation is a partnership based on trust, listening, and determining needs. The ultimate goal is to have a healthy Lab.

Being partners with their veterinarians is a somewhat new idea to owners and to the veterinary community. Ten to 15 years ago most owners left the worries of their pets' health care to their vets. But the team approach is growing. Today owners are more aware, more educated, more concerned about their dogs' health.

What are your responsibilities as a member of your Lab's health care team? Will you don a mask and gown and perform surgery? Absolutely not! But that's what some owners envision when they think about managing their dogs' health. Taking an active role in your dog's health care is much simpler than that.

Learn as much as you can about your Lab—breed particulars, proper grooming, natural temperament, and appropriate training techniques. Learn about dogs in general: normal canine antics, roles as companions and workers, the variety of breeds, and common illnesses and diseases. Read books and magazines, surf the Internet, chat with other Lab owners, and consult with trainers and veterinarians. *Listen* to your vet. He's your primary source of information for healthcare concerns.

If you put in some effort, you'll be a better owner, according to veterinarians. An educated owner is likely to be a good owner.

Know what's normal for your Lab as a pup, adult, or oldster. If you know what's normal, you'll be able to spot changes. The more observations you make and the more understanding you have of your dog, the more useful information you can share with the vet. In fact, studying your Lab helps your vet diagnose illness. An accurate and detailed history help the vet piece together why an animal is having a particular problem. If you take an active role in your Lab's health care and partnering with your vet, you'll reap a plentiful harvest. The firm commitment you give your Lab is something to feel good about, and you'll sleep soundly at night, knowing you've attended to all your Lab's needs with care. You're showing your love for a wonderful companion.

Preventive Medicine

You've heard the adage: An ounce of prevention is worth a pound of cure. This saying rings especially true when it comes to preventing poor health and illness in your Lab. Preventive medicine—providing your Lab with care *before* something goes awry—is another important aspect of medical care every Lab needs.

Take Thee to the Clinic

The cornerstone of preventive care is regular veterinary visits. This may seem obvious, especially if you're a new owner of a Lab pup or adult. You've just had your pet checked or have an appointment scheduled for next week. But later on, when the newness of owning a Lab wears off, you may forget just how important these visits are.

Once or twice a year your vet should listen to your Lab's heart and lungs; check his eyes, nose, and mouth; feel for

Did You Know?

Tests conducted at the Institute for the Study of Animal Problems in Washington, D.C., revealed that dogs and cats, like humans, are either right- or left-handed.

suspicious lumps and bumps; take his temperature; check his internal organs and external joints; order tests; and check for internal parasites. Vaccine boosters may be in order, depending upon your Lab's individual vaccine schedule. These exams are invaluable! They give the vet a chance to evaluate your Lab's overall health and to spot potential health problems. Medical problems caught early are more easily treated and less expensive in the long run. And remember that because dogs age at a different rate than people, a once-a-year exam for your Lab would be like you having a physical every five years. Think how much your health can change in five years!

Make it a priority to take your Lab to the veterinary clinic every year or more often if advised by your practitioner. Senior dogs or those with chronic health problems may require more frequent examinations.

A Shot in the Arm

Another essential part of preventive medicine for your Lab is vaccinations. Vaccinations prevent dogs from getting a host of nasty diseases, such as rabies, parvovirus, and distemper. Vaccinations are given to boost the animal's immunity—or ability to fight—a particular disease.

There are two types of vaccines: modified live virus and killed virus vaccine. Some veterinarians think that modified live virus 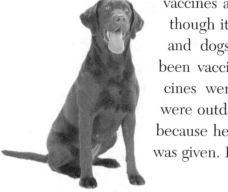 vaccines are most effective and longer lasting. Although it's not common, vaccines occasionally fail and dogs contract disease even though they've been vaccinated. This is usually because the vaccines weren't given correctly, were mishandled, were outdated or the dog didn't develop immunity because he was sick or immature when the vaccine was given. It is much more common to have vaccine

Sample Vaccination Schedule

This chart shows a possible vaccination schedule. Contact your vet as soon as you bring your puppy home to schedule his first checkup and to set up the perfect vaccination schedule for your pet.

8 Weeks: Distemper, hepatitis, leptospirosis, parainfluenza, and parvo (DHLPP), usually combined in one injection.

12 Weeks: DHLPP, possibly Lyme disease and bordetella

16 Weeks: DHLPP, rabies, Lyme disease (if begun at 12 weeks)

20 Weeks: Parvo booster for pups considered at high risk

1 Year after last vaccination: DHLPP, rabies, and bordetella and Lyme, if previously given

failure when the owner or breeder vaccinates—so it's not recommended. Your veterinarian knows how to properly give vaccines, handle them, and store them. And his pre-vaccination exam will tell him if there's a chance your dog has an illness that might prevent the vaccine from working properly.

Young pups receive special antibodies from their mother's milk that protects them against disease. Once the pups are weaned, they lose this protection, which is why, beginning at six to eight weeks, pups need to start a series of vaccinations to build immunity. Even after beginning vaccinations, young pups are vulnerable to disease. Many vets recommend limiting puppy's exposure to other dogs until his first series of shots is complete.

To remain effective, vaccinations must be current. That means after your Lab pup's initial shots, he'll require boosters yearly or as directed by the veterinarian. Some vaccines are required by law. Many states mandate a yearly rabies vaccine—dogs must show proof of rabies vaccination to be licensed.

Good Food

Okay, were you really paying attention last chapter? If so, you'll know why good food acts as preventive medicine for your Lab. Here's a reminder why that's so.

Food is the fuel required to nourish your Lab's body. The body needs a special balance of nutrients to make energy and sustain good health. If that balance is upset, either by lack of food or the wrong foods, health problems can arise. A deficiency or excess in any nutrient can lead to illness.

Your Lab needs good food to be in top health—a proper diet that supplies all the nutrients appropriate to his life stage. If you feed your Lab properly, he's probably going to be healthy. If you don't feed him properly, his health will suffer.

Get Up and Go!

In addition to a proper diet, your chubby-prone Lab needs adequate exercise to maintain good health. If your Lab doesn't get enough exercise, she'll gain weight—that's a guarantee. And an overweight Lab is an unhealthy Lab.

You can prevent the health problems associated with obesity by encouraging (as if you need to) your Lab to get up and go. For activity suggestions see chapter 8, "Family Life." Pick something you both enjoy, and get busy!

Heartworm Prevention and Routine Dewormings

It's fairly common for dogs to have internal parasites, such as hookworms, tapeworms, whipworms, roundworms, or heartworms. All survive by living off their host, your Lab. If your dog is infected with any internal parasites, his health will suffer. Internal parasites literally suck the life out of their host.

Heartworms, which are spread via mosquitoes, are especially dangerous. Fortunately there are medications on the market that prevent infestation. Heartworm preventive medicine makes good sense, especially in areas with heavy mosquito infestation. Ask your vet if heartworm preventive is necessary for your Lab, in your area. A test is required before giving the dog medication to make sure he isn't already infected. Make sure you ask your vet about the heartworm test and preventative for your dog—a heartworm infestation is fatal unless treated. And treatment is both expensive and hard on your dog.

Routine doses of deworming medicine may be necessary for your Lab to prevent ill health from hookworms, tapeworms, whipworms, and roundworms. Most once-a-month heartworm preventatives also keep your dog free of most of these parasites, except tapeworms.

Flea Control

There's no doubt about it. Fleas are extremely irritating, annoying pests. But did you know that if left uncontrolled, a flea infestation on your Lab can actually cause poor health? A heavily infested Lab can become anemic from all the biting and bloodsucking. And if your Lab ingests a flea while biting and scratching, he could become infested with tapeworms. Fleas frequently harbor immature tapeworms in their intestines; they acquire the parasite by eating tapeworm eggs. Once the dog swallows an infested flea, it too becomes infested.

As if that isn't bad enough, fleas are also the cause of flea bite dermatitis. Some animals are highly allergic to the flea's bite—and it only takes one chomp. The result is an itching-scratching-chewing cycle that's hard to break. The pet is miserable, and he looks bad, too. The coat thins from all the chewing and scratching, and the skin is red, irritated, and ripe for a secondary bacterial infection.

The best way to prevent these maladies is to keep fleas under control on your Lab. It's not easy, but it's the best way to prevent severe problems later on. Ask your veterinarian to recommend a flea control program for your Lab.

Grooming and Teeth Care

Labs don't need much grooming. They look great as is. But grooming can actually be a great addition to your preventive medicine program. Brushing is good for the Lab's skin: it removes dead hair, increases circulation, and promotes oil production. More important, the time you spend brushing and fussing over your Lab gives you an opportunity to check the dog for signs of ill health. Do you see any lumps or bumps? How about a tender ear, the beginning of an ear infection? The sooner you notice anything unusual, the better. You can call your vet and begin immediate treatment.

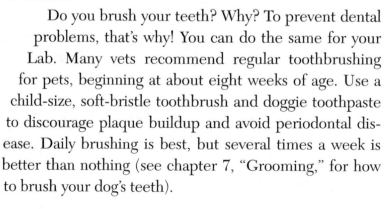

Do you brush your teeth? Why? To prevent dental problems, that's why! You can do the same for your Lab. Many vets recommend regular toothbrushing for pets, beginning at about eight weeks of age. Use a child-size, soft-bristle toothbrush and doggie toothpaste to discourage plaque buildup and avoid periodontal disease. Daily brushing is best, but several times a week is better than nothing (see chapter 7, "Grooming," for how to brush your dog's teeth).

Safety

Just as the parents of young children must be on red alert for dangers surrounding their little ones, so must you be aware of potential dangers to your Lab in your home, yard, and environment. You can't foresee the future, but being on your toes can prevent injuries and accidents that will cause you and your Lab pain and heartache.

First, be mindful of your Lab's curious nature. He'll want to investigate everything! You'll have to supervise your Lab carefully to keep him out of trouble.

You'll need to pet proof your Lab's environment (see chapter 2, "Welcome Home!"). Take this seriously—you really can prevent tragedy by thinking ahead.

Store all toxins (medicine, household cleaners, paint, antifreeze) up and away from your curious Lab, and teach her not to chew anything but owner-approved toys. Labs love chewing, and pups find electrical cords irresistible. These are deadly!

When you're out, keep your Lab on a leash. If there's some kind of interesting trouble to find, your Lab will find it. A curious and wandering Lab could be bitten by a wild animal, stung by an insect, eat a poisonous plant, or cut by walking on a piece of glass.

Labs love to swim, but be careful where you let your dog take a splash. Make sure the Lab can walk in and out of the body of water easily, and be sure the water isn't polluted.

Spaying and Neutering

Spaying or neutering is another important link in preventive medicine. Surgically altering your Lab so she can't breed has many health benefits. For example, female dogs spayed before

Breeding Myths—Common Misconceptions About Breeding Dogs

○ Females need to birth one litter to calm down.

○ "Mother" dogs are sweeter and gentler than females that never have puppies.

○ Children should experience the miracle of birth close up.

○ By breeding my dog, I'll produce a puppy just like him/her.

○ By selling puppies, I'll offset some of the money I've spent on my dog.

the first heat cycle are less likely to develop breast cancer, and spaying eliminates the chance of pyometra, a potentially fatal uterine infection. There are no behavioral or health benefits to allowing your female Lab to first have a litter, then spaying her.

Unneutered male dogs are at higher risk of developing prostate problems and certain cancers. When neutered, male dogs are less likely to roam, looking for a mate, and possibly getting hit by a car or getting into a fight in the process.

A spayed or neutered pet is a more contented pet than one left intact. Altering before puberty can prevent some aggressive behavior. Spaying or neutering doesn't make a Lab overweight.

But that's not all. Spaying or neutering your Lab will prevent unwanted litters that add to the already overpopulated world of homeless animals. "But my Lab is a purebred," you say. Well, even purebreds shouldn't be bred. Approximately 30 percent of the eight to 12 million animals entering humane shelters in the United

Myths About Spaying and Neutering Your Dog

- ○ It is unnatural to sterilize a dog.
- ○ Males are no longer "macho" and become wimps.
- ○ Females will never calm down.
- ○ Males will no longer protect their homes and owners.
- ○ Females will not be as friendly.
- ○ Both males and females will become fat and lazy.
- ○ Both males and females will lose their playfulness.

States are purebred, according to the American Humane Association. There simply aren't enough good homes to go around for purebreds and mixed breeds alike. Do your part to stop pet overpopulation! Spay or neuter your Lab.

Dogs are usually altered at five to eight months of age; they tolerate anesthesia well at this age and heal quickly. Some veterinarians alter much younger pups, eight to 12 weeks of age. Although early spay/neuter surgeries are not widespread, they do have a following, especially among humane workers concerned about pet overpopulation. Altering a young puppy before it has a chance to breed ensures he won't grow up to add the population of homeless animals.

Consult with your veterinarian about the right time to spay or neuter your Lab. If you're adopting an adult from a shelter or rescue organization, the procedure has probably already been done. If that's the case, you're already on the way to preventing illness in your Lab's future.

Signs Your Lab
Is Feeling Under the Weather

Do you suspect your Lab is a little under the weather? Below are some signs that may indicate your Lab isn't feeling well and needs to see her veterinarian:

○ Acts tired and sluggish and would rather stay in bed. Even refuses fetching a ball;

○ Isn't hungry—refuses several meals in a row;

○ Drinks an excessive amount of water;

○ Throws up several times;

○ Diarrhea or blood in stools;

○ Whimpers when touched;

○ Drools excessively;

○ Loses weight but isn't on a weight loss program;

○ Gums are very pale or very red;

○ Coat looks dull and feels rough;

○ Tummy looks bloated;

○ Eyes or nose is runny;

○ Scoots or bites or chews at rear end;

○ Coughs and sneezes a lot; or

○ Limps or walks abnormally.

Sick Calls and Emergencies

Trauma or injury can befall your beloved Lab in the wink of an eye. Although it's certainly not something you want to think about, you must. Because what will you do if your Lab suddenly becomes ill?

When to Call the Veterinarian

If your Lab is sick or injured, do you know when to call the veterinarian? Some owners panic if their pet limps for 30 seconds; others ignore a red, runny eye. Knowing when to call the vet can go a long way toward your Lab getting the right care at the right time.

Generally call the veterinary clinic immediately if you notice:

○ Wounds that expose bone or are actively bleeding or bleeding from the mouth, which could indicate internal bleeding;
○ Difficulty breathing;
○ A temperature higher than 104 degrees Fahrenheit (See chapter 5)
○ Paralysis, trouble walking;
○ Eye injuries, unequal pupil size, or irregular eye movements;
○ Straining to urinate but not passing urine;
○ Broken bones;
○ Sudden onset of severe diarrhea or vomiting;
○ Shock or convulsions;
○ Burns;
○ Non-productive vomiting;
○ Painful or swollen abdomen;
○ Gums that are white, blue, grey, or very pale pink rather than bright pink;
○ Bloody diarrhea;
○ Blood in vomit or urine; or
○ Profound depression.

Call within 12 to 24 hours if you notice:

○ Minor wounds that aren't actively bleeding;
○ Depression or loss of appetite;
○ A slightly elevated temperature;
○ Moderate lameness;
○ Runny eyes or nose;
○ Straining to urinate but passing urine;
○ Diarrhea or vomiting that lasts longer than 24 hours;
○ Mild coughing or any abnormality that worries you.

In the event of trauma or the sudden onset of illness in your Lab, you may have to render first aid. This is a common term, but what exactly does it mean? First aid is the initial help following an illness or accident that can save a dog's life, although it's not a substitute for professional care. The objectives of first aid are to (1) preserve life, (2) relieve suffering, and (3) prevent the illness or injury from becoming worse until the animal can be treated by a veterinarian.

To know whether or not you must administer first aid, first assess your Lab's illness or injury. The following conditions require immediate attention:

❍ Bleeding;
❍ Difficulty breathing;
❍ Shock (The signs of shock are shivering, listlessness, weakness, cold feet and legs. A dog in shock may also have pale gums and mucus membranes and a weak pulse.);
❍ Poisoning;
❍ Heatstroke; and
❍ Burns and frostbite.

Emergencies happen without warning, so it's a wise dog owner who prepares for the unexpected. Study first aid basics. Keep on hand a canine medical book, such as the *Dog Owner's Home Veterinary Handbook,* by Delbert Carlson, D.V.M., and James Giffin, M.D., and your vet's phone number (day and night) by the telephone. And don't forget to prepare a first aid kit (see chapter 2, "Welcome Home!" and see chapter 5, "Common Health Concerns," for more information on first aid and emergency care).

On the Road to Good Health

Exactly what the vet will do to restore your Lab's health depends on the type of illness or injury and varies among individual veterinarians. You can expect the veterinarian to examine the ill or injured animal, run tests if necessary, and then develop a treatment plan. A hospital stay may be required, or you may be asked to treat or medicate your Lab at home. Follow-up visits may be in order.

It's important to remember that a reputable veterinarian has your Lab's best interests in mind when she's treating the animal. Be sure to follow through on the doctor's orders. If your Lab needs medication three times a day, make sure it's administered three times a day. Let the doctor do her part, and make sure you do yours. Your Lab depends on you!

> It's important to remember that a reputable veterinarian has your Lab's best interests in mind when she's treating the animal. Be sure to follow through on the doctor's orders.

Administering Medications

The thought of giving their pet medicine often makes pet owners cringe. But if you know a few tricks of the trade, it's not as difficult as you might think. Besides, Labs are great patients. Most are fairly easy to treat and medicate.

Pills, tablets, and capsules. Don't be tempted to crunch up Labbie's medication and serve it with breakfast. Medications are often bitter tasting, even to Labs. Chances are breakfast and the medicine will go uneaten. Instead, simply open the Lab's mouth and place the pill at the very back of his throat. Then close his mouth and hold it shut. Stroke the dog's throat gently until he swallows. Be sure to place the pill in the center of the back of the throat. If you place it too far on either side, your Lab can work the tablet forward and spit it out.

Liquids. A large-size sterile plastic syringe (sans needle) is ideal for administering liquid medications. Draw in the measured amount of medicine, tilt the Lab's head back slightly, and place the syringe into the dog's mouth between the cheek and molars. Hold the Lab's mouth shut and squirt the medicine in a little at a time. Mmmm!

Eye ointments. Ophthalmic medications are simple to use, too. Pull down the dog's lower eyelid and squeeze a dab of ointment onto the eyelid's inner surface. Rub the eyelid gently to distribute the medication. Eyedrops can be applied by holding the dog's eye open (top and bottom) and dropping the medication directly on the eyeball. Don't touch the eyelid or eyeball with ointment tubes or droppers.

Ear medications. Hold your Lab's ear up vertically so you can see the ear canal. Squeeze the ear ointment deep into the ear, but be sure not to touch the inside of the ear with the tube so you don't accidentally injure the delicate ear canal skin. Keep holding the ear flap up with one hand, and with the other, gently massage the base of the ear to distribute the medicine. Be prepared once you let go, though. Most dogs will shake dramatically after having their ears medicated. You could end up with ear medicine on you as well as in your Lab's ears.

Costs

The reality of owning a Lab is that it requires money. You'll need to pay for veterinary care along with everything else, such as food, dishes, and training fees. The good news is that routine annual care for a healthy Lab isn't terribly expensive. The Humane Society of the United States estimates that the average dog owner spends $135 a year on medical care. Puppyhood can be more expensive, with vaccines alone costing $200 the first year, $65 a year thereafter.

The bad news is that emergency services, long-term treatment for a chronic condition, or care from a veterinary specialist can be quite costly, adding up to four digits very quickly. For example, one year of chemotherapy treatment for a dog suffering from cancer can cost as much as $3,000.

Yikes! That Much $$?

According to the *American Veterinary Medical Association 1997 U.S. Pet Ownership and Demographic Source Book,* total veterinary medical expenditures for dogs were estimated to be approximately $7 billion in 1996; some 95.22 million dogs visited the veterinarian. The average cost of those office visits was $73.60, an increase of $23.64 from 1991. Seven billion dollars is no small change. But why does veterinary care cost so much?

Although it's less costly than human medicine, veterinary medicine is no less sophisticated (a canine CAT scan, or computerized axial tomography scan, used to detect abnormalities deep within the

> **Did You Know?**
>
> Big dogs have larger litters than smaller dogs, but smaller dogs generally live longer.

How to Make an Insurance Claim

It's your responsibility as a policyholder to make the best use of your insurance plan. Take these steps to get the most for your money:

1. Designate a file for pet insurance forms.

2. Always take a claim form with you to the veterinarian's office. Many companies require a veterinarian's signature.

3. Make copies of receipts. A receipt must accompany every claim form. Some companies require only copies; others require originals. Keep a copy for your records.

4. Make copies of completed claim forms. If a question or payment issue arises, a copy to review on your end of the phone line will be reassuring.

5. Note an acceptable payment period on your calendar. Reimbursement may slip your mind, and it may be delayed in cases where a problem is encountered and you forget to inquire about the payment's status.

6. Mark claims paid and date received. Leave a paper trail that's easy to understand. Looking back a year later, you'll be glad for the notations.

©1999 Solveig Fredrickson

body, usually abnormalities in the brain, in dogs costs $300 to $700; a human CAT scan costs $750 to $1,000). Expensive technical procedures are available for animals just as they are for people; for example, hip replacements for dogs with dysplasia; magnetic resonance imaging (MRI), which is used to detect tissue abnormalities; and eye surgery. You name it, a medical treatment is available for your Labrador Retriever. All these sophisticated treatments require highly trained individuals to perform them and high-tech equipment. These factors, along with economic inflation, contribute to the high cost of veterinary care.

The Money Talk

Some people consider it socially unacceptable to discuss veterinary fees, but the best advice is to talk about them openly. Ask the veterinary staff for a list of services and their fees. How much is an office visit, basic vaccinations, or spaying or neutering? What will the vet charge to test your Lab for heartworms, and how much is the monthly preventative? Know what your individual vet will charge for his services and procedures so you won't be shocked when you receive the bill.

In addition to asking about customary fees, communicate with your veterinarian. Make an effort to develop a relationship with this important member of your Lab's health care team. If you're concerned about specific treatment costs, tell him. Perhaps the veterinarian can suggest less expensive treatment options, such as rest and medication for a short period, before ordering more expensive tests. Some veterinary clinics offer three- and six-month, same-as-cash payment plans or longer-term interest financing. And don't forget to ask for a discount. Some veterinarians offer discounts on certain services for seniors or regular clients.

There's no shame in discussing treatment costs with your veterinarian. It's a fact of life vets are very familiar with. They know there's a limit to what families can pay for their pets, and they know the money comes out of pocket. Most veterinarians are willing to work with owners concerned about costs.

Pet Insurance and Rainy Day Savings

With the increase in veterinary costs and the increase of owner commitment to top-of-the-line

Ten Questions to Ask Every Provider

Before choosing a pet insurance or membership plan, be sure to get straight-forward answers to all your questions. If it makes you more comfortable, get the answers in writing.

1. Does your policy follow fee/benefits schedules? If so, please send me your detailed coverage limits. In the meantime, please give me examples of coverage limits for three common canine procedures so I can compare them to my current veterinary charges.

2. Does your policy cover basic wellness care, or does it cover only accidents and illnesses? Do you offer a wellness care endorsement that I can purchase on top of my basic plan for an additional fee? What other endorsements do you offer, and how much do they cost?

3. Under your policy's rules, can I continue taking my Lab to its current veterinarian, or do I need to switch to another veterinarian?

4. Does your policy cover hereditary conditions, congenital conditions or pre-existing conditions? Please explain each coverage or exclusion as it pertains specifically to my Lab. Is there a feature where pre-existing conditions will be covered if my Lab's pre-existing condition requires no treatment after a specified period? What is that period?

5. What happens to my premium and to my Lab's policy if your company goes out of business? What guarantees do I have that I won't be throwing my money away?

6. How quickly do you pay claims?

7. What is your policy's deductible? Does the deductible apply per incident or annually? How does the deductible differ per plan?

8. Does the policy have payment limits over a year's period or during my pet's lifetime? How do the payment limits differ per plan?

9. What is the A.M. Best Co. rating of your insurance underwriter, and what does that rating mean?

10. Is there a cancellation period after I receive my policy or membership? How long do I have to review all my materials once I receive them, and what is the cancellation procedure?

©1999 Solveig Fredrickson

care for pets has come pet health insurance, medical plans designed to defray the costs of hip replacement surgery, for example, which could run $3,500 out of pocket. Although only 1 percent of U.S. pets are covered by such plans, some owners, who will do anything to save a pet, are interested in pet health insurance. In Great Britain 10 percent of the nation's pets have health insurance, and in Sweden 17 percent of pets are covered.

Most plans cover only accidents or illness—no well-doggie checkups, immunizations, parasite treatment, or genetic conditions—which is why not many pets in the United States have health insurance.

Still, pet health insurance can be a lifesaver if the unforeseen should happen: your Lab is diagnosed with cancer, or she needs extensive surgery. Although most pet owners can afford the low cost of caring for a healthy animal, an ill pet is another story.

Shop carefully for pet insurance. Check out yearly costs and deductibles and know which treatments and exams are and aren't covered, whether preexisting conditions are covered, and so on. To learn more about pet insurance policies currently available, see the resources section in appendix A.

Another plan is to buy some self-insurance. Simply set up a rainy day savings fund especially for your Labrador Retriever. Use it for routine care or unexpected treatment. According to the Humane Society of the United States, the average cost of owning a dog is $1,200 a year, including food. If you can squirrel away $100 or more a month, you'll have a nice nest egg when you need it.

Common Health Concerns

The Labrador Retriever is a hardy, robust breed. Most Labs are very healthy and require little medical attention other than preventive care. But the Lab isn't Superdog, able to leap tall buildings in a single bound and 100 percent immune to the ailments, diseases, and maladies that can befall canine companions. As a responsible Lab owner, you need to know about the health conditions that are especially prevalent in the Lab breed and some of the common ones that can affect all dogs.

You'd have to read volumes for a comprehensive look at canine health problems. This chapter is meant to be an introduction to the health issues the average Lab owner may face during her dog's lifetime.

Parasites, Inside and Out

Let's begin by taking a look at a few of the creepy crawlies that commonly affect dogs. Dogs are susceptible to what are called *internal* and *external parasites*. These parasites make their living by staying inside or outside the dog's body. Most dogs are infested with internal or external parasites at some point during their lifetime. It's important to keep your Lab free of all parasites; if left untreated, they can make your dog very ill. But an infestation isn't necessarily a sign that your Lab is weak or diseased. Internal and external parasites are a very common fact of life with dogs (and cats). The important thing is to learn what they are, how to recognize the signs of infestation, and how to get treatment promptly.

> Most dogs are infested with internal or external parasites at some point during their lifetime.

Internal Parasites

Internal parasites are just that: organisms that live inside your dog's body, usually in the intestine, but also the heart. You can usually tell a dog is infested with some type of internal parasite when you notice:

○ Unexplained weight loss;
○ A shiny hair coat has turned dull;
○ Overall poor condition;
○ Lethargy and weakness;
○ Coughing;
○ Shortness of breath;
○ Diarrhea or dark, bloody stools;
○ What appear to be bits of rice in the dog's feces.

Let's discuss internal parasites one at a time. First, there are *roundworms*, or ascarids, one of the most common internal parasites found in dogs. Adult roundworms thrive in the dog's intestine, growing from one to seven inches long. How do they get in your Lab's intestine? Dogs pick up roundworms by coming in contact with dirt or soil that contains roundworm eggs. Your Lab is sniffing the yard, picks up eggs on his nose, and ingests them. The eggs hatch in the intestine, and the larvae make their way to the lungs via the bloodstream. The larvae then return to the intestine and grow into adult roundworms.

Roundworms are especially common in puppies. In fact, most pups are born with roundworm larvae acquired from the dam during gestation. Pups can also ingest roundworm larvae from nursing.

Although the idea of larvae and adult worms inside your Lab's body is certainly repulsive, they aren't necessarily a severe health risk to the adult dog. Severe infestations in pups can be more serious and even lead to death.

Dogs infested with roundworms usually have a dull coat and potbelly. The dog may also vomit, lose weight, and have diarrhea, and you may see worms in the stool or vomit. Roundworms look like small, white earthworms or spaghetti that moves.

Roundworms can affect people, usually children. But because people aren't the usual host for this parasite, the larvae don't grow into adults. Instead they migrate throughout the body and may cause fever, anemia, an enlarged liver, or pneumonia.

A dog with roundworms must be treated by a veterinarian. The vet will determine if the puppy or adult dog has roundworms by checking a stool sample under the microscope. Then the vet will prescribe medication, commonly called a dewormer. Pups are usually dewormed several times to make sure larvae don't grow into adults. For an exact deworming schedule for your Lab pup or adult, consult your veterinarian.

Hookworms are another creepy crawly that can affect your Lab. A dog becomes infested with hookworms by coming in contact with soil or feces that contain hookworm larvae. The larvae migrate to the intestine, where they grow into adults, which are small, thin worms one-quarter- to one-half-inch long. They attach to the wall of the small intestine and make their living by drawing blood from the host. A dog infested with hookworms passes eggs in its feces, thereby continuing the chain for future infestations.

Hookworms can affect adult dogs but are probably more common in pups, who can acquire them through the dam's milk. A severe hookworm infestation causes bloody, dark stools and anemia and can be deadly to small pups. In adult dogs, hookworms usually cause diarrhea, anemia, and weight loss.

Hookworms can be detected in the feces, which is how the vet detects a hookworm infestation. Deworming is essential but fairly simple—the vet will prescribe a dewormer medication. Continued treatment may be necessary for small pups with severe infestations.

You've probably heard about *tapeworms,* those nasty parasites that can grow up to several feet long inside a dog's small intestine. The tapeworm head fastens to the intestine wall and the worm makes its living off the host. The tapeworm body consists of segments that contain egg packets. The segments, about a quarter-inch in length, are passed in the feces and look like rice.

The most common type of tapeworm that affects dogs is acquired when the dog ingests a flea that has immature tapeworms in its intestine. Fleas become infested by eating tapeworm eggs. The immature tapeworms travel to the intestine and grow into adults.

Dogs can also become infested with tapeworms by eating uncooked meat, raw fish, or dead animals.

Surprisingly, tapeworms don't have severe effects on dogs. Even a severe infestation causes only mild diarrhea, weight loss, or loss of appetite. Tapeworm segments are also noticeable in the feces.

Although the ill effects from tapeworms are mild, they must be eradicated from your Lab's body for her to enjoy the best health. Following a veterinary diagnosis of tapeworms, deworming is essential.

Another internal parasite your Lab may acquire is *whipworms*. Whipworms are two to three inches long and have a whiplike appearance. Adult whipworms live in the large intestine and survive by fastening to the intestine wall. Whipworm infestations are less noticeable than those of other internal parasites, partly because the female whipworm lays fewer eggs. Sometimes this makes a whipworm infestation difficult to detect. Heavy infestations do occur, though, and dogs with whipworms lose weight, have diarrhea, and are in poor condition.

A dog with whipworms must be treated by a veterinarian, although several checks may be necessary for an accurate diagnosis.

Heartworms are another internal parasite your Labrador Retriever might get. Heartworm infestation begins when the larvae from an infested mosquito is injected into the dog as a mosquito feeds. Once inside, the larvae grow into adult, sexually mature worms. This takes three to four months. The worms make their way into a vein and are carried to the right side of the heart, where they remain. Adult heartworms are four to 12 inches

Did You Know?

Dogs and humans are the only animals with prostates.

in length and can live up to five years in the dog's heart. These adult worms reproduce, producing microfilaria, or immature heartworms; a female can product up to 5,000 microfilaria a day.

To complete the parasite cycle, the microfilaria must go to a secondary host, the mosquito. Once ingested by a mosquito, they develop into infective larvae. The infective larvae then move to the mouth of the mosquito and are ready to infect the new host—your Lab—when the mosquito comes calling for a blood meal.

At first, a dog infected with heartworms has no symptoms. In fact, dogs can have heartworms for several years before showing signs. A heartworm diagnosis is made when the vet finds either microfilaria or anti-heartworm antigen in the blood. Heartworms eventually take a toll, and the dog may begin to cough, be short of breath, and be unable to exercise. The sick dog is tired, weak, in poor condition, and loses weight. As the number and size of the heartworms increase, the dog's breathing is labored even when she's resting. Eventually, without treatment, she may suffer congestive heart failure, liver failure, or kidney failure and will die.

Once a dog infested with heartworms shows clinical symptoms, treatment is difficult and potentially dangerous. The medications used to kill heartworms and their larvae are extremely toxic, and the dog must be strong enough to withstand the treatment. Occasionally adult worms are surgically removed in those dogs too ill to withstand the medication. Because of the risks associated with treatment, hospitalization is usually necessary.

The good news on heartworms is that you can get preventive medications for your Lab. Depending on where you live and the prevalence of heartworms, the vet may recommend a heartworm preventive for your Lab. These drugs kill microfilaria before they grow into adults. Many vets recommend daily doses beginning several weeks before and after mosquito season. Another preventive may be prescribed once a month to kill young worms that have accumulated. If you live in an area where mosquitoes are year-round pests, some vets recommend starting pups on heartworm preventives at nine to 12 weeks of age and continuing for the remainder of the dog's life. Although effective, heartworm preventives can have mild to severe side effects, so be sure to discuss them with your veterinarian.

Your Lab must be tested for the presence of heartworms before starting on preventive medication and tested once or twice a year thereafter. The test is to make sure the dog is microfilaria-free; otherwise, she could have a fatal reaction to the medicine.

The only fail-safe way to keep your Lab from being infested by heartworms is to keep her from being bitten by a mosquito. That's impossible, but you can minimize opportunities for mosquitoes to bite her by keeping her indoors when the little buggers come out to feed in the evening. Spray your yard and kennel areas for mosquitoes. Also, mosquitoes thrive and breed in swamps or areas of brackish water and are more common in coastal areas. Steer your dog clear of these areas if possible.

> The good news on heartworms is that you can get preventive medications for your Lab.

Protozoans are one-celled organisms, invisible to the naked eye; they're responsible for a number of conditions in dogs. Of all the protozoan diseases found worldwide, only two are common in pet dogs: coccidiosis and giardiasis. An infestation by a protozoan parasite usually results when the dog ingests the cyst form, or oocyst, of the protozoan. These cysts then migrate to the bowel, where they mature and eventually shed in the feces.

Coccidia is an internal protozoan parasite that's most common in puppies, although adult dogs can be affected. Coccidiosis is usually found in young dogs in overcrowded, unsanitary, or cold, damp conditions. Pups can be infected by their mother or pick up the parasite in a contaminated environment; it spreads quickly through a kennel. Coccidia can lie dormant, causing the pup no ill health, but become active during a period of stress. Infected pups usually have mild diarrhea at first. As the infection progresses, the pup may have mucuslike, bloody diarrhea, become anemic and weak, and lose appetite. Pups and dogs that become sick but recover can become carriers, harboring the organism quietly in their intestines and infecting others.

Veterinary treatment is essential for coccidiosis. The vet will provide supportive treatment, such as stopping the diarrhea. A drug to kill the protozoan will be prescribed.

A clean kennel is a healthy kennel rings especially true with coccidiosis. Good hygiene helps prevent it, and once a dog is infected, it's essential to keep it from spreading. Infected pups and dogs must be isolated from other dogs, fecal matter picked up, and the area cleaned with boiling water or disinfectant to kill oocysts. Once *coccidia* is established in the environment, it can be very hard to kill. If you're having trouble, consult your vet.

Giardia, the cause of giardiasis, is another protozoan parasite that affects dogs (and people). The giardia parasite is usually waterborne—found in lakes, streams, or rivers. The most common sign of giardiasis is diarrhea, mixed with mucus and blood. The diagnosis of giardiasis is made when the giardia protozoan is seen under the microscope during a fecal examination.

Treatment is essential, and the veterinarian will prescribe medication to kill the giardia parasite. Because giardia can spread to people, families with infected pets must be very careful to treat the animal and clean up feces.

External Parasites

What goes inside also goes outside, sort of. Your Lab can be infested not only with internal parasites but also with external parasites, such as fleas, ticks, skin mites, and ringworm. Here's the scoop on what you might find crawling in, around, or under that lovely Lab coat.

You may not see them, but surely you've felt them, especially if you live in a climate that's warm all year. We're talking *fleas,* those biting bugs that just love to chew on pets.

> Fleas have to make a living, too, and they do it by biting your Lab and feeding on his blood.

Fleas have to make a living, too, and they do it by biting your Lab and feeding on his blood. If you're nearby, you're likely to get bitten, too. Flea bites itch, and they're very irritating to your dog. A Lab with fleas can be seen biting, scratching, biting, scratching, and so on. In most cases, a flea infestation causes only this mild discomfort, but some dogs are highly allergic to the saliva of the flea. The result is flea allergy dermatitis, a condition marked by red, irritated skin, hair loss, and misery. Secondary bacterial infections can also occur.

As if that isn't enough, since the flea is the intermediate host of the tapeworm (these bad guy parasites all have to work together, you know), most dogs with a lot of fleas also end up with tapeworms.

How can you tell if your Lab has fleas? Your Lab's biting and scratching are a major clue, and flea dirt—small, sand-size black-and-white grains—is a big indicator. Flea dirt is flea feces and flea eggs. The fecal matter is actually digested blood, your Lab's blood. When dampened on a white piece of paper, flea dirt turns reddish brown.

You may also see the flea in person. It's a small, dark brown bug that looks like a dot. It doesn't fly, but it jumps. And boy, can fleas jump! Some sources say more than 100 times their own body length. Fleas thrive in a warm, humid environment, which is why they love living on dogs' bodies. And the higher the temperature and humidity, the more they reproduce. Fleas mate right there on your Lab; a female can lay some 2,000 eggs in a lifetime. The eggs either stay on the dog and hatch or fall off in your yard, the dog's crate, or your carpeting and hatch. Once the eggs hatch into larvae, they feed and continue developing into a pupal stage. If conditions are right, adult fleas follow in two to three weeks, although fleas can remain in the pupal stage for several months without a meal. Once the fleas are hungry adults, they search for a host—your Lab as he walks by.

There are many, many ways to control fleas on your dog and in your home and yard: pesticide-based flea dips, shampoos, topical treatments such as Advantage, Spot-on, and Frontline, flea collars, sprays, foggers, and powders. Your veterinarian can prescribe anti-flea pills or you can buy natural products, such as herbal collars, flea traps, and flea combs. The selection of flea control products is seemingly endless, but it has to be. Fleas are tough to eradicate.

Regardless of what type of products you use, remember this: It's a battle to get rid of fleas, and you've got to fight constantly, especially if you live in an area that's warm year-round. You've got to plan a three-pronged attack and do it all at the same time:

1. Eliminate fleas on your Lab;
2. Eliminate fleas in the house (including your Lab's bedding); and
3. Eliminate fleas in the yard.

For example, on the day you take your Lab to the grooming shop for a flea bath, fog the house and spray the yard. If you just bathe your Lab and fail to get rid of the fleas in the house and yard, then as soon as Labbie returns home the fleas will hop back on. You're right back where you started—you still have fleas and your wallet is a lot lighter. So, remember that your fight against fleas has to include the dog, house, and yard all at the same time.

But getting rid of fleas isn't a onetime battle: just a flea bath and good spraying of the house and yard once a year in the spring. Ha! Fighting fleas is a series of consistent battles. For example, spray the yard once a month, vacuum the house every day (to pick up flea eggs and live fleas wandering about), fog the house every six weeks, spray your Lab and wash bedding once a week, and flea comb every day. The newer veterinarian-prescribed topicals can minimize the battle, however. Many Lab owners find that a once-a-month application of Frontline or Advantage is all they need to keep Labbie flea-free. Whatever you choose to use, ask your vet to help you devise a flea control plan that works for you.

It's a constant struggle to keep the flea population to a minimum. But don't grow weary. What you'll find if you keep up the good fight is that the battle is easier and your Lab is healthier and happier. And that is, after all, your ultimate goal. *Ticks* are another external parasite you may someday find on your Lab. Several species of ticks live on dogs, but the brown dog tick is the most common. Dogs usually pick up ticks while romping outside in wooded or grassy areas. You're most likely to find ticks on your Lab's head, ears, and neck and between his toes. If you've heard that ticks are bloodsuckers, you're right. The female tick imbeds into the dog's skin, feeds, and becomes engorged with blood.

Ticks are carriers of several diseases, most notably Lyme disease and Rocky Mountain spotted fever. Lyme disease is spread by the bite of ticks infected with *Borrelia burgdorferi*, a spiral-shaped bacteria. The deer tick and the western black-legged tick are the most common carriers of Lyme disease. This disease is most common from May through August but can occur anytime. A dog with Lyme disease appears to have arthritis: he's lame, and his joints may be swollen and tender. He may also be lethargic and feverish. Lyme disease is sometimes difficult for vets to diagnose, but when it's pinpointed, antibiotics are usually curative. If you live where ticks are prevalent, ask your vet to recommend a tick control program.

Rocky Mountain spotted fever is also carried by ticks, most commonly wood ticks and dog ticks. When ticks infected with *rickettsia* bacteria bite a dog, the result can be fever, loss of appetite, and sore joints. In people, Rocky Mountain spotted fever acts like the flu, causing fever, vomiting, achiness, and chills. Antibiotics are prescribed to treat the condition in both dogs and people.

If you find a few ticks on your Lab after a walk in the woods, the best thing to do is remove them. Grab the tick with a pair of tweezers—don't touch it with your bare hands—and pull it out as quickly as possible. Get as close to the skin as you can so you remove the tick, head and all. Do not attempt to injure the tick. This might cause it to eject blood and saliva, increasing the risk of infection.

If the Lab is covered with ticks, give the vet a call. He or she can suggest a spray or dip to use at home or will suggest bringing the Lab into the clinic for dipping.

As if ticks aren't bad enough, there's also a tiny bug called a *mite*. This insect parasite can crawl onto your Lab and cause a miserable condition known as mange.

There are two types of mange: sarcoptic and demodectic. The veterinarian diagnoses mange after examining a skin scraping under the microscope and identifying the mange mite.

Sarcoptic mange causes *severe* itching in pets. The horrible itching is caused when the female mites bite and chew into the skin to lay eggs. Eggs hatch in about a week, and the baby mites grow into adults and begin to lay eggs themselves. Sarcoptic mange mites seem to prefer the skin on the dog's ears, elbows, hocks, and face. Hair falls out in these infested areas, and the skin becomes crusty and red.

The signs of demodectic mange are similar, minus the itch. A dog infested with the *Demodex canis* mite has a localized or generalized form of this condition. The localized form of demodectic mange usually occurs in young dogs up to a year old. The dog's hair thins in patches, often around the eyelids, lips, mouth, and front legs. In the generalized form, the hair thins in larger areas—on the dog's head, legs, and body. Sores develop and can become infected.

Treatment is essential for both types of mange. Dogs with sarcoptic mange can be bathed in insecticides to kill the mites or given oral medication. Several treatments will be necessary. Cortisone is often prescribed to soothe the itch.

Many cases of the localized form of demodectic mange heal by themselves in a few months, although topical medication may be prescribed. Dogs suffering from the generalized form aren't so fortunate. Treatment is necessary, but it takes time, and a cure isn't always possible. The dog may be clipped and bathed in a strong dip to kill the mites. Antibiotics

Did You Know?

Dogs have extremely sensitive hearing and a sense of smell up to 1000 times better than humans to compensate for their relatively poor eyesight.

may be prescribed to treat secondary skin infections, but cortisone usually isn't because it can worsen the condition.

Another mite that lives inside pets' ears is the ear mite. These tiny bugs, about the size of the head of a pin, feed on skin debris in the ear canal. The symptoms of ear mites are unmistakable: intense scratching and head shaking caused by the severe itching. Inside the ear you'll see reddish brown or black waxy debris.

The veterinarian makes a diagnosis of ear mites by looking at some of the ear wax under the microscope. Ear mites are highly contagious among dogs and cats and must be treated. The ears will need to be cleaned of debris and treated with medication that kills the bugs. The medication doesn't destroy eggs, so the treatment continues for several weeks until all eggs are hatched.

If you ever see a red, circular or ring-like pattern of hair loss on your Lab's skin, she may have *ringworm*. No, ringworm isn't actually caused by a worm, like tapeworms or roundworms, but most often is caused by the fungus *Microsporum canis*. Ringworm is a skin disease transmitted to dogs from other animals or people or picked up from fungus spores in the dirt.

Ringworm usually grows in circular patches a half inch to two inches across. It causes scaly skin, hair loss, and sores. The vet diagnoses ringworm by examining skin scrapings under the microscope or by growing a fungal culture of the suspicious hairs. Treatment includes bathing the dog in an anti-fungal solution, or giving an oral medication. Since the spores are infective—and an infected dog will shed them liberally throughout his environment—you'll also need to treat the house and kennel to prevent reinfection. Your veterinarian can recommend treatments for different areas of your home.

Since ringworm is contagious between dogs and people, be very careful about handling a dog with the condition. Children are especially susceptible, so if the family Lab does have ringworm, kids should avoid contact with the dog until the condition is under control.

Common Diseases

In spite of the best preventive care, kennel hygiene, and current vaccinations, your Lab may come down with one or more infectious disease. Here are the most common.

Bordetella

Most cases of *bordetella bronchiseptica,* caused by the *Bordetella bronchiseptica* bacterium, are often, but not always, found in dogs recovering from a viral respiratory infection. This bacterium attacks the dog's already weakened immune system, causing continued, usually mild, respiratory illness. The *B. bronchiseptica* bacteria is often identified in dogs diagnosed with kennel cough.

Fortunately there are two vaccines, intranasal and injection, available to fight against bordetella. The intranasal vaccine is believed to give a more immediate and longer-lasting protection against the disease. Pups living where bordetella is prevalent can be vaccinated with the intranasal vaccine as young as two to four weeks; the injection vaccine is given at eight to 12 weeks.

Brucellosis

Brucellosis is a condition that is especially feared among dog breeders. Caused by the bacterium *Brucella cania,* brucellosis causes reproductive failure in dogs—late miscarriages, stillborn pups, and pups that die shortly after birth. A male or female dog

Taking Your Lab's Temperature

If your Lab is ill, the veterinarian will want to determine his temperature. He may ask you to take a reading at home before bringing the dog to the clinic. For the most accurate reading, the temperature must be taken rectally. You may need an assistant to help because this can be uncomfortable to the dog. You can use either a rectal thermometer or a modern plastic digital thermometer and shake it down before inserting it.

1. Lubricate the thermometer with petroleum jelly.

2. Ask the Lab to stand, and have your assistant keep him standing.

3. Raise the tail and gently insert the thermometer. Usually 1½ - 2" is deep enough!

4. Don't let go! Hold the thermometer in place for about three minutes.

5. Remove, wipe clean of fecal matter, and read. Normal is between 100 and 102.8 degrees F. Temperatures under 99 degrees and over 104 degrees are considered emergencies.

6. Clean the thermometer with alcohol and put away.

with brucellosis may become sterile with little outward signs of disease. Because the condition can be passed when mating, testing is recommended before breeding dogs.

A dog with an active brucellosis infection may have enlarged lymph nodes, fever, and swollen joints. The male dog's testicles may swell, then atrophy.

There is no vaccine to prevent brucellosis or an effective long-term treatment. Antibiotics may be prescribed, but a relapse can occur once the medication is stopped.

Coronavirus

First recognized in 1971, canine *coronavirus* affects dogs of all ages and is usually quite mild. It can, however, be devastating to pups or dogs with weak immune systems. The virus is transmitted via feces, urine, and saliva and can spread rather quickly. Symptoms include depression, lack of appetite, bloody vomit, and yellow-orange diarrhea.

Dogs or pups infected with coronavirus are treated with fluid therapy to prevent dehydration, medication to stop diarrhea, and antibiotics to control secondary infections.

Vaccines are available to prevent coronavirus, and many vets recommend vaccinating dogs in frequent contact with other dogs.

Distemper

Distemper is a highly contagious disease that affects pups and adult dogs. The virus that causes distemper is similar to the virus that causes measles in people. Distemper is most common in unvaccinated pups three to eight months old but can afflict any dog, especially if he's in poor condition, for example, underfed and undernourished.

The distemper virus usually attacks the dog's epithelial cells, which are found in the skin, eye membranes, breathing tubes, and mucus membranes of the intestines. The brain is also affected.

Not all dogs respond to the distemper virus in the same way. Some become very ill, some mildly ill. How sick the dog gets often depends on his condition before he became infected. Secondary bacterial infections are common.

Treatment for distemper varies but can include antibiotics to avoid a secondary bacterial infection, intravenous fluids for dehydration and medication to control diarrhea. Usually all that can be done is to support the dog with fluids and good nursing care until the illness has run its course. Antibiotics are often given to prevent secondary infections. The success rate varies, but the earlier the dog is treated the better the chance of a positive outcome.

Fortunately vaccines can prevent distemper.

Hepatitis

Infectious canine hepatitis is a very contagious viral disease that affects dogs of all ages, but infected pups suffer the most severely. This disease can be prevented by keeping your Lab's vaccination up-to-date. A dog with canine hepatitis will have a variety of symptoms, from mild to severe. It's spread easily from dog to dog via urine, feces, and saliva. Don't confuse canine hepatitis with human hepatitis. Each disease is species specific, which means that canine hepatitis is transmitted only from dog to dog.

Canine hepatitis has several forms. In the fatal fulminating form, the dog becomes ill suddenly, may develop bloody diarrhea, and dies. This is most common in puppies.

A dog with the acute form of canine hepatitis will develop a fever and have diarrhea and vomiting. Jaundice, yellowing of the eyes indicating liver infection, may be seen. Both kidney and liver failure can follow the initial episode. Many dogs develop a mild case, however, and recover within several weeks.

Mild cases of canine hepatitis result in a loss of appetite or lethargy.

Dogs that survive canine hepatitis may develop a clouding of the cornea of one or both eyes called blue eye. It usually clears up in a few weeks. Blue eye can also occur after a dog is vaccinated against infectious hepatitis.

Infectious Tracheobronchitis

Infectious tracheobronchitis, also called kennel cough or canine cough, is caused by several viruses that result in a harsh, dry cough. The cough may last for weeks and be followed by infectious bronchitis, a further infection of the lungs.

Infectious tracheobronchitis earned the name of "kennel cough" because of the rapid way it can spread through kennels. Kennel owners, however, prefer not to have kennels labeled as the cause of the cough. Canine cough is the current politically correct slang term. Most kennels require proof of vaccination against the condition before they'll board a dog.

Several viruses and bacteria, alone or in combination, cause canine cough. There are vaccines available that are effective against some strains of canine cough. However, vaccinating will not prevent all cases. Kennel cough is usually more annoying than dangerous, producing a deep, honking cough that can last for up to eight weeks. Because secondary lung infections are possible, your veterinarian may choose to treat with antibiotics. And dogs are often given cough suppressant medication to help ease their discomfort.

Parvovirus

Parvovirus is a highly contagious, often deadly virus that attacks dogs. Parvo, as it's commonly called, is transmitted dog to dog via infected feces but can be carried on the feet or skin of an infected dog. Parvo is most serious in young pups, although it is often fatal in unvaccinated dogs of any age.

The first signs of the diarrhea-syndrome parvovirus are lack of appetite, depression, vomiting, and bloody diarrhea. The dog usually has a high fever and appears in pain.

A less common syndrome strikes the heart muscle and is most common in young dogs. Affected pups will stop nursing, whine, or gasp for breath. Death may come suddenly. Pups that survive often have long-term heart problems.

Parvo can be treated, but the outcome varies depending on the age of the dog and severity of the disease. Treatment can include intensive fluid therapy, medication to stop diarrhea, and antibiotics.

Immunization is available and is highly recommended to prevent this devastating disease.

Rabies

The well-known *rabies* virus can affect any warm-blooded animal, including dogs and people. The virus is spread usually through a bite or wound. In the United States, rabies vaccination is required by law for dogs and cats, which accounts for the low incidence of the fatal disease among domestic animals and people. Rabies is found occasionally in wild animals such as skunks, bats, or foxes. The only way rabies can be definitively diagnosed is through an examination of brain tissue in the dead animal.

There are two forms of rabies: furious and paralytic. The average incubation of the virus in dogs is from three to eight weeks but can be as short as a week or as long as a year.

The signs of rabies are caused by inflammation of the brain, which will make a normally friendly dog irritable and withdrawn. Shy pets may become overly affectionate at first, but soon the animal becomes withdrawn, stares, and avoids light, which hurts his eyes. Fever, vomiting, and diarrhea are common.

The furious form is the "mad dog" type of rabies. An animal with furious rabies is vicious and aggressive. It shows no fear and will run and snap in the air.

An animal with the paralytic form of rabies becomes paralyzed around the head. The mouth drops open, and the tongue hangs out. A rabid animal may show any type of odd behavior. Once an animal shows signs of rabies, it's always fatal.

A rabies vaccination for pets is required by law either once a year or every three years, depending on where you live.

Illnesses and Emergencies

Emergencies happen without warning, so it's a wise dog owner who prepares for the unexpected. The following is a list of common emergencies and illnesses you might encounter as a Lab owner. Remember to keep your vet's telephone number or pager number (day and night) posted by the phone just in case.

> Emergencies happen without warning, so it's a wise dog owner who prepares for the unexpected.

Allergies

There are three common types of pet allergies. First, your Lab could have an allergic reaction to flea saliva, which causes the itchy condition flea bite dermatitis. Dogs who are allergic to the flea's saliva experience a hypersensitive reaction when bitten by fleas. Not only does the dog experience itch misery but her skin becomes crusty, red, and thick.

The second type of pet allergy is food allergies. With this type of allergy the pet is allergic to some food, such as meat, eggs, fish, or grains.

Allergic Emergency!

When Lab enthusiast Linda Power took her chocolate Lab, Rusty Mist, to the veterinary clinic one afternoon for her first yearly shots, she didn't think much of it. Rusty received her vaccinations, and Power brought her home. "She seemed all right, playing catch and having fun like a normal 18-month-old Lab puppy," says Power.

Power had to attend a meeting that evening, but her husband stayed home with Rusty. He didn't notice anything unusual about the dog, and when Power got home, her husband said Rusty had been sleeping. "But the funny thing was, she didn't come to greet me when I got home," said Power, "bouncing off the walls 'cause 'Mom's home,' like she usually did. So I went to check on her."

Power called Rusty, who was resting on the cool bathroom floor. "She slowly came to me," said Power, "and her beautiful chocolate face was swollen so badly that she looked like a Shar-pei instead of a Lab!"

Like all mothers faced with a crisis, Power called the vet. It was 10 P.M., so, of course, her regular clinic was closed. She called a nearby emergency clinic, which was closing in an hour. Power told the veterinarian she'd be there in a few minutes. "This emergency clinic was about 15 miles away, and I think we made it in record time," said Power.

The emergency veterinarian determined that Rusty had suffered a severe allergic reaction to the leptospirosis vaccine she'd received earlier in the day. The vet administered medication to stop the allergic reaction and said if Rusty didn't develop hives, she could go home within half an hour. As fate would have it, "She got hives!" says Power. "Have you ever seen a dog with hives? She had bumps all over her, and her fur was sticking up where the bumps were. A Lab with hives is not a pretty sight. So, she had to spend the night."

Rusty got better overnight, and Power picked her up early the next morning. "We were there at precisely 7 A.M., and she was sure happy to see us. I don't think she was any happier, though, than we were to see her."

It took three days for the swelling around Rusty's head and face to go away. But if Power had waited any longer to get Rusty to a clinic for treatment that night, the ending wouldn't have been so happy. They could have lost her.

"Thank God for emergency veterinary hospitals," says Power.

And like people, pets may become allergic to pollen and other airborne irritants such as dust or mold.

What's interesting about pet allergies is how they're manifested in pets. Dogs react differently than people. Usually when dogs are allergic to something, they get itchy skin. People develop runny noses, itchy eyes, sneezing and congestion, and skin or respiratory problems. But when a dog gets itchy and starts scratching and licking, owners don't necessarily suspect allergies. Common sites of itching include the ears, face, paws, front legs, flanks, on the rump over the tail, and the underside. An allergic pet can develop intense itching that leads to hair loss; raw, oozing sores; and bacterial infections.

The degree of itching and subsequent damage the animal does to its skin shows the degree of the allergic reaction. A mild allergic reaction will produce mild scratching. An intense allergic reaction will cause more scratching.

Most seasonal itching problems are from either flea, pollen, or mold-related allergies. If the itching season is short for an individual pet, it may be possible to control the problem with antihistamines or other medications. If the problem persists longer, desensitization treatments may result in long-term improvement without the constant use of medications. Food trials can also be done to rule out food allergies.

In addition to flea, food, and inhalant allergies, pets can experience acute allergic reactions. Insect stings or vaccines are a common cause of an immediate hypersensitivity reaction; the response is within minutes of exposure, and the pet often develops hives and may also develop trouble breathing or collapse—which is a true emergency and requires veterinary help.

Did You Know?

Dogs see color less vividly than humans but are not actually color-blind.

Not all itching is caused by allergies, so it's important to consult your veterinarian to determine the underlying cause of your Lab's problem. Your veterinarian will ask for a detailed history of your Lab's symptoms and will do a physical exam. He may conduct basic screening tests (skin scrapings, bacterial/fungal cultures, or a skin biopsy). Your veterinarian may also recommend more definitive allergy testing to make a detailed determination of your pet's immune responses to a number of allergens specific to your region. Results from these tests can prove invaluable in developing the best treatment plan for your pet.

How do you spell relief? Although there's no cure for allergies, effective treatments offer substantial relief. Traditional approaches to the relief of allergy symptoms include topical products (medicated shampoos, creams, or sprays), oral antihistamines (often given in conjunction with fatty acid supplements), and cortisone-type drugs. As an alternative, your vet may suggest immune therapy, a long-term approach to desensitize your pet through a series of injections (extracts of the offending allergens). Although immunotherapy is by no means a quick fix, it offers the best opportunity for long-term allergy relief without the potential side effects of allergy drugs.

Bleeding

If your Lab is badly wounded, her bleeding may be arterial (squirting of bright red blood) or venous (oozing of dark red blood). You must stop the bleeding. There are two basic techniques to do this: direct pressure and a tourniquet.

First, try to control the bleeding with direct pressure. Apply several pads of sterile gauze over the wound and press firmly and evenly. Be aware that if your Lab is

Handling an Injured Lab

If your Lab is injured, he may growl or snap when you attempt to touch or move him. Don't be offended by this unusual behavior. Your Lab is feeling pain, and this is the way he shows it. Remember this before handling your injured Lab, and take a few steps to prevent injury to yourself.

First, talk to your dog quietly and calmly. He may be excited or anxious—aren't you when you're injured? Move slowly, and keep talking in a soothing voice.

Next, muzzle your hurt Lab. If you don't have a muzzle available, improvise with a man's necktie, a stocking, or a long strip of soft cloth. Loop the cloth over the Lab's muzzle and tie a half knot on top of the dog's muzzle, then tie another half knot under the chin. Wrap the material behind and below the ears and tie a full knot at the base of the dog's head. If your dog is having trouble breathing, avoid a muzzle if at all possible.

To transport your severely injured Lab to the emergency clinic, use a stretcher. A flat board, a sheet of plywood, for example, works well. If something like that isn't available, use a large towel or blanket. You don't want to injure your Lab more seriously, so be very careful moving him onto the makeshift stretcher. Slide one hand under your Lab's rear and the other hand under his chest. (You may need a helper if your Lab is especially large or you're especially small.) Slowly inch the dog onto the stretcher and cover him with a towel.

Drive carefully but quickly to the veterinary clinic. Have someone ride next to your Lab, keeping him calm and still. Call ahead so that the staff expects you, and have them come out to help carry in the dog.

wounded, she's in pain. You may need someone to restrain the dog gently but firmly while you apply pressure to the wound. Don't wipe the wound or apply hydrogen peroxide, both of which will only destroy blood clots and increase bleeding, or ointments which can seal infection into a wound. If blood soaks through the pad, don't remove it—this could disrupt clotting. Simply place another pad on top and press.

If bleeding on a leg or tail doesn't stop or at least slow to a trickle when you apply pressure, try a tourniquet. Use this only as a last resort, though. Use of a tourniquet is likely result in limb loss. To apply a tourniquet, wrap the limb or tail with one-inch-wide gauze or a wide piece of cloth slightly above the wound and tie a half knot. Don't use a narrow band or rope. Place a pencil or stick on top and finish the knot. Twist the pencil slowly until the bleeding stops. Fasten it in place with tape. Cover the wound with sterile gauze, and quickly take the dog to the veterinary clinic for treatment. Your should release the pressure on the tourniquet for 30-60 seconds every five minutes to try to preserve the limb.

Bloat

Bloat, or gastric dilation volvulous, is the swelling, followed by the twisting, or torsion, of the dog's stomach. Bloat is a medical emergency—50 percent of dogs that suffer from bloat die. Signs of bloat include a sudden onset of abdominal pain, vomiting, attempting to vomit but producing little or nothing, restlessness, and inability to get comfortable. The dog will often lie on her chest with her rump in the air. The abdomen may look swollen and often sounds like a ripe watermelon when thumped with your fingers. The gums often are quite pale. In order to save your dog, seek medical help immediately.

Bloat most commonly affects dogs in the prime of life, between four and seven years of age. It's more common in male dogs and in large, deep-chested breeds such as the Lab. Dogs that suffer bloat tend to eat large amounts of kibble and may have a history of digestive upset.

The incidence of bloat in Labs is higher than in some breeds, but there are common-

sense ways that may prevent the condition. Break up your Lab's daily ration into several small meals. Don't allow him to drink a lot of water right after he eats kibble, and dampen his kibble slightly before serving so that it expands. And don't allow your Lab to exercise immediately before or after eating.

Burns

Dogs can be burned and frostbitten, just like people. For first- and second-degree burns (redness and slight swelling to blisters and extreme tenderness), immerse the burned area in cool water. Don't apply butter or human medicines—they'll only contaminate the burn. Gently dry the burn, bandage it, and call the vet.

In third-degree burns, the skin appears white, hair comes out easily, and the pain is severe. In such cases, call the vet immediately. Don't apply anything except to lightly cover the area with a nonstick dressing.

Frostbite usually affects a dog's toes, ears, tail, and scrotum. The skin is pale white but becomes red and swollen when warmed and circulation returns. Frostbite looks very similar to a burn. Move the dog to a warm place and warm the affected area slowly and gently with cloths soaked in warm water or moist heat packs. Don't rub the area or use excessive heat. Call the veterinarian right away.

Choking

Your Lab may choke, usually when something becomes lodged in her throat or windpipe. Severe coughing and respiratory distress are the usual symptoms when food or a foreign object is stuck in the windpipe or a bronchus, one of the windpipe's lower branches. Often the dog can cough up the obstruction quickly, but if she can't, call the vet and get to the clinic immediately.

Swallowing Fire

When Ike the black Lab came to live with Mary Lynn D'Aubin at six weeks of age, D'Aubin decided it was time to replace the old cedar fence around the yard. "We decided that we should replace the rickety fence before the pup realized he could knock it down just by leaning on it," says D'Aubin.

On Easter weekend the fence builders came, and sacks of concrete mix littered the yard. Ike helped by "supervising": checking every hole, every ditch, every noise. Ike's normal Lab curiosity got the better of him, and he began to dig into a sack of concrete mix and, not surprisingly, tasted the contents.

Sadly, that temptation to taste was like swallowing fire. The lye in the concrete burned Ike internally. "This was one sick pupper," says D'Aubin. "He was foaming at the mouth and crying. When I tried to open his mouth to see, it looked like raw hamburger in there."

D'Aubin took Ike to the emergency clinic right away. "Poor lil' guy spent Easter Sunday in the ER, with IVs and subcutaneous injections of fluids to stabilize him." Then on Monday, D'Aubin took Ike to his regular vet, who filled him full of barium to coat all the inner surfaces burned by the lye in the concrete mix. "He had burns in the mouth, throat, and tummy," says D'Aubin.

Fortunately, after several days of a special diet, Ike was back to normal—and getting into other stuff! "He was a terrible chewer and destroyer of outdoor lawn furniture, garden hoses, sprinklers, pool sweeps," says D'Aubin. That finally stopped when D'Aubin acquired a female yellow Lab, Babsie. "She never chewed like Ike did, and Ike stopped his destructive dog stuff once he had Babsie to play with. But I tell you, that first year was chaos!"

Diarrhea

It certainly isn't a pleasant subject or sight, but at some time during your Lab's life, he may suffer diarrhea. Frequent, loose, unformed stools aren't a sickness but a sign of something else. Because diarrhea can indicate an underlying unhealthy condition, it should be investigated and treated.

Diarrhea has many causes, including a change in diet or water, stress, eating garbage or other no-nos, toxic substances, food allergies, or infectious disease.

Mild diarrhea, lasting no longer than 24 hours, can be treated at home. Consult with the vet for an exact treatment, but she will usually recommend withholding food, giving the dog water or ice cubes to drink, or administering medication to stop the diarrhea. Once the diarrhea subsides, a bland diet (rice and cooked hamburger, for example) may be recommended.

Bloody diarrhea, diarrhea with mucus, or diarrhea that lasts more than 24 hours must be treated by a veterinarian. If the diarrhea is accompanied by other signs of illness, such as lethargy or fever, consult the vet right away.

Difficulty Breathing

Your Lab may have difficulty breathing for several reasons, including chest injuries or foreign objects lodged in the windpipe. The dog may gasp for breath, be anxious or weak, or lose consciousness.

If your Lab has difficulty breathing, act fast—you may need to perform artificial respiration. There are two methods of artificial respiration: chest compression and mouth-to-nose. Keep in mind that you shouldn't attempt artificial respiration on a conscious dog.

Chest compression works by applying force to the chest wall, which pushes air out and allows the natural recoil of the chest to draw air in. Chest compression is the easiest type of artificial respiration to perform. Mouth-to-nose is forced respiration. It's used when the compression technique fails or when the chest is punctured.

Don't confuse artificial respiration with cardiopulmonary resuscitation, or CPR. CPR combines

Heart Massage

Heart massage is done when there's no pulse and dog is not breathing. If he is breathing, the heart is beating whether the owner can detect a pulse or not.

1. Feel for a pulse or heartbeat.

2. Open the dog's mouth and check for obstructions.

3. Lie the dog on his right side and remove his collar and harness.

4. Place your thumb on one side of the sternum (breastbone) and your fingers on other side just below the elbows. For large dogs, place the heel of the hand on the rib cage behind the elbow, which is directly over the heart. If possible, do the same thing with your other hand, on the other side of the chest.

5. With your hands in this position, squeeze firmly to compress the chest. Do so five to six times. Wait five seconds to let the chest expand. During this time give a breath.

6. Continue until the heart beats on its own or until no pulse is felt for five minutes.

You may need two people to combine heart massage and artificial respiration: one person to massage and one to respirate. But if you don't have help in an emergency situation, perform one mouth-to-nose respiration after five cardiac massages without breaking the rhythm of the massages.

artificial respiration with heart massage for an unconscious animal whose heart and breathing have stopped.

Electric Shock

Lab puppies are playful and curious and love to chew on everything. Unfortunately this makes them prone to electric shock—the result of chewing on electric cords. A burned mouth is usually the result, but circulatory collapse and difficult breathing can re-

Performing CPR

Chest Compression Respiration (done when the dog's heart is beating, but he's having trouble breathing). Use only in dire emergencies as it can damage the lungs, ribs, and heart.

1. Lie the dog on his right side and remove his collar and harness.

2. Open the dog's mouth and check for obstructions.

3. Place the palms of the hands near the edge of the rib cage and press down sharply. Release quickly. If done properly, the air should move in and out. If it doesn't, perform mouth-to-nose respiration.

4. Continue until the dog breathes on his own or as long as the heart beats.

sult. What happens is when puppy bites the cord and gets a jolt, the electric current wreaks havoc on the lung capillaries, which in turn leads to fluid in the lungs.

Whether the pup suffers a burned mouth or falls unconscious, immediate veterinary attention is essential.

The good news is that you can prevent electric shock by hiding away electric cords and watching puppy closely when he's in the house. Never allow him to wander around unsupervised. The temptation to chew is overwhelming! And if an electric cord is exposed, chances are Labbie will chew. Teach your Lab pup to chew only on his toys, and make sure you have plenty of well-made chew toys on hand.

Eye Injuries

Your Lab is squinting and pawing at her eye, or the eye appears teary and red. If this is the case, chances are your Lab has injured her eye. Probably the most common eye injury is a foreign object such grass, dirt, or seeds that get stuck in the dog's eye. A foreign object in the eye can be painful and very irritating. Often a veterinary visit is required to remove it, especially if the object becomes lodged behind the third eyelid (a protective membrane that cleans and lubricates the dog's eye).

If a dog has a foreign object in her eye, she will often suffers corneal abrasion or a scratched cornea. If treated promptly, the cornea usually heals quickly. If not, the injury can lead to a corneal ulcer, which is very painful and potentially serious. A corneal ulcer requires veterinary treatment to prevent eye loss.

Trauma to a dog's eye can result in eye displacement—the eye comes out of the socket. This is an emergency condition. Cover the eye with a moist, clean cloth (if your dog isn't fighting you) and take the dog straight to the vet.

Fishhooks

Because Labs love to swim and frequently accompany their owners to lakes, rivers, and streams, they're at risk of being stuck by fishhooks, usually in the lips or mouth, from sniffing or mouthing everything in sight. Fishhooks can also become imbedded inside the Lab's mouth, which will cause the dog to cough, gag, or salivate. Take a look inside with a flashlight, then call the vet.

Wherever it's imbedded, a fishhook must be removed. It's best not to attempt this yourself—let the vet remove it. Removing the hook is extremely painful and anesthesia or sedation is usually required.

Fractures

Dogs can fracture, or break, bones, usually as the result of a trauma, such as being hit by a car.

Fractures are simple or compound. A simple fracture doesn't break through the skin, but in a compound fracture, the bone is exposed. Young pups tend to suffer what's called greenstick fractures—cracks instead of complete breaks.

If you suspect your Lab has broken a bone, the most important thing you can do is keep him still to prevent further injury. Splinting a limb can prevent a simple fracture from becoming a compound fracture.

Surgery, splints, or casts may be necessary to treat the break.

Heat Stroke

Like all dogs, Labs don't tolerate heat very well. Dogs cool their bodies by panting, exchanging hot air for cool air. When the air temperature is close to the Lab's natural body temperature of 100 to 102.5 degrees F, it's difficult for the dog to cool down. The dog becomes overheated, which can cause heatstroke, a potentially serious condition that can lead to death.

Overheating and heatstroke can happen easily. A dog left in a parked car in hot weather or confined in a hot kennel with no shade is susceptible. Snub-nosed breeds such as Bulldogs and Pugs are especially prone to overheating. Dogs that exercise in high humidity—even with temperatures as low as 80—may also be at risk for heat stroke.

The signs of heatstroke include rapid panting, dark-colored gums and tongue, thick, ropy saliva, exhaustion, vomiting, and collapse.

If you suspect heatstroke in your dog, your immediate goal is to cool him down. If the dog seems only mildly affected, move him to a cooler environment, such

Did You Know?

The tallest dog on record was 42 inches tall at the shoulders and weighed 238 pounds.

as an air-conditioned home, or wrap him in moistened towels. Take the dog's temperature, and if it's over 104 degrees F or the dog seems ill, hose him down with cool water (not cold) from a garden hose or immerse him in a tub of cool water. Even if you succeed in bringing his temperature down, get him to your vet as soon as possible. Apparently recovered dogs may develop kidney or liver failure if not properly treated.

Overheating and heatstroke can be easily prevented. Give your Lab the same consideration you would yourself during hot weather. Stay inside in air-conditioning if you have it. Don't exercise at high noon. If you do go out, make sure you carry along plenty of water and insist that Labbie take a big drink every 15–20 minutes. Don't leave your Lab in a parked car. If your Lab stays outside, give him a kiddie pool filled with cool water and plenty of shade.

> Give your Lab the same consideration you would yourself during hot weather.

Hit by Car

Labs and cars don't mix, which is why it's so important that you keep your Lab on a leash while you're out and about. Some dogs are tempted to chase cars, but nip this behavior in the bud. The car will always win, and the outcome is potentially disastrous for the Lab.

What should you do if your Lab dashes in front of a car and is hit? Get to the emergency clinic ASAP. Some dogs get by with minor breaks after being hit, but chances are good the animal is seriously injured. The dog must be treated for shock and transported carefully.

Insect Bites and Stings

Inevitably your active and outdoorsy Lab will find herself face-to-face with a wasp, bee, yellow jacket, spider, or other stinging or biting insect or arachnid. In most cases, the encounter is harmless. Labbie explores, and stinging insect flies away. But dogs can and do get stung by these critters, and it hurts! It can cause a severe reaction and illness.

The stings of bees, wasps, and yellow jackets swell and are painful. That's usually the extent of the damage, but if stung repeatedly, a dog could experience shock. And just as some people are highly allergic to insect bites and stings, so are some dogs, and they'll react severely to bites and stings.

Spider bites can be toxic, especially those of the black widow and Missouri brown spider. The bite itself is painful and can result in fever, labored breathing, and shock. Scorpion and centipede stings are no fun, either. The stings hurt and can make the dog very ill.

When it comes to insect bites and stings, the best advice is to identify the attacker and call your veterinarian. Ask for instructions on what to do at home to make your dog comfortable immediately. The vet may advise you to apply a paste of baking soda or ice packs to the sting, or he may want to examine the dog right away. If your Lab has an extreme reaction to a bite or sting, get to the clinic pronto.

Poisoning

A poison is any substance that can be harmful to your dog. Your Lab may be poisoned when she ingests or comes in contact with a toxic substance

First-Aid Kit Essentials

❍ Your veterinarian's phone number

❍ An after-hours emergency clinic's phone number

❍ The National Animal Poison Control Center's hotline number: (800) 548-2423 or (900) 680-0000

❍ Rectal thermometer

❍ Tweezers

❍ Scissors

❍ Penlight flashlight

❍ Rubbing alcohol

❍ Hydrogen peroxide (three percent)

❍ Syrup of ipecac and activated charcoal liquid or tablets (poisoning antidotes)

❍ Anti-diarrheal medicine

❍ Dosing syringe

❍ Nonstick wound pads, gauze squares, and roll cotton to control bleeding

❍ Adhesive tape

❍ Elastic bandage

❍ Styptic powder (in case nails are cut too short)

such as household cleaners, antifreeze, rat poison, gasoline, plants, or even chocolate. Labs are especially at risk for poisoning because of their curious nature and willingness to taste and smell *everything*. Be extremely careful not to allow your Lab access to potential toxins. Poison-proof your house, and keep your Lab on a leash when outdoors to minimize any chance of poisoning.

The signs of poisoning vary but can include an irritated mouth, excessive drooling, vomiting, diarrhea, skin rash, seizures, or coma. If your dog appears to be poisoned or you know she has nibbled or licked something toxic, call your veterinarian immediately! There's no time to waste. If possible, identify the poison and tell the vet what it is. This will help her determine treatment for your dog.

Once you get the vet on the phone, ask for instructions. Induce vomiting or give charcoal, which will help rid the poison from the dog's system or delay its absorption, only if directed by the practitioner. Follow doctor's orders carefully because it can mean life or death for your dog.

For more information about poisoning, call or have your vet call the ASPCA National Animal Poison Control Center hot line at (800) 548-2423 (for emergencies only) or (900) 680-0000 (non-emergency questions). The ASPCA NAPCC charges a fee for consultation—usually $35 per case—so have a credit card handy when you call.

Seizures

Dogs can suffer seizures or convulsions very similar to those seen in people. A seizure is a sudden and uncontrolled burst of electrical activity in the brain that results in foaming at the mouth, jerking of the legs, chewing, and collapse. There are two types of seizures: grand mal and petit mal.

Seizures can be caused by head injury, hypoglycemia (low blood sugar), heavy internal parasite infestation, poisoning, kidney and liver failure, and so on. Frequent or periodic seizures can indicate epilepsy, a recurrent seizure disorder.

What should you do if your Lab suffers a seizure? Stand aside, wait for the seizure to take its course, and call the vet. Most seizures are over within five minutes. Your veterinarian will probably want to examine the dog to determine the cause and decide whether the dog is suffering from epilepsy.

Shock

Shock is the collapse of the circulatory system. It's usually the result of severe injury, blood loss, or allergic reaction. If your Lab is injured, she

Signs and Treatment of Shock

Shock actually comes in three stages. Early shock results from the body's initial attempt to compensate for a decreased flow of fluids and oxygen to the tissues. The signs of early shock include:

○ Increased heart rate (more than 60 to 100 beats per minute)

○ Normal to increased pulse

○ Redder than normal mucous membranes

○ A normal capillary refill time of one to two seconds (test capillary refill time by pressing on your dog's gums, removing your finger, and counting the time it takes the gums to change from white back to pink)

○ Either a low or, in the case of infection, a high, body temperature.

The middle stage of shock occurs when the body encounters difficulty compensating for the lack of blood flow and oxygen. Signs of the second stage of shock include:

○ Increased heart rate

○ Weak pulse

○ Pale mucous membranes

○ Longer than normal capillary refill time

○ Low body temperature

○ Depressed mental state

○ Cool limbs.

The end stage, or terminal shock, occurs when the body can no longer compensate for the loss of oxygen and blood. Indicators of terminal shock include:

○ Slow heart rate

○ Weak or absent pulse

○ Prolonged capillary refill time

○ Slow respiratory rate

○ Depressed mental state or unconsciousness.

Treat your dog by assessing her vital signs and by administering CPR, if necessary. Control any bleeding. Wrap your dog in a blanket and elevate her hind end slightly by putting another blanket under her rear. (If you suspect your dog has a broken back, however, do not elevate her rear.) Get her to a veterinarian immediately.

may experience shock. A dog in shock will have a decreased supply of oxygen, which results in unconsciousness; pale gums; weak, rapid pulse; or labored, rapid breathing.

Shock must be treated right away because it can be fatal. If you suspect your Lab is in shock, stop any bleeding and administer CPR as necessary. Cover the animal with a blanket or towel, don't give her water because she might choke, and transport her to the veterinary clinic right away.

Vomiting

Another less-than-pleasant symptom your Lab may experience in his lifetime is vomiting. Many illnesses and diseases can cause vomiting, so it's a sign that must be investigated.

One of the most common causes of vomiting is overeating and/or eating too fast. This can happen in Labs who love to gobble their food as soon as it's served. Eating grass or something else irritating to the stomach is another common cause of vomiting.

If the Lab vomits a few times, appears well, and doesn't vomit again, it usually isn't cause for concern. Repeated vomiting, vomiting blood, projectile vomiting, or vomiting foreign objects, and vomiting that produces nothing, especially if your dog's stomach feels hard or painful, *is* cause for concern. Pay attention to when and how often the vomiting occurs, and call the veterinarian.

Lab-Specific Health Concerns

Certain health conditions affect Labs more often than other breeds. You should be aware of these conditions when selecting a Lab puppy or adult. That way, you can ask questions about the health of the dog, her parents, and the rest of her family. Some of these conditions are genetic and can be tested or screened for.

Cold Tail

Cold tail is a benign condition most commonly seen in Labs and other retrievers. Also called limber tail, it's a malady that causes the dog's tail to go limp, and the dog may bite at the tail. It isn't cause for alarm and usually goes away in a few days on its own. Very recent studies have shown that cold tail is a problem with the muscles in between the vertebrae in the tail.

Cold tail is painful, and the dog tries not to move his tail. "They tend to try to hold the tail still, which is hard to do if you're a Labrador," says Autumn Davidson, DVM, National Labrador Retriever Club medical adviser, diplomate of the American College of Veterinary Internal Medicine, and associate clinical professor, school of veterinary medicine, University of California at Davis. Dr. Davidson also owns, breeds, and shows Labs and works with Guide Dogs for the Blind in San Raphael, California. "Unfortunately, it's a condition most veterinarians aren't aware of. So when they see it, they often think it's something more serious," she adds.

Cold tail isn't thought to be genetic, although it's associated with breeds with heavy tails.

Ear Problems

The Lab's love of water, combined with drop ears, makes him a perfect candidate for ear infections. Yeast love warm, moist environments like the Lab's ear. But the Lab isn't necessarily prone to ear problems. "Any dog with a flop ear like a Labrador has a predisposition toward getting an excessive amount of wax and an overgrowth of yeast in the ear," says Dr. Davidson. "I don't think it's necessarily a Labrador problem, but an anatomic ear problem. In most cases, if good ear hygiene is performed, starting when you get the puppy, most serious ear problems can be avoided."

Dr. Davidson advises a weekly cleaning with a commercially prepared ear cleaner to prevent problems.

Many Lab owners use the following home remedy to clean their Lab's ears:

2 tablespoons boric acid

4 ounces rubbing alcohol

1 tablespoon glycerin

> The Lab's love of water, combined with drop ears, makes him a perfect candidate for ear infections.

Dampen a cotton ball and wipe out each ear once a week or so. The mixture works by raising the pH level inside the ear, making it less friendly to bacteria. It's not a remedy for existing ear infections, though. In fact, it can lead to further irritation in an infected ear. Never put anything in a red, inflamed, or painful ear. Consult a veterinarian.

Epilepsy

Epilepsy is a recurrent seizure disorder that may be acquired or inherited. To establish a diagnosis of epilepsy, the attacks must be recurrent and similar. Labrador Retrievers can be afflicted with epilepsy. "Epilepsy is a problem in the breed," says Dr. Davidson. "There is an increased incidence of epilepsy in Labradors as compared to the average dog of its size."

Over the past years, reputable Lab breeders have been making an effort toward breeding away from epilepsy. Dr. Davidson says there is a subtle trend away from epilepsy in the Lab, but it's still a condition that must be considered when breeding or buying a Lab.

Studies of epilepsy in dogs are underway at the University of California at Davis School of Veterinary Medicine to help understand and treat the condition. Results are yet to come.

Eye Problems

Labrador Retrievers can suffer from a variety of inherited eye conditions, including progressive retinal atrophy, cataracts, and retinal dysplasia.

Progressive retinal atrophy, which affects the retina and results in partial or complete blindness, occurs in many breeds of dogs, including mixed breeds. The disease manifests itself differently in different breeds. The most common form of PRA in the Collie can be detected at an early age (six weeks); PRA in Irish Setters is also early onset. In Labrador Retrievers, the age of onset is much later, typically four to six years, making it difficult to isolate carriers in the breed. "Historically, because PRA has been a late-onset condition in Labradors, it's been difficult to eradicate," explains Dr. Davis. "These dogs have often been used for breeding before the condition was found." However, researchers at Cornell University, in conjunction with a private company, have just developed a genetic marker test that can be given at any age, puppy or adult. While not considered a "perfect" test because it can give some false positives, but no false negatives, in terms of identifying PRA carriers and affected dogs, the DNA test can give Lab breeders more information than previously available.

Electroretinography can be used to detect early signs of PRA. The dog to be tested is anesthetized while lenses are placed on the eyes to record the retina's reaction to light. Sometimes ophthalmologic examination by a vet certified by the American College of Veterinary Ophthalmology (ACVO) can pick up cases of PRA, and confirm them with electroretinography if there's any doubt.

All dogs with PRA eventually go blind, either completely or nearly so, but carriers show no symptoms. The symptoms are subtle, starting with night blindness and some pupil dilation and progressing to blindness. Annual screening is always recommended for dogs, especially breeding stock. Lab PRA usually affects the central retina, and affected animals may have some vision restored, although it's quite poor.

Cataracts are relatively common in dogs and many are hereditary. An ACVO-certified veterinarian can easily detect these cataracts. A mild haziness or cloudiness in the eyes in older animals is often not cataracts. Hereditary cataracts can be detected early, so all potential breeders should be screened.

Cataracts may be stable or progressive. With stable cataracts, an owner may never be aware that the dog is afflicted. With progressive cataracts, the dog often adapts very well to the gradual loss in vision until a certain point. Cataracts can be diagnosed by ophthalmoscopic examination, but blindness is usually the end result. If a more detailed examination is needed, a slit lamp examination must be performed. Surgery is the only option for cataracts that seriously impair vision. Most surgery involves removal of the lens, and implants are possible. Recovery and prognosis for dogs with cataracts is usually quite good. Cataracts in Labs tend not to be progressive, but they can cause other problems, such as inflammation in the eye. For

Did You Know?

The average gestation period for a dog is 63 days.

the most part, total blindness isn't as likely in Labs with cataracts as in other breeds.

Labs may have eyelid abnormalities such as *entropion* (eyelid rolls in) or *ectropion* (eyelid rolls out). They're genetic and do require surgery for correction.

Retinal dysplasia is another eye disease that affects Labs. The retina is the light sensitive portion of the eye, and dysplasia is an abnormality in development. RD is present at birth so it is a congenital, not progressive, disease. There is controversy surrounding the several forms of the condition, one in which dogs are born blind, another in which dogs have subtle eye lesions that disappear with maturity. Research for RD is ongoing. RD is considered a serious disorder in Labs. Ideally, pups should be examined by an opthalmologist at six to eight weeks (before leaving the breeder's home) and adult Labs should be screened once a year.

Eye diseases, both those present at birth and those that develop later in a Labrador's life, are recorded by the Canine Eye Registration Foundation (CERF), an organization that works in conjunction with the American College of Veterinary Ophthalmologists. Prospective buyers should ask to see each parent's CERF number, which is evidence that the dog has been screened and found free of heritable eye disease. The CERF registration is good only for 12 months from the examination date; then the dog must be re-examined by an ACVO diplomate and reregistered to maintain an up-to-date CERF number.

Laryngeal Paralysis

Laryngeal paralysis occurs when one or both sides of the larynx don't open and close properly. The result is loud, distressed breathing; coughing; and a muted bark. If the condition is severe, it can lead to heat exhaustion because the dog is unable to pant normally and cool off. Laryngeal paralysis can be hereditary, or it may occur later in life for many reasons. The exact cause is unknown.

One treatment for laryngeal paralysis is surgery to open the laryngeal folds. But if the surgery is done improperly, the dog is at risk for aspiration pneumonia because he can more easily draw food and water into his lungs by mistake. This surgery is best done by a surgeon who is experienced with laryngeal surgery. Post-surgery prognosis is usually fair to good, with the dog returning to normal function.

"[Laryngeal paralysis] isn't a common condition, but it's a condition that occurs more commonly in elderly Labradors than in the average elderly dog," says Dr. Davidson. "So there's probably some breed tendency but also some familial tendency within the breed."

Laryngeal paralysis is difficult to screen for. Reputable Lab breeders record pedigrees in which the condition has occurred and attempt to avoid repeating those pedigrees.

Obesity

Here it is again, the *o* word! Obesity. As we've seen, Labs gain weight easily and can become obese if overfed and underexercised, especially as they grow older. An overweight Lab is susceptible to several health conditions, including impaired heart and breathing functions, heat exhaustion, increased surgical risk, and skeletal stress, and she may not live as long.

Remember, don't overfeed your Lab, and keep her active to burn calories. If Labbie does get fat, consult with your veterinarian. She can help you plan a weight loss program for your Lab.

Orthopedic Disorders

Hip dysplasia is a common cause of lameness in dogs. It's most common in large breeds, in dogs weighing more than 35 pounds. Hip dysplasia is a developmental problem. Over time, how the thighbone fits into the hip socket changes for the worse. The thighbone and hip sockets no longer match perfectly or work smoothly, causing impaired hip function. Because of the poor fit and loose ligaments, the joint can develop arthritis early in life. The dog may have trouble getting up from lying down or sitting or may be lame and lose muscle tone in the rear.

Hip dysplasia is considered a heritable condition, and Labradors are one of the breeds that have an increased incidence of it compared to the general dog population. Although the condition is genetic, whether or not dogs develop hip dysplasia can be modified by diet—by not overfeeding during puppyhood to slow growth—and the dog's physical activity.

Elbow dysplasia (ED) is another degenerative joint disease that affects dogs, including Labs. It is the single most common cause of elbow pain and foreleg lameness in the Labrador Retriever. Dogs with elbow dysplasia often begin to show lameness in their front legs at about four to six months of age; they may limp when trotting or be unable to bear weight on their front feet. A dog with elbow dysplasia usually stands with its elbows facing outward. ED is usually diagnosed by a series of radiographs; if it's a subtle case it requires an experienced veterinarian to detect the symptoms. Surgical treatment is one option, medical management with analgesics is another option. Each case has to be handled individually. Untreated dogs often develop severe arthritis, causing lameness and pain as they age.

Osteochondrosis dissecans and *osteochondritis dissecans*, commonly called OCD, affect large breeds that grow rapidly, usually between four and 12 months of age. It can strike the shoulder, hock, elbow, and stifle joints. It's caused by a defect in the cartilage maturation to bone. The condition may be hereditary and may require surgical treatment.

Since orthopedic disorders can be genetic, dogs with these conditions and normal dogs from families with a high incidence of the problem, shouldn't be bred. More important, all dogs should be screened for joint disorders before breeding. Currently screening is done by taking x rays of a dog's joints, most commonly the hips, elbows, shoulders, and hocks.

The x rays can be sent to the Orthopedic Foundation for Animals, a nonprofit foundation that provides a standardized method of evaluating and registering the x rays. For a fee, the OFA's panel of expert radiologists will review a dog's x rays. If the conformation of the hips (or another joint) is deemed normal for that breed, the dog is then certified and given a number. The OFA certifies dogs 24 months or older and primarily certifies hips and elbows.

The Wind-Morgan Program of the Institute for Genetic Disease Control (GDC) in Animals at the University of California, Davis, School of Veterinary Medicine, is another nonprofit program offering registry and screening of orthopedic disorders in dogs. The GDC certifies hips and elbows but also reviews radiographs of shoulders and hocks.

Why is it important to review the x rays of potential breeding stock for any breed of dog? Genetic studies have shown that breeding radiographically

Did You Know?

An average of 800 dogs and cats are euthanized every hour in the United States.

Elizabethan Style

Although wearing an Elizabethan collar may sound stylish, its purpose is medicinal. Hopefully your Lab won't need one, but if she suffers an injury, a wound, or a skin problem that mustn't be scratched, bitten, or pawed, the Elizabethan collar will do the job. Named for the high neck ruff popular during the reign of Queen Elizabeth, this lampshadelike collar prevents your Lab from turning her head to chew and makes scratching nearly impossible. The size of the collar is tailored to fit the size of the dog.

The Elizabethan collar is effective, but it's not always well received by its wearers. It's a bit bulky, and certainly looks funny. Always the good sport, the Lab usually accepts even this with her natural good humor.

normal dogs produces less joint disease than when affected dogs or dogs of unknown status are bred.

What all this means is that before you buy a Lab pup, ask to see the certification of both parents from the OFA, GDC, or both of these organizations. "The minimal expectation is that the parents have been found to be clear of the disorder," says Dr. Davidson. Additionally, says Dr. Davidson, x rays, preferably hips and elbows, better yet, hips, elbows, shoulder and hocks, should be registered with one or more of the registries so there is validation. Certification, plus an ethical breeder, means less chance of acquiring a pup with an orthopedic condition. However, says Dr. Davidson, "The latest trend is to try and screen as many of a breeding dog's family members to find out what its genetic package is."

Ruptured Cruciates

Labs often can suffer from ruptured cranial cruciate ligaments (knee or stifle joint), usually sustained while running to retrieve, jumping and twisting. Surgery is usually necessary to repair the knee, followed by rest and restricted activity for several weeks.

"Any heavy-muscled, large breed dog—the Rottweiler, the Golden Retriever, the Labrador—those shape of bodies seem to have a predisposition toward ruptured cruciate ligaments in the knee," says Dr. Davidson. The latest research shows the condition is related to the angles that produce stress on the ligaments in the leg; combine that with the fact that these breeds are very active and athletic.

The shape and angle of a dog's legs are determined by genetics. "So I think it is a valid concern that dogs that have cruciate ligament injuries at a young age should probably not be used for breeding," says Dr. Davidson.

Tricuspid Valve Dysplasia

Tricuspid valve dysplasia, or TVD, is a newly recognized heart condition in the Labrador Retriever. "It's a heart condition that we've found in the last five years to have a definite increased incidence in the Labrador Retriever breed," says Dr. Davidson.

Dogs are born with TVD, which is a malformation of the tricuspid valve on the right side of the heart. It can be present in a mild or severe form; some dogs have no signs, others die.

TVD can be detected by ultrasound in Labs about 4 months of age. Because of the large variety of expressions of this disorder, some mild, some severe, it is not known the mode of inheritance or how widespread it is in the breed.

"The problem we're having now is deciding if dogs with borderline tricuspid valve anatomy should be used for breeding," says Dr. Davidson. She estimates it's going to take a few generations to see if dogs with mild malformations produce more problems than dogs with normal tricuspid valves.

Myopathy

This disease affects the muscles and/or the nervous system of both black and yellow Labs. The first signs are seen early in life, between six weeks and seven months of age, and are usually simply an stiff gait when walking or trotting, or excessive tiredness after exercise. As time passes, most dogs get worse and often collapse after exercise, and have trouble walking, trotting and running. Later their muscles may atrophy and they may have trouble standing up and swallowing food or water.

There is no treatment for this disease, but giving the dog lots of rest and keeping him out of chilly weather does improve the signs. It is inherited as a recessive trait, which means that both parents of the affected dog carry the genes for the disease. Affected dogs and their parents should not be bred.

Basic Training for Labradors

By Liz Palika

In This Chapter

❍ When to Begin Training
❍ The Teaching Process
❍ What Every Good Dog Needs to Know

When you go for a walk around the neighborhood, does your Lab pull on the leash? Does he try to drag you toward every other dog you meet? Does he jump on your neighbors when you stop to say hello? These are all very natural behaviors for a healthy, active, social Labrador Retriever, but they are also unnecessary, annoying, and potentially dangerous behaviors that can be changed (or at least controlled) with training. Your Lab pulls on the leash because he wants to go and you're not walking as fast as he'd like to walk. He pulls you toward the other dogs in the neighborhood because Labs are very social dogs. He wants to see who those dogs are so that he can greet friends and meet the new dogs. Your Lab wants to jump on the neighbors so he can greet them face-to-face, a very natural reaction.

However, just because these are natural behaviors doesn't mean they should continue. When your Lab pulls you down the street on the leash, he's endangering you; you could fall and hurt yourself. Or the constant pulling could injure your shoulder. But he's also endangering himself—the constant pulling could injure his neck and shoulders. Greeting every dog that walks down the street isn't a good idea, either—not all dogs are friendly, and many dogs will react aggressively to a strange dog charging across the street toward them. Jumping on people is a very bad habit and could soil or rip clothing, scratch skin, or cause even more injuries if your Lab knocks someone down.

With training, your Labrador Retriever can learn to control himself so that he's not reacting to every impulse. He can learn social rules, such as to sit when greeting people (so he's not jumping on everyone) and to walk nicely on the leash. When your Lab learns to behave himself in public, he's a joy to take for a walk instead of a monster, and you'll be more likely to take him places because you'll enjoy it more.

Quincy is a black Labrador Retriever owned by Tracy Weldon of Carlsbad, California. Like most Lab puppies, Quincy was very social, very happy, and very enthusiastic about life. When she greeted people, her whole body wagged and wiggled! But like most Labs, Quincy was also very strong and could easily knock people over in her enthusiasm. With training, though,

A well-trained dog will accept your guidance even when he would rather be doing something else.

Basic Commands
Every Dog Should Know

Sit. Your dog's hips should move to the ground while his shoulders stay upright.

Down. Your dog should lie down on the ground or floor and be still.

Stay. Your dog should remain in position (sit or down) when you walk away from him. He should hold the stay until you give him permission to move.

Come. Your dog should come to you on the first call, no matter what the distractions.

Walk nicely on the leash. Your dog can walk ahead of you on the leash but should not pull the leash tight.

Heel. Your dog should walk by your left side with his shoulder by your left leg.

Quincy learned to restrain herself when she was excited. Oh, her tail still wagged at ninety miles an hour, but she would sit still for petting and learned never to jump up on people. Today Quincy is a certified therapy dog and regularly visits nursing homes and Alzheimer's facilities, where she is a welcome and treasured guest.

Training doesn't apply just to social rules when out in public; it can also help you teach your Lab to behave himself in the house. Does your Lab raid the trash cans? Does she get up on the furniture when she shouldn't? Does she chew on your shoes and the kids' toys? Does she dig up your backyard? There's no reason why you should have to put up with these behaviors when training can help.

When to Begin Training

Ideally, training should begin the day you bring your Labrador Retriever home. You can begin to train an eight- or nine-week-old

Characteristics of a Trained Dog

A trained dog knows:

❍ The appropriate behaviors allowed with people (no biting, no mouthing, no rough play, and no mounting);

❍ Where to relieve himself and how to ask to go outside;

❍ How to greet people properly without jumping on them;

❍ To wait for your permission to greet people, other dogs, and other pets;

❍ How to walk on a leash nicely so that walks are enjoyable;

❍ To leave the trash cans alone;

❍ To leave food alone (on the counters or coffee table) that isn't his;

❍ Not to beg;

❍ To chew on his toys and not your personal things;

❍ To play with his toys and not the kids' toys;

❍ That destructive behavior is not acceptable;

❍ To wait for permission before going through doorways.

A trained dog is a happy dog, secure in his place in the family.

puppy that biting isn't allowed, to sit for every meal, and where he should go to relieve himself. When your puppy is 10 weeks old, you can start attaching a leash to his collar and let him drag it around for a few minutes at a time so that he gets used to the feel of it. Puppies have a very short attention span but are willing and eager students, especially when you make training fun.

Keep in mind that your adorable Lab puppy is going to grow up to be a big, strong dog. Don't let the puppy do anything now that you'll regret later. For example, if you teach the puppy to cuddle with you on your lap, will you still want him to do that when he weighs 65 pounds?

If you adopt an older Lab puppy or an adult, you can still start training right away. Your Lab will need time to get used to your household, especially if she was in a shelter, a stray, or at a breeder's kennel. But the training will help your new dog learn what you expect of her and make that adjustment easier.

Start teaching your new Lab the rules you expect of her right away. For example, if you don't want her to get up on the furniture, never allow this behavior. Don't make excuses like, "Oh, this is a new house, and she's upset. We can teach her to stay off the furniture later." If you don't want her up on the furniture, she needs to learn right away what your rules are. Breaking bad habits later is much harder!

Start training early so that your puppy learns good behavior instead of bad habits.

Is It Ever Too Late?

Do you have a three-year-old Labrador Retriever who isn't as well behaved as you'd like? It's not too late—you can still train him. The problem with starting training later is that you have to break bad habits as well as teach the new behaviors. With a young puppy, you're starting with a clean slate and can teach the proper behavior before he learns any bad habits. If you've ever tried to stop a bad habit yourself (smoking, for example), you know that it can be very difficult. But with most Labrador Retrievers up to about seven years of age you can, with consistent training and lots of patience, control most bad habits.

Kindergarten Puppy Class

The ideal time to start a group training class is as soon as your Lab puppy has had at least two sets of vaccinations. Many veterinarians may recommend that you wait even longer—ask your vet. Most kindergarten puppy classes recommend that puppies start any time between 10 and 12 weeks of age. These classes provide you with instruction on how to teach your puppy and include the basic commands—sit, down, stay, and come—all geared to the puppy's short attention span. During puppy classes, your dog will also spend time socializing with other people and other puppies.

If your dog is older than eight or nine years of age, you'll have limited success at changing bad habits. Your dog will be able to learn the basic commands heel, sit, down, stay, or come without too much trouble. But you'll have limited success with breaking bad habits in an older dog—especially if he's had those bad habits for years. For example, if your dog has been jumping on people for eight years, you can probably change that by teaching him to sit instead. As an older, heavier, and possibly arthritic dog, he's going to be less apt to jump anyway, and the praise he gets for sitting will make it more worthwhile. But if your older dog has been raiding the outside trash cans for eight years to steal food, your chances of changing that behavior are very small because he's getting rewarded for the activity (by the food he finds) each time he does it. You'd be better off concentrating your efforts on preventing the trash can raids from happening rather than on changing your dog.

Sometimes behavior problems are just impossible to solve. A habit may be too deeply ingrained or the dog's desire too strong to curb. I speak from personal experience. One of my Labs learned at a young age that there was food in the kitchen trash

Basic Obedience Training Class

Most dog obedience instructors invite puppies to join the basic class after they graduate from a puppy class or after the puppy reaches four months of age. Dogs older than four months who have never attended a puppy class also begin with the basic class. In the basic class the traditional beginner commands are taught: sit, down, stay, come, and heel. In addition, most instructors spend time discussing problem behaviors, such as jumping on people, barking, digging, and chewing. A group class such as this helps your Lab learn to control himself around other dogs and people—serious distractions!

can. Ursa, who passed away at the age of 13½, was never reliable around food, even as an old dog. My husband and I had a standing joke that Ursa must have died of starvation in a former lifetime because she'd eat any food she could find. She didn't care what kind of trouble she got into—food was to be eaten! Because of this, I could never trust her in the house alone.

Basic Dog Psychology

People and dogs share a long history. Archeologists have found evidence of human domestication of canines in archeological sites dating back thousands of years. Why did this relationship develop? Perhaps wolves, who are efficient predators, had hunting skills early humans could use. But why did the wolf decide to cooperate with humans? Perhaps some kindhearted person adopted an orphan wolf pup, and the wolf grew up as a semidomesticated animal that considered the people around it as its pack. This wolf could have warned its human pack of trespassers and other predators, helped on the hunt, and provided companionship. In

Private Training

Experts usually recommend private training for dogs with behavior problems the owner can't handle alone. The trainer can tailor the private instruction, which is one-on-one either at your home or the trainer's facility, to your dog's specific problems.

return the wolf would have received companionship, a steady supply of food, and shelter from the weather. No one knows if this is what really happened, but we do have the end result—domesticated dogs who have been human protectors, helpers, and companions for thousands of years.

Families and Packs

In the wild, wolves live in packs. The pack consists of a dominant male, a dominant female, several subordinate adults, a juvenile or two, and the latest pups. The adults all hunt for the puppies and help to protect, rear, and care for the pups. Every pack has an important set of social rules—including limiting the breeding to the two dominant adults—that all members of the pack must obey. The leaders usually initiate the hunt and then direct where and when the hunt will take place. They eat first and best, with the subordinate animals grabbing what they can until the leaders finish and move away. The leaders decide where the pack's den will be, and the rest of the pack follows. These and other rules help keep order among the pack members and minimize disruption in the pack, unless one of the members decides to move up in the pack order. If an older wolf becomes disabled, dies, or leaves the pack or if a younger wolf gets ambitious, the more dominant wolves may posture or fight until they establish a new pack order.

Because of their pack heredity, dogs fit into the social structure of a human family. Of course, although family life resembles a pack in many way, it's very different from a traditional wolf pack in others. Our families often include an adult male and adult female who serve as leaders, but many households today have only one adult. Other adults are seldom part of the immediate human family, and juveniles (teenagers) and children may or may not be present. Family members rarely adhere to the rules of the household as strongly as wolves follow the social rules of the pack. For example, in a wolf pack, the leaders eat first. In our families, people eat any time, often simultaneously, and the order of eating holds no significance to us. These family rules or lack of rules can confuse dogs.

> Archeologists have found evidence of human domestication of canines in archeological sites dating back thousands of years.

What Does it Mean to Be Top Dog?

"Top dog" is a slang term for the pack leader. In a wolf pack, the top dogs are the dominant male and the dominant female, often called the alpha male and alpha female. In your family pack, the top dogs should be you, as the dog's owner, and any other human in the family.

During adolescence, a Labrador with a particularly bold personality may make a try for leadership of his (or her) family pack, but this is uncommon, since Labs aren't usually as aggressive as some other breeds. Adolescence usually strikes at sexual maturity,

Don't let your dog use his body language to show dominance. Your dog should recognize you (and your children) as above him in the family pack.

usually between eight and 12 months of age, and may last for a few months. During this stage of development, the dog is growing up and taking his place in the world.

If the owner is less dominant than the dog or if the owner is unaware of the signals the dog relates to dominance, the dog may actually think he's in charge. For example, eating first is an important signal to the dog. When do you feed your Lab? Many dog owners feed the dog first to get him out from underfoot while they're cooking. If you feed your dog before you eat, he could interpret this as a weakness on your part, even though it means nothing to you! Going first is important, too. Who goes through first when you open the door? Have your dog wait for you.

A dog who takes over can make life miserable around the house. This is when you'll see growling, snapping, and biting at people; sexual behavior (marking and mounting); and other dominant behaviors. The dog may growl whenever you try to make him do something—such as move off the furniture—and the growl may escalate to a snap or bite. Your dog can't be the top dog in your household; after all, it's your house!

Although it's very important that your dog regard you as the leader, or top dog, don't take everything he does as a dominance challenge. Most of the time your Lab doesn't care about his and your position in the pack; he knows you're in charge. After all, he knows you're important—you supply the food! But for dogs

You Are the Top Dog!

○ Always eat first, even if it's just an apple or carrot.

○ Always go though doorways before your dog does. Block the dog with your leg or foot to keep him from charging through ahead of you.

○ Go upstairs ahead of your dog. Don't let him charge ahead and then look down at you.

○ Give him permission to do things. If he picks up his ball, tell him,

"Get your ball! Good boy!" even though he was going to do it anyway.

○ Practice your training regularly.

○ Command your dog to roll over for a tummy rub daily.

○ Don't play rough games—no wrestling or tug-of-war.

○ Never let your Lab stand up and put his paws on your shoulders.

who do have a dominant personality, training during adolescence is critical.

The Teaching Process

Training your dog isn't a mysterious process, although sometimes it might seem that way. Teaching your dog consists primarily of communication and rewarding the behaviors you want—or interrupting the behaviors you don't want—to continue happening. For example, you're in the kitchen, fixing lunch, and your dog follows you into the kitchen. Watch her out of the corner of your eye and see if she moves toward the trash can. If she sniffs it, in a deep, growling tone of voice tell her, "Leave it alone!" When she reacts to your voice by stopping the sniffing and backing away, tell her in a higher-pitched tone of voice, "That's good to leave it alone!"

Did you notice I specified different tones of voice? Because dogs are verbal animals, the tone of voice you use in communicating with them is very important. When your 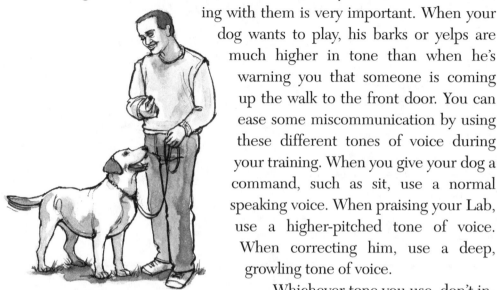 dog wants to play, his barks or yelps are much higher in tone than when he's warning you that someone is coming up the walk to the front door. You can ease some miscommunication by using these different tones of voice during your training. When you give your dog a command, such as sit, use a normal speaking voice. When praising your Lab, use a higher-pitched tone of voice. When correcting him, use a deep, growling tone of voice.

A treat can be a wonderful training tool to help teach your dog to pay attention to you. When he looks at you, praise him, give him the treat, and then follow through with other training.

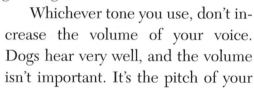

Whichever tone you use, don't increase the volume of your voice. Dogs hear very well, and the volume isn't important. It's the pitch of your voice that matters to a dog. Likewise, don't say something to your dog and then giggle. If you do, he's not going to take you seriously. Don't laugh at him no matter how cute he looks with the sofa cushion stuffing hanging out of his mouth.

Keep in mind, too, that your Lab wasn't born understanding English, French, or German. Therefore, you need to consistently use your tone of voice and your actions to teach him what our verbalizations (words) mean. For example, to teach him what sit means, say the word as you take a treat and hold it above his nose, moving it slowly back over his head toward his tail. As his head goes up, his hips will go down. When his hips touch the ground, praise him with the words, "Good to sit!" and give him

Training Vocabulary

You'll encounter certain terms that you need to understand to train your Labrador Retriever. Your basic canine training vocabulary consists of the following terms:

Positive reinforcement. Anything your dog likes that you can use to reward good behavior, including verbal praise, food treats, toys, and petting.

Praise. Words spoken in a higher-than-normal tone of voice to reward your dog for something he did right; part of positive reinforcement.

Lure. Something your dog enjoys that can help direct him to do something or to assume a position; usually to learn a new command. A lure can be food treats or a toy.

Interruption. Immediately stopping your dog the moment you catch him in the act of doing something. This might consist of a verbal command issued in a deeper tone of voice, such as "No! Leave it alone!" or a sharp sound, such as clapping or dropping a book to the floor.

Correction. Letting your dog know that he's made a mistake. This could consist of a deeper-than-normal tone of voice, an interruption, or a snap-and-release movement of the leash. A correction should be enough to get your dog's attention, and that's all.

the treat. The treat is called a lure. It helps your dog to move in the right direction. The lure also becomes part of your positive reinforcement, letting the dog know he has done something right.

Timing is also very important when you're teaching your dog. Praise her (in a high-pitched voice) as she does something right and correct her (in a deeper voice) as she's making a mistake. In the kitchen trash can example, you need to let your Lab know she's making a mistake *as she sniffs the kitchen trash can*, not when she walks into the kitchen and not when you walk into the

Corrections should be given as the dog is making the mistake, not after the fact.

kitchen and find trash all over the floor and your dog gone. Correcting after the fact doesn't work!

During the training process, don't hesitate to set your dog up for success. We all—dogs and people—learn more from our successes than our failures, and your Lab will be more likely to try again if she succeeds. To set your dog up for success, think about what it is you want to teach her, and then make sure both the environment and your actions support that objective. For example, if you want to keep your Lab off the furniture, ask her to lie down at your feet *before* she jumps up on the sofa. If you want her to stop jumping on people, ask her to sit *before* she jumps on your neighbor.

Don't rely too heavily on corrections to teach your dog. You can let your dog know that she's made a mistake when you catch her in the act—her nose in the trash can—but don't correct her after the fact. She may associate the correction with many things—the trash on the floor, you catching her in the kitchen, or even the trash—but she may not associate the correction with the act of dumping over the trash can.

Although a properly timed correction can let your dog know he's making a mistake, it doesn't tell him what's right to do. For example, if you want to teach your Lab not to jump on people and you correct him, "No jump!" when he begins to leap at someone, he may learn not to jump at them, but you aren't teaching him how to greet people. Your training must address that problem, too. Teach your Lab to sit to greet people. Once he knows how to do that, correct him when he jumps up.

The Training Process

To teach a new command:

○ Show the dog what to do with a lure, your hands, or your voice;

○ Praise him for doing it and reward him with the lure, if you used one;

○ Correct him for mistakes only when he knows and understands the command and chooses not to do it.

To correct problem behavior:

○ Prevent the problem from happening when possible;

○ Set the dog up for success by teaching him to do something else and then rewarding it;

○ Interrupt the behavior when you catch the dog in the act. Let him know he made a mistake;

○ Show him the appropriate behavior.

Teaching Your Dog to Be Handled

Your Labrador Retriever can't care for herself—that's your job. So you must be able to comb and brush her, check for fleas and ticks, and look for cuts, scrapes, bumps, and bruises. When she's hurt or sick, you need to be able to take care of her, whether it's cleaning and medicating her ears when she has an ear infection, caring for her stitches after spaying, or washing out her eyes if dirt gets in them.

It's important to teach your dog to trust you before you need to medicate her. From the day you bring your Lab home, whether as a puppy or an adult, one thing you can do every evening is to teach her to accept social handling. Sit on the floor and invite your Lab to lie down between your legs or in front of you. Roll her over so you can rub her tummy to help her relax. When she's relaxed, start giving her a massage. Begin massaging at her muzzle, rubbing your fingers gently over the skin, and at

Make a Negative into a Positive

Jessie, a yellow Labrador Retriever from Orange County, California, protested any time her owner had to medicate Jessie's ears. Unfortunately Jessie had an ongoing problem with her ears and needed to have them cleaned out and medicated a couple of times a day. When Jessie's owner called me for help, I had her bring Jessie and her medication to me. I watched one of their horrible sessions. Jessie obviously hated this handling and fought with every ounce of her being, even though the ear cleaning didn't appear to be painful—she was just used to fighting. I went in the house and came out with a big spoon and a big jar of peanut butter. I had Jessie sit and offered her a glob of peanut butter. While she licked it, I told her owner to start cleaning one of Jessie's ears. Jessie wiggled, but she was so focused on the peanut butter, she put up with the cleaning. Within a few minutes, it was all over—both ears done—and Jessie was licking the last of the peanut butter off her lips.

the same time check her teeth. Then move up her head, touching the skin around her eyes, looking for a discharge or problem in her eyes. Move up to her ears, stroking the ear flap, massaging around the base of each ear, and while you're there, look inside the ear for potential problems. Continue in the same manner, massaging your dog all over her body, from her nose to the tip of her tail. If at any time your Lab protests, go back to a tummy rub for a moment or offer her a little bit of peanut butter.

A tummy rub can help relax your dog if he's over-stimulated. You can also follow through with any needed grooming. In addition, this is a wonderful time for bonding with your dog.

Do this exercise daily and incorporate your grooming in it.

A Side Benefit of the Lab Massage

There's a welcome side benefit to the daily Lab massage. By the time you're through massaging your Lab, she'll be totally relaxed, like a limp noodle! So massage your dog when you want her to be quiet and relaxed. If she's over-active in the evening when you'd like to relax and watch a favorite television show, turn on the TV and start massaging her. She'll fall asleep, and you can watch the rest of your show!

Comb and brush one side, then roll her over and do the other side. Trim her nails after you've massaged her feet and checked them for cuts and scratches.

If your dog needs medication or first aid treatments, you can do that while massaging, too, so that the treatment doesn't turn into a big fight. It simply becomes part of the daily massage.

The Importance of Good Socialization

Socialization is a vital part of raising a mentally healthy, well-adjusted Labrador Retriever. Introducing a young Lab to a variety of people of different ages and ethnic backgrounds will help make him a social dog who is unafraid and happy to meet people on a walk. Dogs who aren't properly socialized may grow up afraid of children, senior citizens, or people of a different ethnic background than their owners. These dogs often become fear biters, and when that happens, the dog is considered dangerous and usually destroyed.

Socialization also refers to meeting other dogs and pets. A well-socialized dog gets opportunities to meet dogs of a variety of sizes, shapes, colors, and breeds and learns how to behave around these other dogs. Ideally, you should also introduce your dog to dog-friendly cats, rabbits, ferrets, horses, and other pets. Why socialize a city dog to horses? San Diego, for example, is a good-sized metropolis, and not many horses live within the city limits anymore. But the police do have a horse patrol for certain areas of the city, including beautiful Balboa Park. Many city dogs meet a horse for the first time when they're walking in the park with their owners and a mounted police officer rides by. Some dogs panic when they see a horse for the first time and frantically try to pull away from the horse and their owner. Other dogs try to attack the horse. A well-socialized dog will sniff toward the horse to identify it, think about it for a moment, and then relax. After all, it's just a horse! The important lesson is that whether it's horses, llamas, or a trash truck, the more your Lab is introduced to, the better.

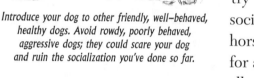

Introduce your dog to other friendly, well-behaved, healthy dogs. Avoid rowdy, poorly behaved, aggressive dogs; they could scare your dog and ruin the socialization you've done so far.

Socialization also includes introducing your Lab to the world around him so that he knows and doesn't fear the sights and sounds of his environment. Let him see and hear a motorcycle going down the street, kids on skateboards and inline skates, the garbage truck on trash day, and birthday party balloons. Walk him past the construction crew working on the house down the street, and let him stop and watch the road crew working on the intersection. The more he sees and hears, the better his coping skills will be as an adult.

Don't introduce your Lab to everything all at once, or you may overload him! You can start socialization when your puppy is about nine to 10 weeks old by letting some friendly, gentle neighbors meet him and cuddle him. Don't allow rough play or handling; interfere if it starts to get too rowdy. Gradually over days and weeks, introduce your puppy to different people, sights, and sounds. Take him to the local pet store when you buy dog food and let people pet him. While there, he can see a shopping cart and follow it with you as you shop. If something frightens your puppy, don't cuddle him and speak softly to him because he'll mistake your soft words as praise for being afraid. Instead use a joking tone of voice to say, "What was that?" Then walk up to whatever frightened your pup and touch it, if you can, to show him it's not dangerous. Don't force him to walk up to it. For example, if your puppy sees a trash can blowing down the street and panics, hold tight to his leash and walk up to the trash can. Ask your puppy in an upbeat tone of voice, "What's this? Labbie, look!" Pat the trash can several times so that your puppy can see you touch it. If he'll walk up to it, praise him for his bravery.

Luckily Labs are by nature very social dogs, but they still need good socialization. Kindergarten puppy class is a wonderful way for Lab puppies to meet other people and other puppies. Most kindergarten puppy classes have playground equipment and toys for the puppies to play with and increase their socialization skills and confidence. Adult Labs can still be socialized, although the best time to do this is during puppyhood.

How a Crate Can Help

Originally built as travel cages, crates have become a popular and valuable training tool. A crate can help you house-train your Lab puppy by confining him to a small place during the night and for a few hours during the day. Because your puppy doesn't want to soil his bed, he'll develop better bowel and bladder control.

A crate helps your puppy develop bowel and bladder control, prevents accidents from happening, and becomes your puppy's special place.

The crate also serves as an effective training tool in preventing problems. If your Lab sleeps in his crate during the night, he can't sneak away to chew up shoes or raid the trash cans. When he's confined while you're at the store, he isn't shredding the sofa cushions. Your crated dog is not only prevented from getting into trouble but also isn't learning bad habits. As he grows up, he can gradually be given more freedom, but not until he's mature mentally and emotionally—about three years old for most Labs!

As you use the crate, it will become your dog's special place. He'll retreat to his crate for a nap when the household is quiet or when he doesn't feel good. He might hide his favorite toys in his crate or go there to chew on a special rawhide. He'll soon use his crate as his refuge.

Many first-time dog owners initially have a problem with the idea of confining their dog to a crate, often comparing it to a jail cell. But dogs are den animals. In the wild, wolves and coyotes give birth in a den or cave and the puppies are confined until their mother thinks they're old enough to venture out. Most domesticated mother dogs are the same way and prefer to give birth in a quiet, secure spot. That's why most breeders provide pregnant females with a whelping box built for that purpose.

Introduce your Lab to the crate by propping open the door (so it can't close accidentally) and tossing a treat or toy inside. Let her reach in to grab the treat and then back out. Praise her for

Choosing the Right Crate

Crates come in two basic styles: solid-sided plastic crates that are used for airline travel and wire crates that look like cages. Each style has advantages and disadvantages. The wire-sided crates provide more ventilation and are good if you live in a very warm climate. But because they're more open, some dogs feel insecure in these crates. Wire crates are usually collapsible and don't take up as much room as plastic crates, but they're very heavy. Plastic crates don't collapse and are harder to store, but they're lighter. They don't allow as much air circulation as the wire crates but do provide more security for the dog. Look at your needs and your dog's personality to choose the right crate style.

The crate should be big enough for your dog to stand up and turn around in as an adult. You'll use the crate for many years, so get one that will be big enough for your adult dog. If you aren't sure what size to get, ask for help at the pet store.

her bravery! Repeat this several times. Then offer her a meal in the crate. Keep the door propped open and set her dinner bowl inside the crate so she needs to step inside to get her meal.

While you're introducing your Lab to the crate, start teaching her a command. As you toss in the treat or toy, wait for her to move toward the crate. When she steps inside, say, "Labbie, crate!" or, "Labbie, go to bed!" At the beginning of crate training, give her a treat each time she goes inside the crate. She'll not only go inside faster and with more enthusiasm but will think of the crate as something positive instead of confining.

The best place for the crate is in your bedroom. I moved my nightstand out into the garage and put the dog crate right next to the bed and use that as a nightstand. That way I can hear the dog and know when she needs to go outside. In addition, she gets to spend eight uninterrupted hours with me. In our busy society, that's important time! She can hear me, smell me, and be with me even though we really aren't doing anything together. It's still time for her to be with me, a member of her family pack.

If you don't want the dog crate in your bedroom, maybe you could put it in one of the kids' rooms. Or maybe you could put it in the hallway outside your room. Whatever you decide to do, don't isolate your Lab by putting him out in the backyard, garage, or laundry room alone. Remember that dogs are social animals—isolation can cause such behavior problems as self-mutilation and destructiveness.

Your Lab can spend the whole night in his crate and a few hours here and there during the day, but preferably no more than three or four hours at a time. After spending the night in his crate, your Lab needs time out of the crate during the day to play, exercise, follow you around, and learn the rules of the house.

What Every Good Dog Needs to Know

No Jumping

Life with your Labrador Retriever will be no fun and downright embarrassing if he doesn't have good social skills. Dogs were domesticated to be friends, companions, and helpers—not pains in the neck! It's not difficult to teach your dog social skills.

Your Labrador Retriever is much too big and strong to jump on people—he could hurt them, scare them, or ruin their clothes—so that should be the first social skill to work on with him. Teach your Lab to sit each and every time he greets people—you, your spouse, your kids, guests, and people on the street (we'll talk about how to teach the sit later in this chapter). Once he knows how to sit, enforce it every time he greets someone.

You can do this in several ways. First, if your dog doesn't have his leash on—say, when you come home from work—then make sure you at least greet him with empty hands. As your dog dashes up to you and begins to jump, grab his buckle collar (which should be on him with his ID tags) and tell him, "Labbie, no jump! Sit!" and with your hand on his collar, help him sit. Keep your hands on him as he sits so that you can help him maintain that position. Praise him for sitting: "Good boy to sit! Yes, you are!"

> Life with your Labrador Retriever will be no fun and downright embarrassing if he doesn't have good social skills.

The leash is also a good training tool to help the dog sit. When guests come to your house, ask them to wait outside for a moment as you leash your dog. (They'll be more than happy to wait!) Once your dog is leashed, let your guests in. Have your dog sit before the guests pet him. If he bounces up, have your guests back off, and don't let them pet him again until you have him sit. This, of course, requires training your guests, too, and making sure they cooperate. If your dog learns that he can jump on some people, he'll never be reliable about not jumping.

You can do the same thing while out on walks with your Lab. Have him sit before you let people pet him. If he gets too wiggly and bounces up, have the people step back for a minute until he's sitting again.

When training young dogs of my own not to jump, I've found that some people won't go along with it. "Oh, I don't mind," they say, brushing paw prints off their clothes. But I don't want my dogs ruining people's clothes, scratching them, or knocking them down. I try to explain to people in contact with my Lab why this training is important, and usually most of them will help.

To Bark or Not to Bark

All dogs bark; it's their way of communicating. Although some barking is acceptable—if someone comes to the front door or a trespasser is climbing over the back fence—too much barking is annoying. Neighbors are quick to complain when a constant barker disrupts the neighborhood. Luckily Labrador Retrievers aren't normally problem barkers, although when Labs do bark, their bark can be very loud!

> The easiest way to make sure your dog doesn't become a problem barker is to control his barking while you're at home.

The easiest way to make sure your dog doesn't become a problem barker is to control his barking while you're at home. Invite a neighbor over and ask her to ring your doorbell. When she does and your dog charges the door, barking loudly, step up to your dog, grab his collar, and tell him, "Labbie, quiet!" If he stops barking, praise him. If he doesn't stop, close his mouth with your hand, wrapping your fingers around his muzzle as you tell him again to be quiet. If he stops, praise him.

Many dogs will learn the "quiet" command with repeated training like this. But some dogs are more vocal and more persistent about barking than others. These dogs need a somewhat stronger correction. Take a clean, empty squirt bottle and put about half an inch of white vinegar in the bottom. Fill the rest of the squirt bottle with water. Squirt the mixture on the palm of your hand and smell it. There should be just a whiff of vinegar smell—not strong—just enough so you know some vinegar is there. If it's stronger, dilute it with more water.

The next time your dog charges the door in a barking frenzy after hearing the doorbell, follow him and quietly say, "Labbie, quiet!" If he stops barking, fine—praise him. If he ignores you,

Bark Collars

Several different types of bark control collars are on the market. Some of these devices give the dog an electric shock or jolt when he barks, some make a high-pitched sound, and one emits a squirt of citronella. The citronella collar works on the same concept as the vinegar-water squirt bottle: the smell is annoying enough to make the dog stop what he's doing. I generally recommend the citronella collar to dog owners. It's a very effective, humane training tool.

squirt a mist of the vinegar water toward his nose (avoid getting it in his eyes). He'll smell the vinegar, and because he has such a finely tuned nose, he won't like it. He'll stop barking, back off, and lick the vinegar water off his nose. Praise him for being quiet! The squirt bottle works as an interruption because it can stop the behavior (the barking) without giving him a harsh correction.

Use the same training techniques (verbal correction, collar, closing the muzzle, or squirt bottle, followed by praise if he responds appropriately) to teach your dog to listen to your "quiet" command around the house. When he reliably follows the "quiet" command in your home, then move the training outside. If he barks at the gate when kids are playing out front, go out there (out of your dog's sight) and be prepared to correct him with a sharp "quiet" as soon as he barks. Always, of course, praise him when he's quiet.

No Begging

Your Lab has no reason to beg while you're eating. Her food appears regularly, and she certainly isn't starving. Some dogs love food, and begging for scraps or a dropped tidbit is normal behavior for them. But begging is a bad habit that usually escalates. It may start with the dog lying under the table, waiting for a tidbit to fall. The dog will then move to laying her head in your lap, hoping to catch the tidbit before it hits the floor. It can lead to stealing food from the children's hands and sneaking food off the table or counters.

Begging is relatively easy to solve. (Later in this chapter you'll learn how to teach your dog the down-stay command.) Once your Lab has mastered the down-stay, use this command to make her hold her position while people are eating. I don't like to exile the dog to the backyard during meals—that just creates more frustration—but you can make the dog lie down in a corner of the dining room and stay there while people eat. If someone in the family can't resist the dog's pleading eyes, then put the dog behind that person during meals so that he or she can't see the dog and won't be tempted to drop a treat. When everyone has finished eating, the dog can then be given a treat *in her bowl*, away from the table.

Teach your dog to hold a down–stay while you're eating. He will learn that he gets to eat when you are finished so he must be patient.

When you first begin this training, make sure you use a leash and collar on the dog. If she has been doing any begging, she's not going to want to give up this very rewarding (to her) habit. Have her lie down and stay where you want her to remain during the meal. Drop the leash next to her and then sit at the table. When the dog gets up from the down (which she'll probably do!), tell her "No!" and put her back in the down-stay at the same place where you originally left her. (Don't let her crawl across the dining room floor!) Your first meal under this new regime will probably be tough; you'll have to correct her several times. But be persistent and firm, and she'll learn the new rules.

No Biting!

Dog bites have received a lot of bad press lately. Every time a dog bite ends up on the evening news, more and more anti-dog legislation is introduced. In some parts of the United States, Great Britain, and other countries, it's now illegal to own certain breeds of dogs.

Luckily Labrador Retrievers aren't on the list of prohibited dogs, but as a dog owner you've still got to take seriously the possibility that your dog will bite. All it takes is one bite, and your dog could be euthanized—plain and simple.

A dog bite is legally defined as when the dog's teeth touch skin. The skin doesn't have to be broken. Vicious intent isn't required, either. If your dog is in the backyard with the kids and grabs the neighbor's son with his teeth, it's a dog bite, even if the dog just wanted to be a part of the play.

You must teach your Lab never to allow his teeth to touch human skin—ever! The dog must not grab at your hand when he wants you to do something or protest with his teeth when you take something away from him. He should never grab your arm or pant leg with his mouth when you play with him. Don't let him mouth you while you're grooming him, petting him, or trimming his toenails. Be consistent and make sure other family members are, too.

It's easy to train young puppies not to use their teeth. Each and every time the puppy grabs skin or clothes, tell him in a deep

No Wrestling!

Dog owners often love to wrestle with their dogs. The owner and dog get down on the floor and roll around, pinning each other and having a great time.

Unfortunately this isn't a good game to play. Wrestling teaches your dog to use his mouth to grab and hold on to people or reinforces a tendency he may already have to do this, a very bad lesson for the dog to learn.

tone of voice, "No bite!" and take your hand away. If he bites during play, correct him and end the game; just get up and walk away. If he bites hard, say, "Ouch!" in a high-pitched, hurt tone of voice and follow it with a deep, "No bite!"

If the puppy persists in using his teeth, take hold of him by his buckle collar with one hand and close his mouth with the other hand as you tell him, "No bite." If he struggles, simply sit down on the floor and hold him on your lap or between your legs until he relaxes. If you let go too soon, he'll simply turn and try to get at you again.

Older puppies or adult Labs who have been using their teeth for any period of time sometimes have difficulty learning the new rules. However, if you are consistent with the training, they are fully capable of learning.

Where to Dig (and Where Not to Dig)

Dogs dig for a number of reasons, all of which are very natural and normal to the dog. Your Lab may think the dirt smells good after a rain or after the sprinklers have been on. She may want to investigate a gopher or mole burrow. If the weather is hot, she

Time-Out!

If your Lab puppy throws a temper tantrum when you correct him—throws himself around and acts like a wild animal—simply take him back to his crate, put him in, close the door, and leave him there for 15 to 20 minutes. Don't yell at him or scold him. This time-out will give him a chance to relax and let you take a deep breath. Most puppies will throw a temper tantrum or two at some point during puppyhood, especially if you ask the puppy to do something or correct him for doing something like biting. As with children, you don't want him to learn that throwing a temper tantrum will get him what he wants.

may decide to dig down to some cool earth to lie in. Your dog has no idea why you get so upset about digging—the concept of a smooth, green lawn with no holes in it is beyond your dog's comprehension!

Because digging is so natural to your dog, it's a good idea to give her someplace where she can dig. If there's a particular spot she really likes, perhaps in a corner behind the garage or next to the back porch, let her have that spot. Frame it off with wood or bricks if you want. Dig it up even more so it's nice and soft, and then bury and partially bury some dog toys and treats to invite her to dig there.

In the rest of your yard, fill in her holes and sprinkle some grass seed over them. If she's dug up a couple of holes repeatedly, fill them in, spread some hardware cloth (wire mesh) over it, and anchor the cloth. Let the grass grow up through this mesh; you can leave it permanently if it's anchored well enough. If your dog tries to redig her hole, she'll hit the wire mesh. She won't be able to dig, and the wire mesh won't feel good on her pads.

If you catch your Lab in the act of digging, you can correct her as you would for any other misbehavior—but don't count on catching her. Most dogs seem to dig when they're alone, usually in the morning just after their owner leaves for work. A strenuous morning run or a good game of catch might alleviate the digging problem. It's worth a try!

> **B**ecause digging is so natural to your dog, it's a good idea to give her someplace where she can dig.

Destructive Chewing

Destructive chewing often starts while the puppy is teething. When his jaws hurt from teething, chewing helps satisfy his need to relieve that discomfort. But the puppy will quickly discover that chewing is fun. It gives him something to do when he's bored—if he chews the corner off a cushion and shakes it, stuffing will go flying everything. What fun!

But chewing is a destructive, costly behavior that must be controlled. Not stopped, but controlled. Your puppy needs to be able to chew, so you'll have to teach him what to chew on and prevent him from destructive chewing.

Prevention is an important part of controlling a chewing problem. Keep closet doors closed, make sure shoes and dirty clothes are put away, and have the kids put away their toys. Don't let your Lab have free run of the house until he's grown up and totally reliable. Keep him close to you and don't let him wander away. When you see him pick up something he shouldn't have, take it away from him as you say, "No! That's mine!" Then take him to his toys and offer him one, saying, "Here, this is yours!"

When your dog picks up one of his toys, rather than something of yours, praise him! Tell him what a smart dog he is and how

Too Many Toys?

If your dog is a chewer, don't try to change his behavior by giving him lots of toys. Too many toys will give him the idea that he can chew on anything and everything because virtually everything is his! Instead, give him just two or three toys at a time. If he likes toys, you can buy him new ones, but rotate the toys so he has only two or three at a time. On Monday, you could give him a rawhide, a squeaky toy, and a Kong toy. On Tuesday, substitute a new rawhide, a rope tug toy, and a tennis ball. By rotating the toys, you can keep him interested in them without overwhelming him.

proud you are of him! Really go overboard. When he learns this is a good choice, he'll be more likely to repeat the behavior later.

Remember that if you find he's chewed something up earlier, don't punish him. After-the-fact corrections don't work.

Other Undesirable Behaviors

Labrador Retrievers are usually pretty good dogs. Unlike some other breeds, their owners don't have to deal with too many problem behaviors. A common problem faced by most Lab owners, especially the owners of young Labs, includes rowdy behavior, such as jumping on people. Training and maturity will help your dog gain self-control.

If your Lab has behavior problems that weren't discussed here, approach them by applying the same methods used to train your dog in other areas. What is your dog doing? When does he do it? Why does he do it? Does he need more training? More exercise? Can you catch him in the act so that you can teach him? Can you set him up so that you can catch him in the act? If you can't catch him in the act, can you prevent the problem behavior from happening?

If you are unable to solve any behavioral problem, don't hesitate to call a reputable trainer or behaviorist for help. Ask your veterinarian for a recommendation.

House Training

Using a Crate to House-Train

As previously stated, a crate is a wonderful training tool to help you house-train your puppy. Puppies are born with an instinct to keep their beds clean and will toddle away from their bed as soon as they are able. A crate builds on that instinct. Confining your puppy to her crate during the night helps her to develop greater bowel and bladder control. Of course, that means you must let the puppy out of the crate and outside as often as she needs to go.

> Puppies purchased from a pet store are often much more difficult to house-train than puppies purchased from a breeder.

Puppies purchased from a pet store are often much more difficult to house-train than puppies purchased from a breeder. Confined to cages, pet-store puppies have no choice but to relieve themselves there. A pet-store puppy has nowhere else to urinate and defecate, so the need to relieve himself overrides the instinct to keep her bed clean. But with patience and persistence, you can crate-train these puppies as well.

House-Training Timetable

Your dog will need to relieve herself after:

- ○ Each meal
- ○ Drinking water
- ○ Playtime
- ○ Waking up from a nap
- ○ Every two to three hours in between

Alert: When you see the puppy sniffing the floor and circling, grab her quick and get her outside!

You can also crate-train an older puppy or adult dog even if the previous owner never introduced him to a crate as a puppy. The process is the same—it just might take longer.

House-Training Guidelines

Of course, you need more than a crate to house-train your dog, whether she's a puppy or an adult. House training also requires teaching the dog where you want her to relieve herself. You should teach her a word (command) so you can ask her to relieve herself when you need her to, when on a trip, for example. Restrict her freedom in the house until she's reliably house-trained.

Just sending the dog outside alone won't work. If you simply open the door and shoo her outside, how do you know whether and where she's relieved herself? She may have spent a half hour chasing butterflies and relieve herself on the carpet. You must go outside with your dog. Tell her to "go potty!" (or whatever command you want to use). When she does what she needs to do, praise her.

Asking to Go Outside

Don't teach a dog to bark when she needs to go outside—barking dogs often cause neighborhood complaints. Your dog does need some way to tell you she wants to go outside, so teach her to ring some bells instead.

Go to a craft store and get two or three bells, about two inches across. Hang them with a string from the doorknob or handle where you want the dog to ask to go outside. Make sure they hang at your dog's nose level. Rub a strong-scented dog treat on the bells and encourage your dog to nose and lick it. When the bell rings, open the door quickly, take your dog outside, praise her, and give her the treat.

Repeat this training three or four times per training session for several days. When she makes the association and starts ringing the bell on her own, reward her with enthusiastic praise instead of a treat and let her outside!

Once she's done her business, bring her inside and give her some supervised time in the house. Put up baby gates or close doors so that you can restrict her activities. Don't consider her house-trained for at least six to eight months. If she has no accidents during that period, it means you're doing everything right!

If you take your dog outside and she doesn't relieve herself, bring her in and put her in her crate for a while, then take her back outside a short time later. If she still doesn't go, put her back in her crate. Don't let her run around the house (even under supervision) unless you know she has relieved herself.

One of the most common mistakes dog owners make in house training their puppy or dog is to give her too much freedom too soon. Many dogs don't want to take the time to go outside to relieve themselves, especially if their family is inside. Instead the puppy will go hide behind a sofa or wander off to a back bedroom and relieve herself there. You may not find the accident for hours, when it's much too late to correct your puppy. By restricting your puppy's freedom to the room where you are, you can keep an eye on her and reduce the chances of an accident.

When Accidents Happen

If you catch the puppy in the act of relieving himself in the house—it's still happening—you can let him know he's making a mistake by saying, "Oh, no! Bad boy," and then taking him outside. But if you find a puddle, don't scold him. It's too late.

While house training your puppy, keep in mind that he has to relieve himself. Urinating and defecating aren't wrong; where he goes can be wrong, especially if he does it in the house. If your puppy misunderstands your correction and thinks that relieving himself is wrong, he'll become sneaky about it. He might sneak to a back bedroom or go behind the sofa. He may hold it for hours when you're nearby and then, when his bladder is ready to burst, go somewhere inappropriate. Make sure he knows you're concerned about where he relieves himself and not about the fact that he does it.

Go outside with your puppy, praise him for going where he should go, teach him a word for it, and be patient. For some puppies, the process could take several months.

Five Basic Obedience Commands

Labs are big, spirited dogs and need training. With training, your Lab can learn to control himself. When he masters the following commands, you can do more things with him, and he'll be a joy, rather than an embarrassment, to take places.

Hold a treat in your hand and let your dog sniff it. Then take the treat up and back over his head. As his head comes up, his hips will go down.

Sit

When your Lab learns to sit, he also learns to control himself and be still. When he learns to sit, you can prevent him from jumping on people. When he sits, he can wait for his meals without knocking the food bowl out of your hands. When he sits still, he can pay attention to you and wait for other commands. This is an important lesson for most bouncy young Labs.

The easiest way to teach a dog to sit is to shape him into the position you want as you say the word "sit." Have your Lab on a leash, and

When your dog sits and his hips are on the ground, praise him.

hold the leash in your right hand. Place your right hand on the front of your Lab's neck, under his chin. Slide your left hand down his back and tuck his tail under his hips as your right hand pushes up and back. (Think of a teetertotter—up and back at the front and down in the rear.) At the same time, tell your dog, "Labbie, sit!" When he sits, praise him.

With one hand on the front of the dog's chest under his neck, push gently up and back as you slide the other hand down his hips. At the same time, tell your dog to sit. Praise him when he does.

Down

When combined with the stay command, the down command teaches your Lab to be still for gradually increased lengths of time. You can have him do a down-stay at your feet in the evening when you'd like some peace and quiet. You can have him down-stay when guests come over so he isn't pestering them. He can also do a down-stay in a corner of the din-

Have your dog sit and then show him a treat. Tell him to lie down as you take the treat from his nose down to the ground in front of his paws.

ing room so he isn't begging under the table. If you drop a glass on the kitchen floor and it shatters, you can tell your dog to down-stay right where he is so he doesn't

As your dog lies down, praise him.

walk in and cut his feet. The down-stay is a very useful command.

Start by having your dog sit. Once he's sitting, show him a treat in your right hand. As you tell him, "Labbie, down!" take the treat from his nose to the ground right in front of his toes. As he moves down, rest your left hand on his shoulder. If he tries to pop back up, your left hand can help him stay down. Once he's down, praise him and give him the treat.

If your dog doesn't lie down for the treat, just scoop his front legs out from under him and gently lay him down. Praise him even though you're helping him do it.

Stay

Stay means hold still in either the sit or the down position. When you tell your dog to stay, she should remain in that position until you come back to her, praise her, and release her.

Start by having your dog sit. Then tell her, "Stay," as you give her the stay hand signal, your open-palmed hand in front of her nose. At the same time, put a little pressure backward (towards her tail) with the leash so that it's helping her remain in place rather than move forward. When you're pretty sure your dog isn't going to move, release the pressure on the leash. After a few seconds, go back to your dog, pet her, and praise her.

Very gradually increase the time you ask your dog to stay and your distance away from her. For the first few training sessions, take one step away and have her hold the stay for 10 seconds. Later that

The signal for stay is an open-palmed gesture right in front of the dog's face.

week, take two or three steps away and have her hold the stay for 20 seconds. Make the increase very gradual so your dog can succeed. If she makes a lot of mistakes, that's a sign you're moving ahead too fast.

Once you train your dog to stay with the sit, you can follow the same steps for the down-stay. Because she's more comfortable lying down and you've already taught the stay, you should be able to increase the time and distance of the down-stay more quickly. Again, though, if your dog makes mistakes, don't increase the time and distance so fast.

Walk Nicely on the Leash

Taking your Lab for a walk should be a pleasurable experience. I enjoy walking my dogs; we visit with neighbors, watch the herons down in the riverbed, and stop to sniff the spring flowers. Our walks are enjoyable because my dogs are well behaved in public. They have learned their manners and don't jump on people, bark at other dogs, or pull on the leash.

It's no fun to walk your dog when he's yanking on the leash so hard, your arm hurts and he's choking himself. Your dog must learn to treat the leash as if it were something fragile and to pay attention to you.

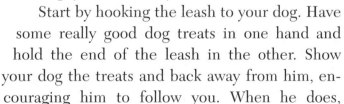

Use a treat and your happy verbal praise to encourage the dog to follow you on the leash as you back away from him. Praise him when he follows you.

When your dog is following you nicely, turn so that the both of you are walking forward together. Keep a treat handy to pop in front of his nose should he get distracted. Praise him.

Start by hooking the leash to your dog. Have some really good dog treats in one hand and hold the end of the leash in the other. Show your dog the treats and back away from him, encouraging him to follow you. When he does, praise him. If he doesn't follow you or doesn't pay attention, show him the treat again and back away. If he's very distracted and ignores the treats, try using a squeaky toy or different treats.

If your dog still fights the leash or ignores you, continue offering the treats and backing away but use the leash to give a snap-and-release correction with the collar. A snap and release is like the bounce of a tennis ball—snap to pull the leash tight very quickly and release to let off the leash tension. The force of the snap should be only enough to get the dog's attention, and no more. When he reacts to the snap by looking at you, praise him, show him the treat again, and encourage him to follow you.

As soon as your Lab will follow you as you back up, turn as you're walking so that you're headed forward with your dog walking close to your left side. If he pulls ahead, let him go as you hold on to the leash and back away. When he hits the end of the leash, act surprised and say, "Wow! How did that happen?" and continue walking. Show him that when he walks with you and pays attention to you, good things (praise and treats) happen, but when he pulls ahead, he'll get a leash correction and a verbal reprimand.

Come

Daily life with your dog is much nicer when you don't have to chase her all over the house to put her outside and or worry about her dashing through the open door to play keep-away with the neighborhood kids. In short, your dog needs to learn to come when you call.

To teach come, hold your dog on a leash with one hand and a box of dog treats in the other. Shake the treats and tell your dog, "Labbie, come!" as you back away from her. When she follows you, praise her and give

Make sure your dog will come to you reliably all the time before you try it off leash.

her a treat. The sound stimulus (the box of treats) is very important to the come command. Continue to use the box of treats until your Lab follows the come command reliably. With some dogs, that might be months.

When your dog responds well to the come command on a short leash, which is usually very quickly, make a long leash—20 to 30 feet of clothesline works well—and practice the same thing with the long leash. Take your dog out to play while letting her drag the long leash, and then call her to come, shaking the treat box. If she comes, praise her and give her a treat. If she doesn't come, use the long line to make her come and praise her anyway—since you made her do it—but don't give her a treat.

Don't try the come command off leash until your dog will come to you reliably on a short and long leash. Dogs learn very quickly that the rules are different off leash!

Training Is an Ongoing Process

As you've seen in this chapter, to train your Lab, you need to understand her. Why does she dig up the backyard? Why does she pull on the leash? Before you can deal with your dog's misbehavior, you need to understand why she does it.

In addition, training is an ongoing process. There's no magic wand you can wave over your Lab's head to make her into a perfectly well-behaved, fully

A well-behaved dog is a joy to own and a pleasure to spend time with.

grown dog. You must make training a part of your life and incorporate it into your dog's daily routine. Have your dog sit when you fix her meals so that she's not jumping on you. Tell her to sit at doors so that she's not dashing ahead of you. Make her lie down at your feet while you're watching the evening news and during meals so she isn't begging under the table.

With understanding, training, and consistency, your Lab will grow up to be a great friend who is a joy to have around.

7

Grooming

The Labrador Retriever is an extremely handsome breed, and Labs require very little grooming to maintain those good looks. It's a natural gift, you could say, and one of the great beauties of owning a Lab. Owners don't have to bother with the laborious, expensive grooming some breeds need, such as the Poodle or the Cocker Spaniel.

That's not to say Labs never need to be groomed. They do. But it's very simple—easy enough to do right at home if you want.

Your Lab's Skin and Coat

Your Lab's skin and coat are unique. To stay healthy and in good condition, they'll require care. Let's look at the basic physiology of a Lab's skin and coat.

A dog's skin consists of three layers: the epidermis (outer), the dermis (middle), and the hypodermis (inner). The skin protects the body from outward trauma and keeps water and nutrients inside. Sebaceous glands secrete oils that lubricate the skin and coat, giving the healthy Lab his shiny, slick appearance. The skin oils also protect him against bacterial and fungal infections.

A dog's skin regulates his body temperature by protecting him from rapid temperature changes outside. But dogs rely on panting to cool off internally since they can't sweat through the skin like people.

The skin is a reservoir for body fat, water, vitamins, and proteins. If a dog is deficient in any of these, chances are you'll see a disruption in the skin.

A dog's skin is thinner than a person's and less acidic. That means soaps and shampoos made for you are unsuitable for your Lab. Use only those shampoos made with the special pH balance of your dog's skin in mind.

The Lab's dense but easy-care coat is an example of form that follows function. The Labrador was originally bred by fishermen in Newfoundland, which means that Labs were, and are, working water dogs. No time for beauty treatments! The short, flat hairs of the Lab's outer coat form a water-repellent shield to help keep the dog dry while he works in water. A soft, downy undercoat keeps him warm. Unlike people, whose hair grows continuously, a dog's hair grows in cycles, going

What's Your Favorite Color?

Not only is the Lab's coat easy care, but it comes in three different colors—black, chocolate, and yellow!

Yellow Labs, sometimes mistakenly called "golden Labs," come in a range of colors, from fox red to light cream. The yellow Lab's eyes are brown or hazel, although black or yellow is allowed according to the American Kennel Club breed standard. Black Labs are all black, although a small white spot on the chest is permitted; the eyes are preferably brown or hazel but can be black or yellow. The color of chocolate Labs ranges from light sedge to actual chocolate. A small white spot on the chest is permitted. The chocolate Lab's eyes are light brown to clear yellow. All Labs regardless of color should have a dark brown or black nose, although some yellow Labs have dark noses that fade to pink during the winter months. No one knows exactly why this happens, but you'll see it in other breeds, such as Huskies and Malamutes. It's not considered a fault.

Some Labs are yellow with chocolate pigmentation or yellow with no pigmentation on the nose or eye rims. These dogs are called "Dudleys." A Dudley may also have a pink nose. This coloration is considered a fault in show dogs and penalized. To tell the difference between a Dudley and a Lab with a faded nose, look at the dog's eye rims and gum tissue. A Dudley will have light pink or tan skin; the regular kind of yellow Lab will have black pigment in these areas.

The only difference between black, yellow, and chocolate Labs is color, despite the many theories and myths about dogs with the individual colors. For example, yellow Labs are the laziest, black Labs are the most active and make good hunters, and chocolate Labs are stubborn. No evidence supports these theories.

How does an individual Lab get her color? Genetics. It all depends on the parents' color genes. You might not think it possible, but black Labs can give birth to yellow Labs and yellow Labs can give birth to black. You can get chocolates from blacks or yellows and vice versa. If both parents are yellow, the pups will always be yellow, and if both parents are chocolate, you'll get chocolate or yellow pups, never black.

Are there any other Lab colors? No, black, chocolate, and yellow are the only colors accepted in the American Kennel Club breed standard. Be wary of anyone selling high-priced rare or unusually colored Labs, such as "pure white" or "silver" or "blue." The only correct Lab colors are black, yellow, or chocolate.

Essential Grooming Supplies

Before you say ready, set, groom, make sure you have these grooming supplies:

○ Toenail trimmers

○ Styptic powder

○ Rubber curry

○ Soft slicker brush

○ Cotton balls

○ Ophthalmic ointment

○ Towels

○ Grooming noose

○ Sponge

○ Small plastic bucket

○ Spray attachment

○ Commercial ear cleaner or boric acid, rubbing alcohol, and glycerin to make homemade remedy

○ Pet shampoo

○ Flea control products

○ Spray-on mink oil or coat conditioner

○ Toothbrush or gauze and tooth-paste

through a growing period, a transitional period, and a resting period. This cyclical growth is responsible for the Lab's usual twice-yearly molt.

Hair growth and shedding are controlled by seasonal changes in length of daylight, seasonal temperature, what your Lab eats, pregnancy, stress, or illness.

Home Grooming

What does grooming your Lab involve? The Lab's beauty-control list isn't long, but figure on:

❍ Brushing

❍ Nail trim

❍ Ear check/cleaning

❍ Bathing

That's about it. No hair trimming, detangling, fluff drying, or special lotions and potions. The Lab is a wash-and-wear breed, and owners like it that way!

Brushing

Plan on brushing your Lab's coat once a week or so. A thorough brushing removes dead hair and dirt and distributes coat oils. Regular brushing will help keep your Lab's coat shiny and her skin healthy. Of course, if she's really dirty, for example, caked with mud after a run by the creek, brush as needed.

Labs shed most heavily in the spring and fall. At those times more frequent brushing may be necessary to remove dead hair. Excessive shedding is abnormal and can be a sign of a poor diet or ill health. If your Lab sheds more than normal, consult your veterinarian.

The favored brush for Labs isn't actually a brush—it's a rubber curry. Also used by equestrians to groom horses, the oval-shaped curry with serrated edges does a great job of removing a Lab's dense coat and feels good. Rubber curry gloves are also a good tool for grooming Labs, and some Lab enthusiasts swear by a metal shedding blade, a saw-toothed device with leather handles. Rake it gently over your

Did You Know?

A Dudley is a yellow Lab with chocolate pigmentation, or can refer to a Lab with no pigmentation on the nose or eye rim.

Lab's body to remove dead hair. During shedding season, a soft wire slicker brush can be helpful to remove excess hair.

The trick to good coat care is how you use the grooming tool you chose. Brushing should be done systematically, starting at the head, for example, and working back to the neck, legs, back, tummy, rear end, and tail. Don't start at one place and skip to another. Develop a brushing pattern and do it every time. You won't lose your place, and your Lab will learn what to expect next. Brush in the direction the hair grows.

Grooming outdoors is best, but if the weather doesn't permit, brush Labbie inside with a large (washable) sheet underneath to catch the hair. Otherwise you'll have hair bunnies wandering around the house.

Don't brush too hard on tender areas, such as the Lab's tummy or legs.

The areas where you'll find the most hair are your dog's hips, flanks, and chest. A Lab who hasn't been brushed in a while may have "packing," thick pockets of dead hair in these areas. If that's the case, a slicker brush may be necessary to remove the hair.

Brushing should precede and follow bathing to remove the most hair. You may also want to mist your Lab lightly after brushing with a spray-on coat conditioner to add sheen to her coat.

Nail Trim

You'll have to tackle nail trimming at least once a month for adult Labs and once a week for pups. If you don't, your dog may develop sore, splayed feet. How can you tell if your Lab's nails are too long? Listen. Do you hear a click-click when the dog walks across a tile or linoleum floor? If you do, that means the nails are touching the floor—and they shouldn't. Or take a look at your Lab's feet while he's standing. Do his nails touch the floor? Time for a trim.

Several types of nail trimmers are on the market. Some are better suited for small- to medium-size breeds; others are made with large dogs in mind. You'll see clippers with one or two cutting edges, clippers with changeable blades, and clippers with extra-large handles. Small-size trimmers will work when your Lab is a pup. Large size are best for adult Labs.

When purchasing trimmers at your local pet supply store, be sure to pick up styptic powder. Styptic powder will stop bleeding if you accidentally cut your dog's nail too short and nick the quick, the part of the nail that contains nerves and blood vessels. Have styptic powder handy while trimming.

Many dog owners cringe at the thought of accidentally cutting to the quick and fear trimming their pet's nails. But don't let this turn you away. You can learn to spot where the quick is and cut right below it. This is easiest in dogs with light nails. For light nails, trim to right below the pink area. With dark nails, you'll have to guess where to stop, but usually if you cut to right below where the nail starts to curl, you'll be in good shape. Be aware that as nails grow, so does the quick. So if your dog's nails haven't been trimmed in a long time, trim a little at a time, very carefully.

To trim Labbie's nails, hold one paw firmly in your left hand (if you're right-handed) and place your thumb on top of the foot. Place your fingers underneath the pads so you can spread his toes. With the clippers in your right hand, clip each nail right below the quick with short, decisive strokes. Don't forget the dewclaws.

If you accidentally cut the quick, don't panic. Simply put down the clippers—keep holding your dog's paw—and grab a pinch of styptic powder between your thumb and forefinger. Apply this to the bleeding nail and hold it there firmly for one minute. Release and check if the bleeding has stopped. If not, apply more powder and press again. Continue until the bleeding stops.

Finish trimming the first paw, then file each nail with a large-size metal file to remove sharp, rough edges that could scratch your legs the next time your Lab is naughty and jumps up on you. Work your way to the next paw, trim each nail, and then file.

> Begin nail trimming while your dog is a pup and do it every week.

A few notes on nail trimming: Start early. Labs, like all dogs, must learn to accept new experiences. Begin nail trimming while your dog is a pup and do it every week. In between trimmings, handle the dog's feet to accustom him to being touched. Labs are so good-natured, they usually don't make a fuss about trimming, but it's wise to teach your dog to accept it from a young age. Labs are very strong, and it's difficult to trim their nails if they decide to resist. No sense in arm wrestling! If you adopt an adult dog who isn't thrilled about trimming, take the time to teach him.

Ear Check/Cleaning

Your Lab's grooming isn't complete without an ear check. Clean, healthy ears are the result of good grooming, so don't forget this task. Each time you brush your dog, make it a point to look inside her ears. Are they healthy? Here's how to tell.

○ Take a good look. A healthy ear is free of debris, dirt, or excess wax. It's not sore, red, or inflamed.
○ Take a good whiff. A healthy ear is odor-free. Ears that are infected or infested with ear mites may smell bad.

❍ Touch your Lab's ears. Do they feel overly warm, or does the dog
seem overly sensitive to having her ears touched? If so, an ear infection could be in progress.

❍ Watch your Lab. A dog with problem ears will frequently shake her
head or tilt it to one side, scratch, and whine. Any of these signs can
indicate trouble is brewing.

A healthy Lab usually has healthy ears, so you probably won't
have to do much cleaning. Each time you groom, wipe your Lab's
ears with a dry cotton ball (don't use cotton swabs) or one slightly
moistened with the following home remedy used by Lab owners:

2 tablespoons boric acid

4 ounces rubbing alcohol

1 tablespoon glycerin

> A healthy Lab usually has healthy ears, so you probably won't have to do much cleaning.

Many vets prefer commer-
cially prepared ear cleaners over
home remedies. Ask your vet to recommend a product or home
remedy best suited to your dog.

It's more difficult to clean a dirty ear, one filled with wax or
brown waxy debris, a sign of ear mites. Dampen a cotton ball
with ear cleaner. Hold up the ear flap with your left hand (or
right hand if you're a lefty), wrap the cotton ball around the index
finger of your right hand, and wipe out all the folds and crevices.
Wipe gently, but be sure to get the ear clean. Change cotton balls
as needed.

If the ear is extremely dirty, you may want to soak the ear
canal with cleaner before wiping to loosen the debris. Hold up the
ear flap and squirt a small amount of cleaner into the ear canal.
Massage the base of the ear for a few moments, then clean with

cotton balls. However, it's important to know that it's not normal for an ear to get this dirty—even if your Lab's been swimming or rolling in mud! When ears are dirty deep inside, red, painful, or smell bad, it's likely he is brewing an ear infection. Taking him to the vet—before any vigorous cleaning—will help your vet make an accurate diagnosis, so she can give proper treatment.

Your dog will probably want to shake as soon as you squirt in ear cleaner or start wiping. No harm in that, but take a few steps back before you allow her to shake. Otherwise you'll have ear cleaner and ear gunk all over you!

If your Lab swims frequently, make it standard practice to dry out her ears afterward to prevent ear infections.

Do your weekly ear check and light cleaning to prevent or identify serious ear conditions. If one of your Lab's ears smells bad, is red, or painful, inflamed, and is filled with dark, waxy debris, don't put anything in it and consult with your vet right away. The sooner you catch ear problems, the sooner your dog can be treated.

Bath Time

At some point, your Lab will need a bath. But because a Lab's coat is short and easy to keep clean, frequent bathing isn't necessary. "This is one of the beauties of owning a Lab," says Laura Michaels of Woodhaven Labs. "They rarely need a bath. If you brush two to three times weekly, you shouldn't have to bathe unless they happen to have a good roll in something disgusting."

Professional groomers usually recommend bathing a Lab no more than once every eight weeks. Too frequent shampooing will strip the natural oils that protect the dog's coat and keep the skin in good

Hold the Soap, Please

Elizabeth Foti's Labrador, Samantha, loves bath time. At least she loves it until there's soap involved. Sam gets bathed much more frequently than most Labs because the Fotis have allergies. "Her vet and my allergist have approved a plan for managing our allergies," says Foti.

Sam knows where she's supposed to go when asked if she wants a bath. She runs into the bathroom and jumps into the tub. The current setup has a push handle to turn on the water; Sam has almost figured out how to push it to turn it on. She frolics in the water for a few minutes (Foti uses a shower attachment), and then the dreaded soap appears. Sam tries to dig up the tub to get away, and the fight is on. "By the time I've finished soaping her, I'm almost as wet as she is," says Foti.

Rinsing is easier because there's less soap and more water. After rinsing, the trauma begins because the water is turned off. "She always tries to turn it back on, so far, with no success," says Foti. "Then I try to towel her off while she tries to shake off the water. Needless to say, our bathroom ends up looking like we have 12 dogs instead of one."

In spite of Sam's aversion to a soapy bathtub, she returns to the tub when she does something naughty. "The really funny thing is that she will run and hide in the bathtub when she's about to get into trouble if we forget and leave her bathroom door open," says Foti. "This is even funnier because her tub also houses the drying rack for our clothes, and she's come out of there wearing my shirts, my socks, and my panty hose draped over her back."

condition. A properly oily coat repels dirt and sheds water. Many Lab enthusiasts simply rinse their dogs in fresh water without shampooing.

But the Lab's love for investigating everything, including things that smell really bad, may necessitate bathing with shampoo. A Lab with fleas may need bathing, too.

You can get your Lab bathed by a professional groomer, but it's a job done easily at home. The trick is to be prepared beforehand.

Many owners scrub their Lab right in the family bathtub. Pups can be bathed in the kitchen sink. A spray attachment is best because you don't want the dog standing knee-deep in soapy water (although most Labs would probably like it). You can buy many kinds of spray attachments made especially for bathing dogs at home. Check out a local pet supply store or pet supply catalog. Don't bathe your dog in the front yard with the garden hose. How would you like to be sprayed with freezing cold water?

You'll need a rubber mat in the tub to prevent Labbie from slipping and, if possible, a way to secure your dog in the tub, such as a professional grooming noose or nonleather collar and leash. The idea is keep your Lab from springing out of the tub midbath if he's less than thrilled about bathing.

Next, ready your bathing supplies before turning on the water. You'll need cotton balls for your Lab's ears, ophthalmic ointment, shampoo, a plastic bucket full of water, towels, and a sponge or rubber curry. Dilute the shampoo with the water in the bucket and throw in the sponge. Once you've got everything within arm's reach of the tub, it's time for the big event.

Secure your Lab in the tub and put a cotton ball in each ear to keep water out. Apply a dab of sterile ophthalmic ointment (available from your vet) in each eye to protect against shampoo irritation. Dampen the dog with warm water, beginning at the top of the head, behind the ears. Keep the spray nozzle close to the dog's body. Work back, soaking the back and the tail. Come back to the front and soak his neck and chest. Then saturate the tummy and legs. Finally, hold the nozzle on the top of the dog's head and carefully dampen his face, but don't spray directly into it.

Make sure you wet your Lab down to the skin—this may take a while due to the Lab's naturally water-resistant coat. Once he's completely wet, pick up your soapy sponge and apply shampoo from head to tail. Be careful not to get soap in his eyes, but don't skimp on shampoo. You want to get your Lab clean. Scrub with the sponge or your hands. You can also use the rubber curry to comb the shampoo through and loosen dead hair. Rinse well, beginning with the head and working back, and shampoo again.

The final rinse is really important. If you don't get all the soap out of the coat, it can leave the coat dull and the dog's skin itchy. In dark-colored Labs, dried shampoo looks like flakes of unsightly dandruff! Rinse until you think all the soap is out, then rinse again. You literally want to hear the coat squeak.

Swipe off excess water with your hands, then towel-dry. Use as many towels as needed. Labs usually love this part and will get excited and jump about.

Keep your Lab inside in a warm, draft-free area until he's dry. You can speed up the drying process by using your hair dryer set on low (high is too hot and can irritate the dog's skin). Brush or curry your Lab again once he's dry.

Anal Glands

Every dog has two anal glands or sacs in the anal area. These sacs are sometimes called scent glands and may be a way dogs identify each other. This explains dogs' propensity for nose-to-rear sniffing. The anal sacs normally empty when the dog defecates, and the secretion that comes out is liquid and brownish. Anal sacs can also be emptied after a sudden contraction of the anal sphincter, which might happen if the dog is frightened or upset.

Did You Know?

Human bites are usually more dangerous than dog bites because a dog's mouth has fewer germs and bacteria.

In some dogs, the anal sacs fail to empty normally. Although this condition is most common in small breeds, it can happen to any dog. Soft stools, a small opening, or overactivity is usually the cause. When the sacs don't empty normally, they can become impacted, which may lead to infection. A dog with anal gland irritation or impaction may scoot on his rear, bite as if in pain, or whine.

Impaction is treated by expressing the glands, a messy and smelly job. Since large, healthy dogs generally don't suffer from impacted glands, you probably won't need to express your Lab's anal glands unless directed by the vet.

Let's Not Forget Manners

Good manners go hand in hand with good grooming. A Lab who accepts grooming graciously is easier to groom than one who puts up a fight. Grooming should be a safe and pleasant experience for all involved, which is why it's essential to teach your Lab from an early age to accept grooming as part of his normal routine.

Along with basic obedience training for your Lab pup or adult, you must teach grooming manners. To be a good grooming student, Labbie must learn to sit, lie, or stand still while being brushed; accept nail trimming; stand quietly while being bathed; sit patiently while his ears are checked or cleaned; jump into the tub or onto the grooming table when asked; and hold still while being towel-dried or blow-dried.

Labs are very smart and anxious to please, so it's not hard to teach them what's expected during grooming sessions. Remember that dogs learn through repetition, correction, and praise. That means you must be consistent in what you expect and ask while grooming, just as you would in obedience training. Be firm, but praise is essential.

Keep your expectations realistic. Don't think a young pup will sit still for hours while you brush and fuss. Keep grooming sessions short for puppies, no more than 15 minutes or so. Expect some squirming, whining, or other theatrics. It's all part of learning that the grooming experience isn't scary or harmful, a primary goal. Teach your Lab that grooming can be fun! Yes, it's a time for brushing and nail trimming, but it's also a time when he'll get your undivided attention. Labs adore that!

> Remember that dogs learn through repetition, correction, and praise.

Pups or adults not accustomed to grooming may fear it. Speak quietly to your Lab when you sense he's afraid. The dog may nip at the "mean" brush, pull away from the nail trimmers, or shy from the loud blow-dryer. Always be firm and gently correct such antics with "no" or "stop." Show your Lab what you expect, and praise him when he complies.

Labs are quite capable of learning good grooming manners. Introduce grooming at a young age, keep it short, positive, and fun, and you'll have a Lab who retrieves the curry and asks for a brushing!

Minimizing the Mess

If you don't already know this, you'll figure it out after one home grooming session with your Lab. Grooming is messy! Figure on shed hair, sloppy wet towels, dirty cotton balls, and dirty clothes. You can minimize the mess, though, by thinking ahead. Here's how.

Invest in a quality vacuum cleaner. This is must for every dog owner, not only to suck up shed hair after grooming but dirt, fleas, and anything else the Lab drags home in between groomings. If you don't vacuum up the hair after brushing your Lab, it will migrate. Before you know it, you'll have a family of hair bunnies throughout the house.

Wear an apron and a specific set of dog-grooming clothes when you groom your Lab. A waterproof apron will help keep you dry when your wet Lab shakes all over you. And if you're wearing old clothes, you won't have to worry about how dirty and hairy they get.

Have a stack of Labbie towels handy for towel-drying your Lab or putting underneath him while he dries. The towels don't have to be fancy or monogrammed—you can buy them from a thrift store.

Keep a trash bag nearby while grooming to toss cotton balls or shed hair into. If you clean up as you go, the mess isn't as overwhelming. Keep a roll of paper towels handy, too, for accidents (puppy may get excited and go potty) or spills.

Machine wash your grooming clothes and towels in hot water and detergent. Don't mix grooming items with the family laundry, or you'll end up with hair all over everything.

Rinse the curry after use, especially if you've brushed a muddy dog.

Wash out the tub and mat with disinfectant cleanser, and be sure to remove shed hair from the drain.

Going Pro

Not everyone has a knack for dog grooming or is so inclined. You may feel overwhelmed by the thought of bathing your Lab,

What to Look for in a Groomer

The groomer you select for your Lab should:

○ Possess certifiable knowledge and hands-on experience;

○ Treat clients with courtesy and listen to their concerns;

○ Handle each dog firmly but gently;

○ Show a genuine love of dogs;

○ Never allow puppies that are not fully vaccinated to be around older dogs.

The grooming facility should:

○ Be sterile and clean;

○ Supply an adequate number of crates in all sizes to house its clients' dogs;

○ Provide a special outside area for potty breaks.

trimming her nails, and brushing her coat. Not to worry! With cash in hand, hire a skilled, kind professional to do the grooming dirty work.

The best way to start your search for a groomer is to ask someone you trust, such as a breeder, rescue volunteer, dog-owning friend, or veterinarian, for a recommendation. Ask why they recommend a particular groomer, if they utilize the groomer's services, and how long they've taken dogs there.

Once you have a few referrals, hopefully for salons pretty close to home, make some calls. Ask about grooming prices (and what's included), how far in advance you need to make appointments, how many groomers are on staff, whether or not the groomers are certified (it's not required by law, but it's a good indication of professional commitment), and if the shop sells products such as shampoos or collars and leashes. Keep notes on each shop.

The next step is to visit each salon. Groomers are usually very busy, so be courteous and let the shop know you'll be stopping by. Otherwise the owner or groomer may be too busy to chat with you for long. Keep visits short, from 10 to 15 minutes. That's long enough to ask a few more questions and form an impression of each shop. Ask yourself

- Is the shop clean? (Don't expect perfection, though!)
- Is the staff friendly and professional?
- Is the shop well organized, with up-to-date equipment?
- Do the groomers handle the dogs carefully?

After making the rounds, it's time to make a decision. Consider the recommendations, along with your positive or negative impressions of each salon. Choose one and call to schedule an appointment. Then sit back and relax. Your Lab will soon be sparkling clean, and you won't have to lift a finger!

The Old and the Young

Grooming your Lab is fairly simple and straightforward. But when she's very young or old, you'll need a slightly different approach.

Grooming the Lab Puppy

As we've seen, you should approach grooming sessions as if they're training sessions. This is especially true with youngsters. To make grooming a fun and positive experience for puppy, do the following:

○ Set aside a certain time and place for grooming. Puppy will quickly learn that when she's placed on the grooming table you have set up in the basement, it's time for grooming.

○ Keep sessions short (10–15 minutes). Pups have short attention spans.

○ Always praise puppy for cooperating.

○ Use obedience commands: sit while brushing, stand while bathing, for example.

○ Be realistic in your expectations of puppy. Learning to sit or stand quietly while being groomed takes time. Don't be surprised if puppy tries to wiggle away, bites the brush, yelps when you trim her nails, shakes her head wildly as you clean her ears, or disregards your commands. In good time, your clear instruction, patience, and praise will encourage even the most rambunctious pup to adopt good grooming manners.

○ Because puppies can chill easily, it's best to dry them right away with a blow-dryer. Don't let puppy outside until she's completely dry.

○ Puppy toenails are sometimes soft and very small, which means the nail can tear when you clip. Make sure the trimmers are sharp, or try using human fingernail trimmers when the pup is very young.

Grooming the Oldster

Grooming is still important for the elderly Lab, but you may notice that he's less patient with grooming, doesn't have the stamina to stand up for long, or is grouchy when his nails are trimmed. Don't be surprised by such behaviors—they're very common. You just need to find positive ways to work around the older Lab's quirks. Here are a few tips:

○ Keep sessions short. (Sound familiar?) Although dogs in their prime can tolerate lengthy grooming sessions, the old and young can't. The older dog may tire more easily or arthritis may make standing for long periods painful. Be considerate of your older Lab's limitations.

○ Be extra gentle when handling an older Lab. The dog's joints don't move as well as they used to, and he may be more touch sensitive.

○ Make sure your dog is comfortable during grooming. Let him lie down every so often so that he doesn't tire too quickly.

○ Pay special attention to his nails. Because older Labs are sometimes less active than younger dogs, their nails may not wear down. More frequent trimming may be necessary.

○ Watch for skin and coat changes in the older dog. He may become sensitive to coat products or develop dry skin as the activity of oil-producing glands decreases. Be on the lookout for lumps, bumps, or other signs of illness, too.

Smells and Sticky Stuff

Sooner or later your Lab will delight you with an incredibly bad odor or a sticky, gooey mess. Labs are naturals that way—they have an ability to find anything that smells bad or sticks in the coat within a 10-mile radius.

> What can you do if your Lab gets sprayed by a skunk? Unfortunately there are no magic cures.

One of the worst offenders is skunk spray. The biting, acid odor is unforgettable on a dog. One whiff is enough to send you running in the opposite direction! Labs, especially those who live in the country or work in the field, are likely to encounter these smelly black-and-white critters. The Lab's curiosity, more than aggression, usually accounts for her getting sprayed.

What can you do if your Lab gets sprayed by a skunk? Unfortunately there are no magic cures.

Commercial products and homemade remedies will help reduce the odor. But the bottom line is the smell has to wear off, and you'll have to live with it until it does.

One favorite remedy for skunk spray that you've probably heard of is tomato juice. Soak the smelly Lab from head to tail in it. Rub the tomato juice into the coat and let it stay on for 15 to 20 minutes. Then shampoo with regular dog shampoo. Repeat this process several times over the next few days. You can also substitute milk or apple cider vinegar for the tomato juice.

Another favorite is a mixture of one quart of 3 percent hydrogen peroxide, a quarter cup of baking soda, and one teaspoon of regular shampoo. Apply and let stand for 10 minutes or so. Shampoo and rinse thoroughly.

If you try a commercial product, follow the directions carefully.

Your Lab may also roll in something dead (very smelly) or party in garbage (also very smelly). After such a romp, a thorough bath, with two or three shampoos, is in order.

Gum, tar, and motor oil aren't strangers to this breed, either. The only problem is how to get them out once they're firmly attached to that wonderful Lab coat.

For gum, groomers still favor two old-fashioned remedies: ice and peanut butter. Freeze the gum with an ice cube to make it less sticky and easier to pry out of the coat or apply a little peanut butter and work it around and underneath the gum. The oil in the peanut butter loosens the gum from the hair shaft.

Did You Know?

Nose prints can be used to identify dogs just as fingerprints are used to identify humans.

Tar is another matter. It can be difficult to remove and may take several treatments. Soak the tarry area in vegetable oil for 30 to 60 minutes (yes, it's very messy) and shampoo in Dawn dish-washing detergent. Follow up with a regular dog shampoo to restore the pH balance. Avoid using petroleum products to remove tar, such as gasoline or turpentine. These are highly toxic to your Lab.

Grease or oil isn't easy to remove, either. Try shampooing in Dawn dish-washing detergent (it's used to remove oil from wild animals saturated by oil spills), followed by a regular pet shampoo. You can also apply baby powder or corn starch to the oily area, then shampoo in pet shampoo.

Pearly White Smile

As we saw in chapter 4, regular teeth brushing should be a part of every Lab's health care. To make regular brushing easy to remember, many Lab owners include it as part of their grooming routine. Brush the coat, then brush the teeth.

The Lab's 12 incisors, four canines, 16 premolars, and 10 molars can suffer from plaque or tartar buildup or periodontal disease. Normally plaque, a soft white or yellow substance that consists of organic and inorganic material, along with bacteria, is deposited on your Lab's teeth (yours, too). If it's not removed, it hardens and becomes tartar. Tartar is yellow-brown in color and usually found along the gum line. Unlike plaque, tartar can't be removed by brushing or wiping—only a dentist can remove it. Plaque and tartar are perfect hosts for bacteria and will lead to infection and disease.

Each time you groom your Lab, take a close look at his teeth and gums. Are his teeth white, or do you see tartar buildup? Are the gums pink or red and bleeding? Does your Lab have extremely bad breath or regular, mild doggie breath? Consult with your vet if you notice tartar buildup, red or bleeding gums, broken teeth, or obvious decay.

Brush your Lab's teeth with a small toothbrush and doggie toothpaste. Don't be tempted to share your toothpaste because it can make your dog sick. Brush his teeth in the same way you brush your own, with gentle, thorough brush strokes. Brush once or twice a week.

Labs are usually very accepting of toothbrushing as long as you teach them to accept it as youngsters. But some dogs just don't like having a toothbrush in their mouth. If you've got one of those dogs, try wiping the teeth with clean, sterile gauze. Wrap the gauze around your finger, moisten it with water, add a dab of toothpaste, and wipe the teeth one at a time.

Feeding a kibble diet helps keep teeth clean, too. Soft or canned food can increase plaque, but a crunchy diet actually cleans the teeth. Chewing on hard biscuits or dental toys also helps.

> Don't be tempted to share your toothpaste because it can make your dog sick.

Safety First

Grooming a Lab is fairly safe for the dog since you won't be handling the scissors or clippers necessary for grooming some other breeds—no cuts or clipper burns to worry about. But your dog might suffer the following minor injuries during grooming.

Bleeding Nail. If you cut a nail to the quick, don't get upset. It's not serious, and your Lab will be fine. Follow the instructions given on page 215 for applying styptic powder.

Shampoo in the Eyes. Apply sterile ophthalmic ointment before bathing, and always be careful not to get shampoo in your dog's eyes. But if it happens, flush out the eye with plenty of fresh water or saline (the kind that contact lens wearers use). Don't apply more ointment. If the eye is red or if the dog squints, give the vet a call. Prevent the dog from rubbing and pawing the eye, which could irritate it more.

Allergic and Toxic Reactions. If your Lab seems extremely itchy after a regular bath or her skin is red, she may be allergic to the shampoo or conditioner used. Call your vet, especially if the dog develops hives. Medication may be required to stop the allergic reaction. Some Labs are highly sensitive to the insecticides used in flea shampoos and dips. Signs of insecticide poisoning include vomiting, diarrhea, drooling, trembling, and pinpoint pupil size. If your Lab shows signs of poisoning after being washed in flea shampoo or rinsed in flea/tick dip, call your vet right away. Ask for immediate instructions and be sure to tell the vet what products you used.

Injuries from Jumping. Never leave your Lab unattended in a bathtub or on a grooming table. A jump off a grooming table or out of a tub could result in a broken leg or other injury.

8

Family Life

In This Chapter

❍ Activities Labs Love
❍ Making Your Lab a Good Neighbor
❍ Kid's Best Friend
❍ Travels with Labbie

Always remember two things about your Labrador Retriever: she adores you, and she needs to keep busy. Repeat that as many times as necessary. As we saw in chapter 1, to make the grade as a good Lab owner, you must satisfy your Lab's need to be a family member and give her creative outlets for her inexhaustible energy. Finding such outlets can seem overwhelming if you're a novice Lab owner. Where to begin? Read on.

Activities Labs Love

Originally bred to be a working dog, the Lab needs activities, formal or informal, to keep her mind and body active. Otherwise you'll have a bored Lab on your hands. And a bored Lab is a dog who will invent her own creative ways to keep busy: dig up the backyard, chew the patio furniture, empty the garbage. You might not appreciate these activities, so here are some other suggestions. Enjoy!

Agility Competitions

Racing against time, agility competitors must maneuver over and around a series of jumps and obstacles. The dogs race against the clock as they jump hurdles, scale ramps, travel through tunnels, traverse a seesaw, and weave through a line of poles. Agility competitors are judged on accuracy as well as speed. This fast-paced, athletic sport is challenging and fun. Events are governed and sanctioned by the United States Dog Agility Association (USDAA).

> Agility is a competitive, athletic sport, but the USDAA promotes dog agility as a community sport, a fun way for individuals and families to spend time with their dogs.

Any dog with good physical ability and a lot of energy is a strong candidate for agility competition. It's a natural sport for the athletic Labrador Retriever. Although some breeds appear more naturally adapted to the sport, more than 100 breeds and mixed breeds have demonstrated agility ability. The sport is open to all dogs regardless of pedigree; mixed-breed and purebred dogs alike are welcome to compete in USDAA events. Agility is a competitive, athletic sport, but the

USDAA promotes dog agility as a community sport, a fun way for individuals and families to spend time with their dogs.

Agility competitors can earn certification titles, such as agility dog, advanced agility dog, and master agility dog, as well as titles offered through the USDAA Junior Handler Program and Basic Performance Program.

Agility is a fun, positive experience for dogs and owners. Enthusiasts can't say enough about it. "I started with Chelsea in agility in the fall of last year, so we've been in training for about 10 or 11 months," says Lab enthusiast Dayna Rousseau. "I think that agility really gives a dog extreme confidence. Shy dogs come out of their shell and timid dogs become brave after training positively in agility. It gives energetic dogs an outlet for that energy. It gives smart dogs something to figure out and make their minds work. It gives not-so-smart dogs something they think they've figured out, even though you may have lured them over that big A-frame at first, and it teaches them how to learn!

"The strong and happy relationship built between handler and dog is absolutely the best result of training in agility. Whether or not you go on to compete, the positive aspects of agility shine within you and your dog!"

If you're interested in agility, attend a few events. Contact a local obedience club and ask for information on agility classes, and find a trainer/coach who is experienced teaching agility. See the resources section in Appendix A for information on contacting the USDAA.

Canine Good Citizen

Would you like to show off your Lab's good manners? And would you like your

Lab to be considered a good citizen? A program sponsored by The American Kennel Club does just that. Administered by dog clubs, obedience clubs, private trainers, or 4-H clubs throughout the United States, the Canine Good Citizen program aims at encouraging all owners to train their dogs.

What does it take to earn a citizen seal of approval? To earn a Canine Good Citizen Certificate, dogs are graded pass/fail on such things as allowing a stranger to approach, walking on a loose lead, walking through a crowd, sitting for examination, reacting to another dog, and distractions. You'll find contact information in the resources section of Appendix A.

Conformation Competition

In conformation competition the Lab's structure, looks, and movement are judged against the breed's "standard of perfection" (according to the AKC, registry, or whatever organization is sponsoring the show). Dogs that most closely adhere to the standard are considered the best dogs for breeding. There are two types of conformation dog shows: specialty and all-breed. Specialty shows are limited to a designated breed or grouping of breeds, such as working dogs or toy dogs. All-breed shows include all breeds. Dogs competing in conformation shows are working for points toward a championship.

To become an AKC champion of record, a dog must earn 15 points at AKC-approved shows. A dog can earn from one to five points at a show. The 15 points required for a championship must be won under three different judges and include two majors (wins of 3, 4, and 5 at one show) under different judges.

AKC conformation shows are divided into five classes: puppy (subdivided into classes of six to nine months and nine to 12 months), novice, bred by exhibitor, American bred, and open. If you're interested in conformation showing, the best place to start is by visiting a breeder with show-quality pups for sale. Then contact a local Lab club to meet experienced conformation show enthusiasts and handlers—they can give you lots of tips.

Field Trials and Hunting Tests

Some 70,000 Labs compete every year in field trial and hunting test events, according to the American Kennel Club. With good reason—the Labrador Retriever is at home in the field, retrieving through brush, water, or open terrain. Field trials are practical demonstrations of the Lab's ability to perform in the field the functions for which they were bred.

AKC field competitors can earn titles of field champion (FC) and amateur field champion (AFC). Each year the number-one field champion is awarded the coveted title of national field champion (NFC). A dog earns the title of FC in the same way she would win a conformation title from the AKC. Different placings earn the dog different point values, with a total of 10 points required for the FC title. A dual champion is a dog that has an FC and conformation championship (CH). A dog earns the title of NFC by beating out an entire field of field champions at a national open competition. The AFC title is awarded to the winning field champion handled by an amateur in a similar contest.

Did You Know?

According to the American Animal Hospital Association, more than 40 percent of pet owners talk to their pets on the phone or through the answering machine.

Retrievers can also compete in AKC hunt tests. One of the major differences between field trials and hunt tests is that field trials are competitive and hunt tests are not. Dogs in a field trial are judged against each other, whereas dogs in a hunt test are judged against a standard and either pass or fail. Hunt tests evaluate a dog's ability at three levels; each succeeding level is more difficult. Beginning hunt tests grade the Lab's natural ability to retrieve a marked bird (one they can see fly and fall), and stay until signaled by the handler to retrieve. As the Lab advances, hunt tests include more difficult scenarios such as double marks (two birds felled in the same run). Labs that complete each level successfully can earn the titles junior hunter (JH), senior hunter (SH), and master hunter (MH). Master hunters that successfully pass five master hunter tests in one year are *invited* to test at the Master National Hunting test. Dogs that make it to this level are exceptional—the best of the best.

The AKC, UKC, and the National American Hunting Retriever Association also offer noncompetitive hunt tests for retrievers.

For more information on what comes naturally to your Labrador Retriever, contact the American Kennel Club, the Hunting Retrieving Club, or the North American Hunting Retriever Association (see Appendix A for contact information).

Flyball

If your Lab is crazy about tennis balls, consider flyball competition. Flyball is a team sport for dogs that was invented in California in the 1970s. In this exciting, fast-moving sport, dogs compete in timed relay teams with four dogs on a team.

The course consists of a starting line, four hurdles spaced 10 feet apart, and a spring-loaded box that shoots out tennis balls. The first hurdle is six feet from the starting line, and the box is 15 feet from the last hurdle for an overall length of 51 feet. Each dog jumps the hurdles, then steps on the spring-loaded box, which shoots out a tennis ball. The dog catches the tennis ball and then runs back over the four hurdles. When the dog crosses the starting line, the next dog goes. The first team to have all four dogs run without errors wins the heat.

Tournaments are usually organized in either a double-elimination or round-robin format. Double elimination is usually best of three or best of five. Round robin is usually best three out of five, and the first team to win three heats receives one point toward their standing in the tournament. Flyball competitors earn points towards flyball titles based on the team's time. If the team finishes the course in less than 32 seconds, each dog receives one point; in less than 28 seconds, each dog receives five points, and in less than 24 seconds, each dog receives 25 points. Dogs can earn the titles flyball dog (FD, 20 points), flyball dog excellent (FDX, 100 points), flyball dog champion (FDCH, 500 points), flyball master (FM, 500 points), flyball master excellent (FMX, 10,000 points), flyball master champion (FMCH, 15,000 points), ONYX award (20,000 points) and flyball grand champion (FGDCH, 30,000 points).

> If your Lab is crazy about tennis balls, consider flyball competition.

Contact the North American Flyball Association, the governing organization for flyball (see appendix A) or www.flyball.org.

Obedience Competition

Every civilized dog should know at least five basic commands: heel, sit, down, stay, and come, according to the *AKC Complete*

Dog Book. Obedience training is essential for Labs. You might say it's the glue that holds together all owner-dog activities. A Lab who knows and obeys basic commands is a trustworthy, livable companion.

Obedience competition is a team activity in which dog and owner perform a prescribed set of exercises (or commands) on which the dog is scored. AKC obedience competition is divided into three levels and titles: novice, companion dog (CD), open, companion dog excellent (CDX), and utility dog (UD).

> A Lab who knows and obeys basic commands is a trustworthy, livable companion.

The novice obedience competitor must heel on leash, stand for examination, heel free, recall, and perform an extended sit and down. The stakes are higher for the open competitor, who must heel free, drop on recall, retrieve on flat, retrieve over a high jump and broad jump, and perform an extended sit and down. The advanced utility competitor must perform signal exercises, pass two scent discrimination tests, perform a directed retrieve and directed jumping, and stand for the judge's examination.

To obtain an obedience title, a dog must earn three legs. To be credited for one leg, he must score at least 170 points out of a possible 200 and get more than 50 percent on each exercise. Dogs that have earned a UD title can earn points toward an obedience trial championship. To become an obedience trial champion, the dog must win 100 points, including a first place in utility with at least three dogs in the competition, a first place in open B class with at least six dogs in competition, and a third first place in either of these competitions.

Obedience competition is an excellent activity for Labs—and owners enjoy it, too. But be aware that Labs sometimes have their own ideas about competition. "I had entered my yellow boy, Dusty, in a trial up by the San Francisco area," says Dianne Mullikan of Rycroft Labradors. "It had been raining most of the weekend, so the ground was muddy and slushy. As I entered the ring, it was cloudy but dry. I did the heeling pattern on leash, and Dusty did okay. As we prepared for the off-leash part, I removed the leash, and Dusty and I went back to the starting place. The judge said 'forward,' and off *I* went. I went sailing through the pattern only to get to the other side of the ring and be told by the judge to stop and call my dog. And there he sat, still in the original spot! You see, there was a great big patch of mud, and Dusty just couldn't go through it. He did a mighty fine recall, though. During our long sits and downs, you could see the rain coming from over the mountains. Dusty did something he had never done before: he broke a sit, so the judge excused us. I couldn't have been happier because as soon as I left the ring and went under cover, the downpour hit. Everyone left in the ring was thoroughly soaked."

Interested in obedience competition? Begin with basic obedience classes, then find a trainer who's experienced in obedience competition.

Tracking Tests

Tracking tests require a dog to follow a trail by scent. Dogs can earn several tracking titles from the AKC: tracking dog (TD), tracking dog excellent (TDX), variable surface tracking (VST), and champion tracker (CT). Dogs either pass or fail tests; they don't compete against each other or against the clock. The purpose of a tracking test is to demonstrate the dog's ability to recognize and follow human scent.

A TD test is 440 to 500 yards long and must include at least two right-angle turns. It must be an hour to two hours old, and the individual laying the track must be unfamiliar to the dog. A scented article is dropped at the end of the track, which the dog must recover.

The TDX track is longer, 800 to 1,000 yards, and three to five hours old. It's more complicated and runs through varied terrain such as tall grass or ditches. Dummy scent articles are placed along the track.

A VST test challenges a dog's ability to follow a track in a more developed area. The VST track is 600 to 800 yards over at least three types of surfaces. The track must be three to four hours old, with up to eight turns.

A CT title is awarded to the dog who has earned TD, TDX, and VST titles.

Labrador Retrievers are well known for their scenting abilities, and they're commonly used by law enforcement agencies to detect illegal drugs, foods, or explosives.

For more information on tracking, start by contacting a local obedience or tracking club.

Search and Rescue

Search and rescue (SAR) is a noncompetitive aspect of tracking. Owners with dogs trained to follow a scent often volunteer as search-and-rescue teams for local, national, or international law enforcement agencies. The training for an SAR dog is intense; it's estimated that every one hour of actual searching requires 10 hours of training. There's no national standard for SAR certification, so individual agencies, the Federal Emergency Management Agency (FEMA), for example, each has its own guidelines.

Pfister the Service Lab

The Labrador Retriever has several characteristics—good temperament, retrieving ability and intelligence—that make it a natural service dog. Labs are trained as Guide Dogs to lead the visually impaired, assistance dogs to the physically challenged and hearing dogs for the hearing impaired. Labs are well accepted as service dogs. They have a positive public image as trustworthy, people-loving dogs. Labs truly enjoy their jobs as service dogs. They see their work as a game—and they love to play.

The road to becoming a service dog is a long one, and it begins with dedicated Lab enthusiasts known as "puppy raisers." Puppy raisers are individuals who volunteer their time to a service dog organization; they raise, train, socialize and love potential service dogs in their home beginning when the dog is very young. Once the Lab is about 15 months old, the puppy raiser returns the dog to the service organization for in-depth, specific training.

Being a puppy raiser is a rewarding—and tough—job. Pat Chesley is a puppy raiser for New Horizons Service Dogs. Chesley shares a challenging experience she had raising a black Lab pup that came to be known as "Pfister." "I brought him home and put him down in the kitchen," says Chesley. "Then I discovered his special talent: He could drink and pee at the same time. It was amazing to watch the liquid go in one end and out the other simultaneously.

"I started referring to him as 'The Faucet' since he didn't have a name yet. Someone suggested calling him Pfister, and it stuck. Little did I know that the name would be prophetic.

"Pfister was the hardest puppy to housebreak I have ever raised. He would come to me and look up at me with his bright, happy Labbie eyes—and pee. I'd rush him outside where he would pee again. I was patient and didn't scold him at first. Then I started scolding him, but it didn't matter, he'd still come to me and pee and then pee again outside. At least he was learning the command to potty with all the trips outside.

"Finally, I realized he was telling me when he had to eliminate by showing me what it was he wanted to do. I hung a bell by the back door, and within a day he had learned to bump the bell with his nose so the door would open to allow him to go outside to take care of business.

"Pfister is now a wonderful service dog. I'm very proud of him."

Labs make excellent SAR dogs. They have a good nose and are hardworking and athletic, all essential qualities. Owners must be equally hardworking and committed.

For more information, contact the National Association for Search and Rescue (see appendix A).

Therapy Dogs

You might call Labs and owners who participate in therapy goodwill ambassadors. Therapy dogs make regular visits along with their owners to nursing homes, hospitals, day cares, and assisted-living facilities. A visit from a friendly dog, especially a Lab, is a welcome sight to those who are lonely, bringing joy and friendship in a special canine way. Pet visits are not only emotionally uplifting to nursing home residents and hospital patients but can encourage healing. Studies have shown that petting an animal can lower blood pressure, and many people, especially those feeling withdrawn or isolated, respond to pets when they don't respond to people.

> Pet visits are not only emotionally uplifting to nursing home residents and hospital patients but can encourage healing.

Not just any Lab can be a therapy dog. Most therapy dogs are certified by an organization such as the Delta Society in Renton, Washington. Therapy dogs must pass physical and temperament tests to prove they're safe and friendly with strangers. Owners and pets attend training.

Lab enthusiast Ellen Morris and her dog, Spottie, had the wonderful experience of visiting at Sterling Manor, a nursing home in Maple Shade, New Jersey, some years ago. Morris and Spottie were visiting Morris's mentor, Ted Squires, a well-known

AKC judge and Lab breeder. Squires had suffered a stroke. "When Ted had his stroke and went into a nursing home for his last days, Spottie and I went to visit him on a weekly basis," recalls Morris. "Spottie was a celebrity at the home and took his time to visit everyone who reached out to him. I would take him off leash as soon as I got in the door. Spottie always would lie at my feet while I visited with Ted.

"One day, I was ready to go and looked down and Spott was gone! I called him and no Spott, so I started looking, getting more and more frantic. I asked the nurses; they hadn't seen him. I called the receptionist and he had not gotten out; he was just gone.

"The room across from Ted's was always darkened, with the bed sides high and draped with quilts, and I had never gone in there with Spott because I had assumed the man was very sick. This day I was frantic so I walked toward the room. As I got closer, I heard giggles and went in. There in the bed was the oldest man I had ever seen and Spottie snuggled up to him. Spott was twice his size. The man was blind and wizened, and all of his wrinkles were turned up into a huge smile. He started to sing and talk to Spott in Italian while Spottie gently cleaned lunch off his face.

"Spottie didn't understand Italian, but he understood love. I looked around, and the nurses were standing in the doorway in awe. They thought the old man was out of it. He just couldn't or wouldn't communicate. Spottie took care of that and was insistent about visiting him whenever we went to see Ted. I took him back for months after Ted died so he could see his friend until I got a call from the home that the old, old man had also gone to the bridge."

For more information about therapy dogs, see appendix A.

Great Games for Kids and Labs

Kids of all ages can have fun with the family Lab. Here are a few ideas to get started. Adult supervision is advised with all activities.

Fetch! Kids can keep a Lab busy for hours tossing tennis balls.

Go for a walk. Inside the house for little kids, in the yard for older children. Leash required, of course.

Swimming. Great on a hot day! Fill up the kiddie pool and jump in.

Soccer. Kids can kick the ball, Labs can roll a ball with their nose.

Junior showmanship. Kids are judged on their ability to handle a dog in the breed ring.

Hide and seek. A parent holds the Lab and the kids go hide with treats. Then the dog is sent to find everyone. (The Lab will need a little help at first, so the kids must call the dog or say its name once or twice until the dog catches on.)

Frisbee. Toss one in the air and watch what happens.

Baseball. Let the Lab be outfielder. Hit a tennis ball with a soft bat (not too hard or far), then wait for the retrieve.

Just for Fun

Organized or formal canine sports are wonderful—but they're not the only way to get active with your Lab. Here are a few informal ideas.

Swimming. Whether its a boat ride (life jackets, please!), walk on the seashore, or dashing in and out of a lake, all Labs love to swim and be near water.

Neighborhood stroll. A brisk walk is good for you and Labbie, so pull out the leash and get going.

Perfect Sunday Morning

Deirdre Hoedebecke is the mother of 7-year-old Heather and 22-month-old Michael. She is also "Lab mom" to several Labs, including Black Jack, Winnie, Lil' Bit and Hercules. It's never a dull moment at the Hoedebecke household with kids and Labs running to and fro. In fact, there are times it's downright hectic. But every now and then there's a calm in the storm. Hoedebecke fondly remembers one special morning:

"Heather and Michael were still in their nightclothes. Heather in a flannel Barbie nightgown and Michael in a little blue sleeper with the feet cut out. They had just finished breakfast and I was cleaning the kitchen. It was quiet except for the sound of Heather attempting to read her Winnie the Pooh book, occasionally asking for help with a word.

"Now normally when it is this quiet it means someone is doing something they shouldn't be. But when I looked up I saw the perfect moment frozen in time. Heather and Michael were sitting side by side on the floor, with the sun shining in the back door. Michael's curls seemed on fire and Heather looked like someone had taken a paint brush and streaked her hair with gold. Lil' Bit had her head in Heather's lap looking up at her. Winnie was resting her head on Michael's shoulder with one of her ears flipped back. Michael had his cardboard version of a Pooh book, too. In front of the four of them with his chin resting on his paws was Black Jack; his fur was gleaming in the sunlight, looking for all the world like an indulgent uncle baby-sitting his nieces and nephews.

"Those are the moments that send me searching far and wide for a missing dog and allow me to forgive the chewed up diapers or stolen loaves of bread. Long after the kids are grown and gone I will always have that picture of a perfect Sunday morning in my heart."

Tricks. How about teaching your Lab the traditional shake and roll over or the not so traditional high five? Check out *The Complete Idiot's Guide to Fun and Tricks with Your Dog,* by Sarah Hodgson.

The Family Lab

The Labrador Retriever is a people lover through and through, which is why this breed is a great family dog. No matter what the family size, with or without children, the Lab wants to be a full-fledged member and participate in everything.

Making Your Lab a Good Neighbor

Are you a good doggie neighbor? Are you considerate of those living nearby? Let's hope so! Because we've all known of or lived next to bad doggie neighbors. You know, those people who stick their dogs in the backyard and let them bark from 1 to 3 A.M. Or take the dog for a walk to defecate in *your* yard. Then there are the neighbors who allow their dog to wander, making mischief in every yard—digging, scattering garbage, chewing up the kids' plastic picnic table. Make it your goal to be a good neighbor and teach your Lab to be one, too.

Basic obedience classes should be a Lab's introduction to Neighbor Relations 101, followed by the the Canine Good Citizen Program, sponsored by the AKC. A dog who knows and understands basic obedience commands is on the road to becoming a trustworthy companion. Suppose you're taking a walk through the neighborhood with your Lab. He walks quietly beside you, then sits nicely as you chat with elderly Bill from across the street. No jumping up and knocking down the older man. Or you're in the house, and Labbie is in the front yard. The dog begins to bark, so you go to the door to say "quiet" and call Labbie inside so he won't continue barking. Your Lab knows and obeys both commands.

Commonsense Rules
for Kids and Labs

Parents must supervise all interactions.

Never leave a baby or small child alone with any breed of dog.

Crate train the Lab, but children should be taught to never go into the dog's crate. Teach the child that the crate is the Lab's special, private room.

Never bother the Lab when he's eating or sleeping.

Never tease and always be gentle. No yelling, feet stomping or arm swinging. Don't poke or pull eyes, ears, nose, tail.

Don't permit snack stealing from kids. Place the Lab in his crate or another room with his own doggie snack during little people snack time.

Don't allow kids to supervise the Lab. Parents must be in charge of doggie discipline.

Basic obedience training, along with your sensitivity to others, is essential if you want your Lab to be known as a good neighbor. Here are three simple good-neighbor rules:

○ No incessant barking.

○ No wandering. Keep your Lab in the house, yard, or kennel run at all times. If you leave the premises, make sure your Lab is on a leash.

○ If your Lab defecates while out for a walk, clean it up.

Kid's Best Friend

If you've heard that Labs are a kid's best friend, you've heard right. "They're excellent with kids," says Lab owner Delores Gleason. Her dog, Thunder, who lived to be fourteen and a half, was especially gentle with children. "Thunder was so good with all kids, including my precious granddaughter, Ashley. Ashley is now six years old, but when she was younger, she would come over and always want to play with Thunder. He was so gentle with her. They loved each other. She would put the leash on him, and they would slowly walk around inside the house. It was so adorable."

The Lab's friendly, happy nature make her highly compatible and trustworthy with kids. But that's not to say every Lab will like children. The hallmark of the well-bred Lab is a good temperament, but some Labs, puppy mill Labs, for example, aren't the result of careful breeding. If dogs with questionable temperaments are bred, the offspring may inherit less than sunny dispositions.

Proper socialization and adequate training accustom a Lab to children. And health status can affect the Lab's attitude toward kids. Older dogs, for example, may be grumpy because they don't feel well.

Then you've got to consider the kids in the family. How old are they? Very young children can be overwhelmed—and knocked over—by a friendly, strong Lab.

Generally, though, if you've got kids, you can't go wrong with a Labrador Retriever. *But you must be prepared to supervise all Lab-child interactions.* That's the key to any successful dog-kid relationship. Parents must supervise to ensure the safety of both child and dog.

The degree of supervision you'll want to impose varies, depending on how old a child is and how old and well-socialized the Lab. Babies and toddlers need constant supervision with pets. Never leave toddlers alone with animals or another child. As a child grows and shows maturity, supervision can be minimized. While babies and young children should never be alone with a Lab, older children, say eight years old, could play in the yard with her. Parents don't have to be right in the midst of the game but close by.

Children need not only ongoing supervision with the dog but also ongoing instruction on how to treat a pet kindly. Kids aren't born even knowing how to pet nicely—they must be taught. The best way to do that is for parents to model the desired behavior. Show the child how to pet with an open hand—no grabbing! Talk to the child and tell him what you're doing and why. Keep lessons short and simple.

> Parents must supervise to ensure the safety of both child and dog. That's the key to any successful dog-kid relationship.

Kids will be kids, though, and forget your instructions. That's where constant supervision comes in. You can observe how the child interacts with the dog and correct his behavior as needed. Having a young child and a Lab can be a lot of work. But it's also a wonderful opportunity for parents to show children how to be kind to animals, an experience that helps children develop empathy for creatures other than themselves.

Travels with Labbie

Imagine yourself relaxing on a tropical island. You're lying in a comfortable hammock on the beach, gazing at the aqua water and pale blue sky. A light breeze cools you. You sip an orange juice spritzer. You don't have a care in the world, other than to choose a restaurant for dinner.

But wait! Where's your Labrador Retriever? Did you bring him with you? Or did you leave him at home? To be sure, there's nothing like going on holiday and getting away from the day-to-day details of life. But before you bolt, Lab owner, you've got to

Kids and Dog Bites

Renowned for its life-is-a-bowl-full-of-cherries attitude, the good-natured Labrador Retriever is hardly a dog you would think of as a biter. Generally, it is not. But there are always exceptions to every rule, especially when it comes to kids and dogs. Children are most commonly bitten by their own family pets, according to the American Humane Association. Overall statistics show that 60 percent of dog bite victims are children; over half are children age 12 or under.

Dog bites can be prevented, of course, by making sure you acquire a Lab with a trustworthy temperament. Buy only from a reputable breeder who is as concerned about temperament as conformation. Scrutinize the temperament of the pup, parents and adult relatives.

Following that, socialize and train the Lab. Set limits on acceptable behavior. Teach the Lab to be a trustworthy member of the family and community.

Do not encourage mouthing or biting by allowing kids to play rough, aggressive games with the Lab. Though they are favorites, games like tug of war and wrestling can encourage aggression. A family pet should never have its mouth on any person, for any reason.

Make sure kids know never to disrupt the Lab when it's eating or sleeping. Kids should also learn never to approach a strange or loose dog, and to remain motionless and avoid eye contact if approached.

Be on the lookout for trouble, such as occasional growls or snaps. Be honest with yourself as to the dog's nature and don't make excuses for bad behavior. Learn to recognize aggression and dominance, and take steps to nip it in the bud.

make a few decisions and arrangements for your dog. Then you can really relax!

To Go or Not to Go

The question isn't whether or not you'll plan a vacation, but whether you'll take your Lab along or leave him at home. The answer to that depends on the type of vacation you are taking and your personal preference.

In general, Labs are good travelers and go almost anywhere quite easily. But not all vacations are cut out for Labs—a honeymoon, for example, or a tour trip to Europe. Use common sense to figure this one out. Visualize the vacation, and place your Lab in the picture. If it's an easy fit, take Labbie along. If not, leave him at home.

Not This Time, Girl

If your holiday plans don't include a four-legged bundle of zest, then you've got some arranging to do. Someone has to take care of your Lab. You certainly can't leave out a feeder like you can for cats and say, "Bye, see you in a few days." First of all, the feeder would be empty 10 minutes after your departure. Then the Lab would go crazy with loneliness and boredom and tear the house/yard/kennel to bits. Besides, it's unsafe to leave a pet unattended.

You have several good choices. You can

❍ Leave the Lab at a reputable boarding kennel or vet hospital;
❍ Hire a pet sitter; or
❍ Ask Grandma to baby-sit.

Boarding Kennel. A boarding kennel is a business that houses dogs and cats, for a fee, while owners are away. Dogs are usually kept in large, indoor-outdoor kennel runs; cats are housed in an indoor cattery. The average cost to board a dog per night is $10.63 (for a dog the size of a Lab, the cost will probably be

Did You Know?

40 percent of dog and cat owners carry pictures of their pets in their wallets.

higher), according to the American Boarding Kennels Association (ABKA). Of the some 9,000 boarding kennels in the United States and Canada, some are good, some not so good. Your goal in choosing a kennel to care for your Lab while you're sipping drinks on that Caribbean beach is to find one that's clean, well-supervised, secure, and adequately staffed.

There are many types of kennels—some large, some small, some plush, others basic. Which type you select depends on what you're looking for and what you can afford. There are good basic kennels that house the dog in an indoor-outdoor run; provide food and water; give medication as needed; clean daily; require pets to be current on all vaccinations, including canine cough for dogs; and may require that the pet be flea-free or dipped for fleas before it can stay in the kennel. More luxurious kennels provide plush beds, daily walks or play sessions, even swimming. Whether you're interested in basic care or some degree of frills, don't hesitate to ask questions about the care your pet will be given. Tour several kennels before making a choice.

To ensure that your Lab has the best of care while you're away, tell the kennel staff as much as possible about your dog: her level of training, likes and dislikes, bad habits, eating schedule. Drop off your Lab and pick her up as scheduled, and notify the kennel of any change of plans.

Just as a mother will pack an overnight bag for her preschooler who's spending the night with Grandma, so must you pack a bag for Labbie, including any special-diet foods, medication, favorite sleeping blankie, and toys. And don't forget your Lab's up-to-date vaccination records. Reputable kennels don't allow overnight guests without current immunizations.

To find ABKA kennels in your area, go to www.abka.com.

Pet Sitter. A pet sitter is a person who comes to your house, for a fee, to care for your pet. This individual may also water plants or pick up mail. Visits average $10.50 each. According to the National Association of Professional Petsitters (NAPP), keeping the pet at home in its familiar environment, eating its regular diet and enjoying its exercise routine, is best for the animal. It eliminates the trauma of being transported and minimizes exposure to the illnesses of other animals.

> Just as a mother will pack an overnight bag for her preschooler who's spending the night with Grandma, so must you pack a bag for Labbie.

You can choose from many professional pet sitters. If you opt to have a pet sitter come into your home, make sure the person is licensed and bonded. Ask for the names of other clients as references. Meet with the individual who will be coming to your home and introduce her to your Lab before you leave your dog in her care.

For a pet-sitter referral from the NAPP, contact 1-800-296-PETS or www.petsitters.org.

Hi, Grandma! This is probably your least likely option. But for those blessed with a parent, family member, or trusted friend who knows and loves your Lab, who better to look after her while you're away? Either Labbie can stay at home while Grandma stays at your house, or you can take the dog to her home. Be sure to offer payment or at least bring home an expensive souvenir from your trip.

I Want to Go!

Labs are good travelers, and rather than leave them at home while vacationing, many owners make room for one more. But

Holiday Hazards

Dangers are present any time of year, but are you aware of extra hazards your Lab may face during holiday seasons?

For example, cookies, cakes and other sweets are a big part of Thanksgiving and Christmas dinners. But don't be tempted to share these goodies with your Lab. Chocolate is especially dangerous because it contains the chemical theobromine. While an overdose of chocolate may sound great to you, your Lab could suffer from chocolate toxicosis if she eats the stuff. This condition can cause severe digestive upset, or at its worst, can be fatal. Candy and sweets are big at Easter and Halloween, too, so keep goodies out of sight and out of reach.

Rich foods are a favorite part of holidays: baked goose, turkey or ham, dressing, mashed potatoes and gravy. All are delicious, but way too rich for your Lab. Don't be tempted to share your dinner!

If digestive upset isn't enough, you've got to worry about all those holiday decorations. Your Lab may try to eat those, too. Or at least taste them. Christmas tree decorations, candles, Easter baskets, Halloween costumes. Supervise your Lab carefully during these times of year to prevent accidental (intentional on your Lab's part) ingestion.

Noise and confusion associated with holidays can be upsetting to the Lab: houseguests, parties, constant doorbell ringing. If your Lab is upset by the commotion (most Labs aren't, they just join in), confine her to a quiet area in the house. On July 4th, you'll be wise to keep your Lab close by. Some dogs are frightened of fireworks and will bolt out the door, never to be seen again.

before adding Labbie to the holiday head count, you'll have to plan in order to make the trip go smoothly. If you're willing to think ahead and your Lab fits easily into the vacation plan, there's no reason you can't enjoy doggie company, too.

Before You Leave Home. Just as parents of young children must pack up a diaper bag for an outing, you'll have some packing to do if you plan to take your Lab on holiday. You'll need food, bottled water, dishes, collar, leash, bedding, toys, identification tags with vacation addresses and phone numbers added. You may also need a current health certification; keep that along with other important travel papers. And, make sure your dog is wearing an up-to-date rabies tag. Don't forget plastic bags so you can clean up after your Lab. It's also a good idea to pack a doggie first aid kit. You never know when an emergency will arise! Bring along anything you can think of that will help keep your Lab happy and comfortable.

Traveling by Car. Car travel is a great way to take along your Lab. But before starting on a 300-mile journey, take time to accustom your Lab to traveling in the car. Take short trips around town, to the park, the store, the veterinary clinic, the grooming salon. That way, your Lab will be less anxious on a longer ride.

Many Lab enthusiasts transport their dogs in crates or use canine safety restraints. Dogs can be injured just like people can if there's a crash. A crate or safety restraint also makes driving safer for you; the Lab is unable to jump into the front seat and startle you, which could result in an accident.

Do not feed your dog or give water for about two hours before driving to help prevent motion sickness, but carry paper towels for cleanup in case your dog gets car sick. Stop every few hours for water and a nature break. Take along a few toys and chews to keep your Lab busy while driving. However, you'll find that Labs, like children, tend to fall asleep while riding in the car.

A word of warning: Never leave your dog alone in the car, even parked in the shade or with the windows cracked, in warm weather. The interior of the car can get hot, quickly, resulting in heatstroke and, possibly, death.

Air Travel. Who said Labradors can't fly? Most anywhere you can fly on commercial airlines, you can buy a ticket for your Lab (there are a few airlines who refuse pets). In the United States, service animals travel free of charge on all airlines; proof of disability may be required (Guide Dogs, signal dogs and assistance dogs).

The United States Department of Agriculture sets minimum rules and guidelines regulating pet travel, though each airline makes its own rules regarding pet travel, and every airline is different. Pets travel either in the cabin in a carrier that stores under the seat or as cargo. Obviously, because of its large size, the flying Lab will travel in a crate placed in the plane's cargo area.

Call the airline before traveling to determine pet travel policies. Some experienced air travelers recommend calling the airline several times to make sure you're getting accurate information. Make an appointment with your veterinarian a few days before you leave to get a current health certificate for your dog and a updated certificate of vaccinations. Some county and national park officials, as well as border patrols, may require a proof of health certificate. Additionally, most destinations require rabies shots, and a few sites, such as Hawaii and England, have quarantines that prohibit pets from visiting.

When traveling to another country, be aware that they may have strict and difficult importation requirements. Contact your vet and the USDA APHIS (Animal Plant Health Inspection Service) or area veterinarian in charge for your state at least one month in advance of departure. (Out of country travel requirements and APHIS can be found at http://www.usda.gov.)

Pets must travel in USDA approved kennels. Airlines usually have several sizes available for rent, though you can buy one at most pet shops or by mail order. If you opt to purchase, ask the airline

Dog Camps

Camp isn't just for kids anymore. If you're a dog owner and you're itching to get back to camp, you can. And bring along your Lab! There are several dog camps in the United States, organized settings for dogs and owners to spend a weekend or a week together learning new skills, attending training classes, enjoying competitions or just having fun with other dog enthusiasts.

A camp of special interest is hosted by the Dog Scouts of America. DSA was founded in 1995 by Lonnie Olson for dogs and people who love them. Any dog can become a Dog Scout. The only requirement is that the dog must pass a test much like the AKC Canine Good Citizen test. An added requirement is that the dog is stable and calm in groups of other dogs. Testing takes place at Dog Scout Camp, which usually takes place once a year for six days. Different topics/activities are offered at Dog Scout Camp every year, including backpacking, water rescue, flyball, agility, herding, and other fun dog activities.

For more information on dog camps, contact:

Dog Scouts of America
5068 Nestel Road
St. Helen, MI 48656
517-389-2000
www.dogscouts.com
dogscouts@aol.com

Camp Winnaribbun
P.O. Box 50300
Reno, NV 89513
775-348-8412

Camp Gone to the Dogs
RR #1 Box 958
Putney, Vermont 05346
802-387-5673

Dog Days of Wisconsin
Summer Camp
1879 Haymarket #24
Waukesha, WI 53186
1-800-226-7436

for the specific USDA requirements. Put extra food and water in a pack on top of the crate. Mark the crate carefully with your flight information; luggage tags work well for this. The Lab should wear a collar with an identification tag that lists your name, address and telephone number, along with vacation information.

Avoid feeding your Lab several hours prior to a flight to minimize air sickness. Exercise your dog before kenneling and boarding, too. Allow time for a brisk walk and a nature break. Sedatives and tranquilizers are usually not necessary for the easy-going Lab. If you think your dog needs them, they should only be used under veterinary supervision.

Fly direct whenever possible. If there is a plane change, check to make sure the dog is boarded on the aircraft. If you have a layover of 30 minutes, try to physically check on the dog, particularly if it is hot or cold outside. In hot weather fly at night, in cold weather fly during the day. Upon arrival, tell the gate attendant there is a live animal on board. Request that it be unloaded first. As soon as you know your Lab is unloaded, head to the baggage claim.

Lab-Friendly Accommodations. Before you embark on your journey, you've got to find out if the destination accommodations you've chosen will be happy to see your Lab. Not all motels, hotels, bed and breakfasts, or campgrounds, allow pets. However, many do. Just make sure you plan ahead. Get a copy of *Vacationing with Your Pet!* by Eileen Barish. This book contains more than 10,000 listings, state by state, of pet-friendly hotels, inns, ranches and B and Bs. Another excellent resource is the Travel Dog website at www.travel-dog.com. This site contains everything you every wanted to know about traveling with your Lab, and includes specific information on hotels, motels, campgrounds, that accept pets.

Wherever you go, you and Labbie must be considerate guests. Don't allow your Lab to sleep on the hotel bed and it's probably best not to leave the dog alone in the room. If you must, leave it in a crate. Pick up after your dog and keep it on leash.

9

A Lifetime of Love and Good Health

In This Chapter

❍ Your Aging Lab—What to Expect
❍ Day-to-Day Comfort
❍ Saying Goodbye

The glory of young men is their strength,
gray hair the splendor of the old.

—PROVERBS 20:29

O ne of the great mysteries of life is that it eventually ends. From a biological perspective, a progressive and irreversible deterioration of cellular and organ function takes place in the tissues of all animals as time passes. Why this happens isn't really known—there are theories— but the effects are well known. It's called aging. As the years pass, your boisterous and lovable Labrador Retriever will age. You may notice changes in his activity level and his ability to hear and smell. Although you can't change the

Ten Good Reasons
to Adopt a Senior Lab

1. Senior Labs are housetrained.

2. Senior Labs won't chew up your shoes (as long as they're well trained).

3. Senior Labs are more settled and mellow than pups.

4. Senior Labs adapt very well in new homes because they've learned what it takes to be part of the pack.

5. Senior Labs know obedience commands.

6. Senior Labs are very loving and affectionate.

7. You know what you're getting when you adopt a senior Lab.

8. Senior Labs aren't as demanding as pups but are just as much fun.

9. Senior Labs sleep all night.

10. Senior Labs join you for naps!

inevitable, you can help your Lab enjoy his golden years by understanding the aging process.

Your Aging Lab—What to Expect

Every dog ages differently and at a different rate. Generally large breeds, such as Labradors, German Shepherds, and Saint Bernards, tend to age more rapidly than small breeds, such as Toy Poodles, Pugs, and Chihuahuas. A six-year-old dog is roughly equivalent in age to a 45-year-old human. At 10, a dog is equivalent in age to a human of 65, and at 12, he's the same as a 75-year-old. At 13, he's like an 80-year-old; at 14, an 85-year-old; and at 15, a 90-year-old.

According to experts at Tufts University, the point at which a dog qualifies as "aged" varies. Veterinarians generally consider small dogs to be senior citizens at about 12 years of age, whereas large dogs reach the senior stage at seven to eight years of age. This roughly corresponds to the 55-plus category in people.

An individual dog's biological age is determined by genetics, environment, disease, and nutritional status. A good diet and appropriate veterinary care throughout a dog's life greatly contributes to his good health as a senior. The condition of the aging pet reflects, in part, the care he received during his lifetime.

For the most part, older dogs are less active, less curious, and more complacent than they were in their youth. The older dog can be forgetful, sleepy, resistant to change, a picky eater, and an excessive barker. Sometimes an older dog is grumpy and irritable, usually when he suffers from poor health. You may notice some or all of these changes as your Lab ages.

Musculoskeletal. As your Lab grows older, so does his musculoskeletal system. Many Labs develop arthritis in their joints and spine. You may notice a decrease in your dog's muscle mass and tone. The neck and body may appear bulky and the extremities thinner. Your Lab's tummy may sag, his back sway, and his elbows stick out. If he's got arthritis, he may limp or hold up the affected limb, or his joints may be painful to move or touch. Such changes in mobility can affect your Lab's behavior. A Lab who can no longer follow his owner from room to room might become depressed.

Did You Know?

The old rule of multiplying a dog's age by seven to find the equivalent human age is inaccurate. A better measure is to count the first year as 15, the second year as 10, and each year after that as 5.

Labs are people lovers, so if they're unable to join in all family activities, they may suffer the effects of isolation.

The musculoskeletal changes your Lab experiences as he ages can be painful. Some dogs show little evidence of discomfort, but others become cranky, even aggressive toward family members. Depending on the Lab's condition, a veterinarian can prescribe medication or therapy to decrease pain.

Vision. It's not uncommon for the older Lab to experience changes in vision. A common change in all older dogs is nuclear sclerosis, a hardening of the central part of the lens that results in a clouding of the lens. Although the dog's overall vision won't seem affected, even in advanced stages, she may have trouble seeing objects close up.

Another common age-related visual change is the formation of cataracts. A cataract is the loss of the normal transparency of the lens of the eye. Any spot on the lens that is opaque, regardless of size, is considered a cataract. Eyes with cataracts have a milky gray or bluish white cast. Dogs of any age can develop cataracts, but they're most common in oldsters. Some breeds or lines of dogs are predisposed to develop cataracts.

Cataracts can cause vision loss, making it difficult for the Lab to navigate her surroundings. Most dogs adjust well to the gradual loss of vision if they are still able to hear. But cataracts in Labs don't tend to be progressive, and so total blindness isn't as likely in Labs as in some other breeds of dogs. Veterinarians can offer surgery to remove cataracts when they interfere with your pet's vision.

Hearing. Deafness due to gradual loss of hearing is another common condition in older dogs. Senile deafness

Senior Health Care

Many veterinarians recommend a geriatric screening for your dog at the appropriate age. A geriatric screening usually includes a physical exam, blood tests, and an electrocardiogram or specialized tests for your dog's specific health conditions. Diseases of older dogs that are not usually seen in young dogs include arthritis, diabetes, Cushing's disease (obesity and muscular weakness caused by malfunction of the adrenal or pituitary glands), cancer, and kidney, heart, and liver disease. Your veterinarian will perform blood tests during a geriatric visit to screen for many of these diseases.

Since dogs of different size age at different rates, screening begins at different ages:

Up to 15 pounds: Begin geriatric screening at age nine to 11

51 to 80 pounds: Begin geriatric screening at age six to eight

16 to 50 pounds: Begin geriatric screening at age seven to nine

Over 80 pounds: Begin geriatric screening at age four to six

Your veterinarian may recommend semiannual visits once your dog becomes a senior. Between visits, be alert to changes in your Lab that could indicate serious illness and require immediate veterinary attention.

- ○ Sudden loss of weight
- ○ Serious loss of appetite
- ○ Increase in appetite without increase in weight
- ○ Diarrhea or vomiting
- ○ Increased thirst without a change in activity level and increased urination
- ○ Excessive fatigue
- ○ Extreme limited mobility
- ○ Coughing and excessive panting

usually comes on gradually at about 10 years of age. You may not notice it at first, although the dog may seem less active and responsive. Senile deaf dogs often retain the ability to hear high-pitched sounds.

Hearing loss in the older Lab can cause problems. Since the older dog can't hear your commands, such as sit or no, he can be more difficult to discipline, and a dog who was previously well trained may be difficult to control. With time and patience, a hard-of-hearing Lab can be taught to respond to hand signals for common commands such as sit, down, and come.

Some deaf dogs bark uncontrollably. Often this behavior is encouraged by the owner, who gives treats to stop the barking. A better idea is to isolate the dog until the barking stops, even if it's only for a short time. As soon as the dog is quiet, let him out and reward the quiet behavior.

A deaf Lab is at increased risk of automobile injury, often in his own driveway, because he can't hear an oncoming vehicle. Of course, not all deafness in older Labs is strictly age-related. It's quite possible his problem is caused by a waxy buildup inside the ear, infection, or even a polyp—a benign growth in the ear. If you notice Labbie can't hear as well as he used to, his vet can help you decide if it's simply old age or a treatable problem.

Kidney and Bowels. Kidney function declines with a dog's age. The aging dog may urinate more frequently because her kidneys can't concentrate waste anymore. Also, the urinary sphincter weakens with advancing age, causing unconcious dribbling, espe- cially when the dog lies down. Both kidney and sphincter problems can make the dog unable to keep from wetting in the house, especially at night. For some older dogs, an increase in trips outside will help in controlling house soiling. If the dog must be left alone for long periods, you might revert to paper training. Also be aware that changes in bowel or bladder habits are often the sign of serious illness, such as kidney disease or liver problems, and should not be ignored. Your vet can help diagnose and treat these conditions.

Loss of sphincter control can result in the dog's defecating in the house. Dogs also respond to stress by soiling the house with stool, and older dogs can't tolerate stress very well. If the source of the stress can be identified, an older Lab can be acclimated to the change, and hopefully the house soiling will subside.

Teeth and Gums. Are you aware that your veterinarian can roughly determine your Lab's age by looking at her teeth? Although it's easiest to tell a dog's age from one year to seven years of age, a vet with a trained eye can detect subtle changes in the teeth from years of biting and chewing. For example, by age three and a half, all cusps are usually worn flat on the upper middle incisors. As time goes on, the incisors are worn flat and the canine teeth are blunted.

Tooth and gum disease, a common malady in older dogs, can interfere with the dog's ability to eat. No teeth, no chewing! That's why proper dental care throughout your Lab's lifetime is essential to ensure that she'll have healthy teeth during her senior years. Regular brushing and periodic cleaning are especially important for the older Lab. Ask your veterinarian to recommend a dental plan for your senior, then stick with it.

Skin and Coat. Because the activity of oil-producing glands decreases, the aging Lab's skin and coat may become dry or scaly. You may also notice that the geriatric dog has a stronger doggie odor. More frequent grooming may be necessary to keep his skin and coat in good

Did You Know?

Two dogs survived the sinking of the Titanic, a Pomeranian and a Pekingese named Sun Yat Sen.

condition and smell at bay. It's also a good time to look for lumps, bumps, or skin problems. The older dog's nails will need to be trimmed more frequently since the less active senior doesn't wear them down.

Heart.   The geriatric dog can suffer from a weakened heart muscle. Acquired valvular heart disease, a common cause of heart disease in dogs, usually affects only dogs over age 12. As the dog ages, the heart valves degenerate. A dry cough is often the first sign of valvular heart disease in the older dog. He may also have less energy and muscular weakness and be short of breath. Although heart disease is always serious, it can usually be treated with medications that make the heart function more strongly.

Cognitive Dysfunction.   Canine cognitive dysfunction syndrome includes several age-related changes in older dogs' behaviors. These behaviors include circling; tremors; stiffness or weakness; inappropriate vocalization; compulsive behaviors; and changes in sleep patterns, house training, interest in food, attention and activity, and awareness of surroundings. The older dog may feel separation anxiety if you leave him alone, for example, or be uneasy with visitors. Like many other aging changes, these behaviors may also be associated with more serious problems, such as Cushing's disease or a brain tumor. Cushing's disease is treatable with medication.

Routine. Older dogs can be very resistant to change. For example, one elderly dog refused to eat out of the new bowl his owner purchased. No matter what food the owner served in the shiny new bowl, the 13-year-old dog stubbornly refused to eat it. When the owner switched back to the old bowl, the dog gobbled up the food!

New routines, locations, or social situations—visitors, children, workers in the home, boarding—can be overly stressful to the elderly dog. Old dogs adjust poorly to emotional and physical stress; their hearts, livers, kidneys, and metabolism are often unable to meet the increased demands stress puts on them.

> New routines, locations, or social situations—visitors, children, workers in the home, boarding—can be overly stressful to the elderly dog.

Day-to-Day Comfort

Now you have an idea of what to expect as your Lab advances in years. But how do you apply this knowledge? How can you best care for your geriatric Lab every day?

First, those aching bones and joints mean your Lab needs softer ground on which to rest. Perhaps in her youth she was content to nap on a tile floor, but in old age an orthopedic bed is in order. Stiffness from osteoarthritis is made worse by sleeping on cold, damp ground or hard surfaces such as cement. You can purchase a bed at a pet supply store or make one yourself with foam rubber (easily found in thrift stores) covered with a machine washable, snugly blanket. Place the bed in a dry, draft-free area of the house—older dogs are sensitive to extremes of heat and cold.

When your older Lab is wet after bathing or an outing in wet weather, reduce stiffness by drying her off thoroughly. "Make sure they don't get wet and stay damp," says Lab owner Leland Perry. "Dry them off, let them dry in the sun. Do not let them curl up and sleep that way in an air conditioned area or into the night."

The arthritic Lab may find it difficult to bend down to eat and drink from bowls on the floor. Consider buying her an eating table that's at neck level for her, with special cutouts for food and water bowls. A senior Lab whose arthritic neck hurts when she bends it will be more comfortable eating from a table.

Although an arthritic Lab may try to avoid activity because it's painful, nothing is more beneficial to an older dog than a regular exercise program, according to Delbert G. Carlson, D.V.M., and James M. Giffin, M.D., authors of the *Dog Owner's Home Veterinary Handbook*. Exercise improves an older dog's muscle tone and strength, keeps her joints moving, and keeps her weight on target. The veterinarian can prescribe medication to reduce arthritic pain so that exercise is possible.

> Exercise improves an older dog's muscle tone and strength, keeps her joints moving, and keeps her weight on target.

Activity is essential, but you'll need to protect your arthritic Lab from injury by modifying her exercise and not allowing the oldster to overdo. "Reduce jumping and all things that can wear down the joints more," says Perry. "Lift them into and out of the car. Avoid stairs. Avoid very rough play. Let the dog choose what he wants. Let them change pace slowly in their walks. Tell them it is okay, you like to enjoy a calmer pace. Sit and rest on the walk."

An aging Lab needs more rest than she did in her younger years. If she's exercising on a regular basis and wants to nap more, let her. Just make sure you have a comfy bed handy! "They sleep more, and it can be very deep," says Perry. "It is lovely to watch their peaceful faces. They love to lie on the grass and watch the birds now rather than chase them. They age so gracefully. If only humans could learn from them and not fight it so, and not give up altogether."

Remember that your older Lab is a creature of habit. She's not likely to appreciate any sudden changes in routine, bed placement, food dishes, or activity. Keep changes in your older Lab's life to a minimum, changing only essentials. For example, if you

Leaving Your Pet in Your Will

Who will care for your pet if you die before he does? Many people neglect to think this could happen, with the result of their beloved pet being placed in an animal shelter after their death. Talk with family and friends and find someone who is truly willing and able to take care of your dog if you should pass. Then speak with your lawyer and include your pet in your will. You may also want to specify a certain amount of money to go to the person caring for your Labbie to offset the costs of food, veterinary care, and other pet-related expenses.

feed your Lab every morning at seven-thirty, then go for a walk, stick to that routine.

If you're planning a holiday away from home, consider hiring a pet sitter to care for your Lab at home rather than boarding the dog. No matter how nice the boarding kennel is, older dogs don't tolerate well drastic changes in their routine. Keeping your old dog at home in the care of a trusted pet sitter is the best option while you're away (unless they've learned to love the kennel previously, of course).

Reduced hearing and failing eyesight are realities with an older dog. Teach hand signals for obedience commands to a Lab who doesn't hear as well as he used to. You can also get the dog's attention by stamping on the floor; the dog can feel the vibrations. Approach your deaf dog slowly so you don't startle him. "If they start to go deaf," says Perry, "start letting them know you are home by walking up and gently touching their heads. Don't step over them without letting them know by a gentle touch on the head or side. They will jump up startled and you can fall. It is important to do this, whereas before your dog would have smelled and heard you."

If you have a Lab with failing or loss of sight, don't move the furniture! Blind dogs are amazingly adaptable as long as everything in their physical environment stays the same. Dogs rely on their sense of smell and hearing much more than sight to navigate the world, and these senses become even more acute when sight fails. The blind dog should never be allowed to run free, and basic obedience commands are essential. Calling to a blind Lab to stop or sit could very well save his life.

An older Lab's failing kidneys and bowels can be troublesome and frustrating to owners. Cleaning up accidents in the house can be like a return to puppyhood. Be patient, take it in stride, and take your Lab out for nature breaks frequently. And of course check with the vet as soon as you realize there's a change in bladder or bowel habits. Not only can your vet help should this be a sign of serious disease, he can often provide medications to relieve overactive urinary sphincters or suggest dietary changes to improve bowels.

Senior Meal

Your senior Labrador needs some special consideration when it comes to diet. Besides serving dinner on a silver platter (old dogs are *so* demanding), you'll need to be very conscious of the number of calories in each of her meals. Older dogs tend to be less active, which means fewer calories are needed to maintain their target weight. Feed a diet too high in calories, and you'll have an overweight Lab. Since obesity is very unhealthy, you've got to keep your Lab at her optimum weight.

One way to do that is to feed her a commercially prepared senior diet. Senior diets generally contain a reduced concentration of fat and calories; some foods also contain extra fiber to further reduce caloric density. Ask your veterinarian if a senior diet is appropriate for your older Lab.

According to current research, a diet rich in protein is also important for the older dog, because senior dogs are less efficient in metabolizing protein than younger dogs. The additional protein is needed to maintain protein reserves and support protein turnover, which help maintain the dog's immune system. Dogs who don't eat enough protein are more prone to suffer ill effects from stress. The specific amount of protein required for senior dogs varies depending on the dog but veterinary researchers recommend that protein constitute 20 to 26 percent of calories for older dogs. Many veterinarians recommend a senior diet that contains about 25 percent protein.

> Older dogs tend to be less active, which means fewer calories are needed to maintain their target weight.

Some dog breeders and owners think that older dogs shouldn't eat a high-protein diet because protein can cause kidney failure. Although a protein-restricted diet may be recommended for a dog suffering from kidney failure, there's no evidence that protein at an appropriate level in a nutritionally complete and balanced diet causes kidney problems in older dogs.

Don't feed your elderly Lab table scraps or excess treats, make sure he gets enough exercise, and don't supplement his diet unless advised to do so by a veterinarian.

A senior dog's appetite may diminish. As a dog ages, his sense of smell or taste may fail, making food less appealing. (If your dog suddenly loses his appetite, check with your vet—a sudden loss of appetite could be a sign of serious illness.) One way to increase food appeal for the senior Lab is to warm his food a bit. Some older dogs like their food "soupy," so add a little water. You can also add unsalted beef or chicken broth to encourage a senior to eat.

Sometimes all the senior dog needs is a little variety in his food. Instead of the same old kibble slightly moistened, add a tablespoon or two of canned food, beef or chicken broth, or a few lightly cooked veggies. Add variety in small amounts to prevent digestive upset. (Avoid high-sodium, canned broth for a dog with heart disease.)

The picky senior can be picky about drinking enough water, too. Older dogs often forget to drink or, due to arthritis pain, avoid getting up and going to the water bowl. Dehydration isn't good for any dog but especially is harmful to seniors, who already aren't as strong as they used to be. Encourage your senior Lab to drink, and make it easy by setting out several water bowls throughout the house and yard. Don't allow your older dog to drink impure water. Although a few licks of rainwater didn't do any harm in a dog's youth, a senior's aging immune system can't handle the stress.

Facing the Inevitable

No matter how healthy and active your senior Lab is and no matter how hard you work at keeping him that way, there's a day in the future that will be tough to face. Eventually your Lab will die, either from old age or an illness associated with old age. The average Labrador lives 10 to 14 years, depending on his genetics, health care, nutrition, and injuries.

There's certainly no reason to be morbid about your Lab's last day on earth. But it's healthy for you to realize that one day you'll be without a boisterous companion who delights and entertains you. And that last day may be a matter of choice. Some old dogs die naturally in their sleep, but many others are euthanized when owners no longer believe the dog has a quality life. What is euthanasia? Commonly called "putting to sleep," euthanasia is performed by a veterinarian in the office or sometimes as a house call. It's an intravenous injection of an barbiturate anesthetic in a large enough dose to cause immediate loss of consciousness and cardiac arrest. Many people think it's a kind way to help a pet die easily and without pain.

Saying Goodbye

You may be faced with making a decision about euthanasia for your elderly Lab. Perhaps he's been getting along okay, with you accommodating his limited mobility, giving him medication to reduce pain, and sticking to a daily routine that doesn't change (that's so important to old dogs!). Senior dogs can enjoy many months or years in relative comfort even though they "aren't what they used to be." But one day you might realize your Lab is no longer enjoying anything. He's restless and seems to be in great pain. The vet can't offer any more help. Or perhaps your Lab is young but very ill, and his chances of improving are slim. His quality of life is questionable. Is it time to consider euthanasia?

The decision to euthanize a pet is a personal one, and it's wise never to make that decision quickly. Get the facts on your Lab's health status from your veterinarian. Know your dog's chances of

Did You Know?

The oldest dog ever documented was an Australian cattle dog named Bluey, who was put to sleep at the age of 29 years and 5 months.

survival and the estimated quality of life he'll continue to have and for how long. Are there any treatments/surgeries/medications that might help? Is hospitalization required? Is your Lab suffering and if so, how much? Can you care for your Lab at home?

Once you get the facts, think carefully over the decision to euthanize or treat, and how much to treat. Talk with a friend who knows you and your dog. It's also helpful to chat with other Lab owners who have faced the same decision. (You can find plenty of support, thoughts, and ideas from members of on-line Lab mailing lists; see appendix A.)

Even after you've gotten the facts about euthanasia and talked it over, don't expect to decide right away. "I do believe in euthanasia," says Dianne Mullikin of Rycroft Labradors, "but it's never an easy decision. I have an old-timer who will be 13 in July. I love him dearly and was quite relieved when I was able to put him on an anti-inflammatory medication to ease his arthritis. He's much more active now, and I know that I've just made him more comfortable. I still dread the day when I have to make a decision about euthanasia. Unfortunately, dogs are fighters and don't want to give up no matter how much pain they're in. That is why we must make the decision."

The decision to euthanize a pet is a highly individual and personal decision. Two Lab owners faced with the same circumstances will make different choices, for different reasons, at different times. Unlike math problems, there's no one right answer. "I've learned that you can never decide or judge a person for their acts," says Lab enthusiast Karla McCoy. "Whether it's to euthanize a pet too soon or let a pet suffer too long before euthanizing, or to treat a condition or not, or to do surgery or not. The best thing you can do is support the decision, no matter what it is. You never know the cir-

Veterinary Teaching Hospital Grief Hotlines

University of California, Davis, California, (916) 752-4200, 6:30–9:30 P.M. PST, Monday through Friday

Colorado State University, Fort Collins, Colorado, (970) 491-1242

University of Florida, Gainesville, Florida, (352) 392-4700 (ext. 4080); takes messages 24 hours a day; someone will call back between 7:00 and 9:00 P.M. EST

Michigan State University, East Lansing, Michigan, (517) 432-2696, 6:30–9:30 P.M. EST, Tuesday, Wednesday and Thursday

Ohio State University, Columbus, Ohio, (614) 292-1823; takes messages 6:30–9:30 P.M. EST, Monday, Wednesday and Friday

University of Pennsylvania, Philadelphia, Pennsylvania, (215) 898-4529

Tufts University, North Grafton, Massachusetts, (508) 839-7966, 6:00–9:00 P.M. EST, Monday through Friday

Virginia-Maryland Regional College of Veterinary Medicine, Blacksburg, Virginia, (540) 231-8038, 6:00–9:00 P.M. EST, Tuesday and Thursday

Washington State University, Pullman, Washington, (509) 335-4569

cumstances that are involved, so you cannot judge. If the pet's quality of life is no longer good, thank God we are able to let them go in peace by a simple injection."

The decision to euthanize can give rise to a multitude of mixed feelings: sadness at the loss of a friend, relief that a beloved Lab isn't suffering anymore. "I miss Thunder Road so much," says Dolores Gleason. "The vet and I helped him to the Bridge February 3, 1998. How I cried as I held him in my arms, but I knew it was his time. It was hard for him to get around, his hearing was almost gone and he had cataracts. I knew it was the best thing I could do for him even though I didn't feel it was the best thing for me. He gave us so much love and happiness, it was the least I could do for him to let him go peacefully to the Bridge."

What are some hints euthanasia might be the most humane choice? Lab owner Rosemary Dunn believes this: "If everything you do to your buddy is painful—IVs, blood tests, and so on—and there isn't any hope that he'll get better, it's time. If you're doing all this stuff to keep him alive for you, it's time. If he's in severe pain, it's time. But you can never second-guess another owner to know what's best for their partner, any more than I would want anyone to question my decision."

How about letting your Lab pass on naturally? Richard H. Pitcairn, D.V.M., author of *Natural Health for Dogs and Cats*, suggests that if the pet appears close to death and seems reasonably comfortable and peaceful, let the process unfold naturally. It is natural, after all. If the pet is restless and crying or has difficulty breathing or convulsions, euthanasia is probably best.

The Grief Factor

Whether you make a decision to euthanize your Lab, he dies naturally of old age, or he dies from illness at a young age, you'll feel sad. Your bond with your Lab friend is real, as real as it is with any member of your family. When that Lab dies, you'll experience real grief and a sense of loss. Normal responses to grief include crying, lack of appetite, insomnia, depression, loneliness, and tightness in the chest and throat.

Just as you experience different stages of grief when a beloved person dies, so might you experience the following stages of grief when your Lab passes on.

Denial. Denial is a very common first stage of grief. You might have the feeling that this isn't real, your Lab isn't really dead. You might feel like you're in shock, numb. Denial is a way that people deal with severe trauma until they can prepare emotionally and intellectually.

Bargaining. This stage can occur even before your Lab dies. You might bargain with God, promising to buy only the best food, products, and health care in exchange for your dog's life.

Anger. Anger might be the next emotion you feel. You may want to blame someone for your dog's death, for example, the veterinarian, who you're sure didn't do enough. You may blame yourself or even God. Anger is sometimes turned inward and manifests itself as guilt. Perhaps you didn't do enough, you might think; you didn't make the right decisions.

Acceptance. In time, you'll accept what has happened. You may still feel very sad and miss your Lab friend, but you'll accept that he's truly gone. Good memories of the Lab fill your mind rather than feelings of loss. You can bear the thought of your loss, and you may think about getting another Labrador someday.

How long each stage of grief lasts varies from one person to the next. There is no normal time period of grief or one correct way to grieve. It's very helpful to be able to share feelings of loss with someone who understands your sadness. Many pet grief counseling groups, hot lines, and web sites offer opportunities to connect with others who have suffered the death of a pet. Many of these groups and sites have trained counselors who can walk you through the process of grief.

Rainbow Bridge

Just this side of Heaven is a place called Rainbow Bridge. When an animal dies that has been especially close to someone here, that pet goes to Rainbow Bridge. There are meadows and hills for all our special friends so they can run and play together. There is plenty of food, water, and sunshine, and our friends are warm and comfortable. All the animals who had been ill or old are restored to health and vigor; those who were hurt or maimed are made whole and strong again, just as we remember them in our dreams of days gone by. The animals are happy and content, except for one small thing; they each miss someone very special to them who had to be left behind.

They all run and play together, but the day comes when one suddenly stops and looks into the distance. His bright eyes are intent; his eager body quivers. Suddenly he begins to run from the group, flying over the green grass, his legs carrying him faster and faster. You have been spotted, and when you and your special friend finally meet, you cling to each other in joyous reunion, never to be parted again. The happy kisses rain upon your face, your hands again caress the beloved head, and you look once more into the trusting eyes of your pet, so long gone from your life but never absent from your heart.

Then you cross Rainbow Bridge together.

—Author unknown

The Rainbow Bridge Web site includes this story, written by an unknown animal lover. The site includes tributes to and photos of deceased pets, a message board, and grief support. For owners who are sad after the loss of a pet, from dogs to guinea pigs, "the Bridge" is the place to go for understanding, sympathy, and help. If you've recently lost a beloved pet friend, be sure to check out this very popular web site, run by Kathie Maffit and a host of volunteers.

But don't forget a hankie!

If your Lab was a family dog, you may be faced with explaining illness, death, or euthanasia to children. What do you say to a child when Labbie dies? Explain the dog's death simply and sincerely, but how you say it and what you say really depend on the child's age. Young children understand and view the world differently than older children. When a child is under the age of five there's a fine line between reality and make-believe. At this age, children need literal, concrete explanations to understand, for example, "Our Lab has died. He won't be coming home anymore." Older children, ages five to 10, have a better grasp of the life cycle. They'll typically ask more questions. Answer them honestly, but spare them any gruesome details that might be more upsetting. Teenagers understand the concept of death and may be very frightened about it. Because they are more mature, they are the most vulnerable to feelings of grief.

Grief counselors advise against lying to a child about a pet's death. Telling a child that the Lab has gone to live on a farm doesn't really answer the child's questions about why the Lab is no longer at home, and it could cause the child to develop fears about being taken away to a farm. It's best to be honest and allow the child to feel sad, too.

The Afterlife

Do dogs go to heaven? That's a question many owners ask when a pet dies. Will they someday be reunited with their Lab in the afterlife?

Theologians and philosophers have explored that question for aeons with, of course, no definitive answer. How can there be? No one really knows. But depending on who you ask—a priest, rabbi, pastor, or monk—you'll hear a different perspective, even within religions.

The Jewish view, for example, is that everything, humans and animals, is endowed by the Creator with a spirit, and every spirit someday returns to the Creator and is rewarded in the afterlife if that spirit has led an exemplary life on earth.

Catholicism teaches that heaven was designed for people, but dogs may be part of the heavenly realm because of their connection to humans. People and dogs are different, however, because people have a soul made in the likeness of God, and animals don't.

Southern Baptists teach that dogs don't have souls. And Scripture doesn't say anything specific about animals in heaven, although a few references in the Old Testament suggest that animals might be there.

Buddhists believe in reincarnation, meaning death isn't the end of our existence. Humans and animals alike take another lifeform, which could be another human or dog. According to Buddhist thought, there is a heaven and we all go there, dogs too, if we're in the right condition. Our karma, or the force generated by our actions, determines where we end up.

So do dogs go to heaven? Only God knows.

Final Plans

Burial plans are an essential part of accepting the loss of your Lab. You've got several options, including burial or cremation at a pet cemetery, letting your vet take care of the burial, or burial at home.

For information on pet cemeteries and services in your area, contact the International Association of Pet Cemeteries at 13 Cemetery Lane, Ellenberg Depot, NY 12935; (518) 594-3000.

If you prefer not to deal with the burial, ask your veterinarian to dispose of the body. You might have to pay a fee, and burial practices vary among clinics, depending on local regulations.

If you have a large yard and city ordinances permit pet burial in residential areas, consider burying your Lab at home. Although it's painful to take care of this yourself, it's also a good way to come to terms with the loss.

A Fresh Start

Although right now you may not believe it, the empty spot in your heart and home after losing a beloved Lab can actually be very positive. True, you won't ever have your old friend back, but you can open your heart to another wonderful Lab who desperately needs a loving, responsible owner.

That may take time—don't rush out immediately to fill the void. Let the feelings of loss come and subside. Accept your Lab's death; face it head-on. Then consider getting another puppy or adult. When exactly should you get another Lab? When you're ready, and only you know the answer to that.

Appendix A: Resources

Boarding, Pet Sitting, Traveling

Books

Dog Lover's Companion series
Guides on traveling with dogs
    for several states and cities
Foghorn Press
P.O. Box 2036
Santa Rosa, CA 95405-0036
(800) FOGHORN

*Take Your Pet Too!: Fun
    Things to Do!*, Heather
    MacLean Walters
M.C.E. Publishing
P.O. Box 84
Chester, NJ 07930-0084

Take Your Pet USA, Arthur
    Frank
Artco Publishing
12 Channel St.
Boston, MA 02210

*Traveling with Your Pet 1999:
    The AAA Petbook*, Greg
    Weeks, Editor
Guide to pet-friendly lodging
    in the U.S. and Canada

Vacationing With Your Pet!,
    Eileen Barish
Pet-Friendly Publications
P.O. Box 8459
Scottsdale, AZ 85252
(800) 496-2665

Other resources

The American Boarding Ken-
    nels Association
4575 Galley Road, Suite 400-A
Colorado Springs, CO 80915
(719) 591-1113
www.abka.com

Camp Gone to the Dogs
RR #1 Box 958
Putney, VT 05346
(802) 387-5673

Camp Winnaribbun
P.O. Box 50300
Reno, NV 89513
(775) 348-8412

Dog Days of Wisconsin
Summer Camp
1879 Haymarket #24
Waukesha, WI 53186
(800) 226-7436

Independent Pet and Animal Trans-
portation Association
5521 Greenville Ave., Ste 104-310
Dallas, TX 75206
(903) 769-2267
www.ipata.com

National Association of Professional
Pet Sitters
1200 G St. N.W., Suite 760
Washington, DC 20005
(800) 296-PETS
www.petsitters.org

Pet Sitters International
418 East King Street
King, NC 27021-9163
(336)-983-9222
www.petsit.com

Breed Information, Clubs, Registries

American Kennel Club
5580 Centerview Drive
Raleigh, NC 27606-3390
(919) 233-9767
www.akc.org/

American Pointing Labrador
Association
P.O. Box 1167
Cambridge, MD 21613
(410) 221-8766
www.pointinglabs.com/apla/

Canadian Kennel Club
Commerce Park
89 Skyway Ave., Suite 100
Etobicoke, Ontario, Canada M9W 6R4
(416) 675-5511
www.ckc.ca

Canine Good Citizen Program
AKC, Attn.: CGC, 5580 Centerview Dr., Ste. 200
Raleigh, NC 27606
(919) 233-9767

Dog Scouts of America
5068 Nestel Road
St. Helen, MI 48656
(517) 389-2000
www.dogscouts.com
dogscouts@aol.com

Friends of Animals
P.O. Box 30054
Hartford, CT 06150-0054
(800) 321-PETS

Federation Cynologique International (International Kennel Club)
13, Place Albert I
B-6530 Thuin
Belgium
(011) 327-159-1238

Hunting Retrieving Club
P.O. Box 3179
Big Spring, TX 79721-3179
(915) 267-1659
www.hrc-ukc.com

International Pointing Labrador
   Association
N. 4758 350th St.
Elmwood, WI 54740
(715) 639-3900
www.pointing-lab.com

InfoPet
P.O. Box 716
Agoura Hills, CA 91376
(800) 858-0248

The Kennel Club
(British equivalent to the American
   Kennel Club)
1-5 Clarges Street
Piccadilly
London W1Y 8AB
ENGLAND
www.the-kennel-club.org.uk/

Labrador Retriever Club, Inc.
P.O. Box 454
Chesterland, OH 44026
secretary@the labradorclub.com

National Dog Registry
Box 116
Woodstock, NY 12498
(800) 637-3647
www.natldogregistry.com/

National Labrador Retriever Club
105 Coles Dr.
Doylestown, PA 18901
(618) 235-8046

North American Hunting Retriever
   Association
P.O. Box 1590
Stafford, VA 22555
(540) 286-0625
www.nahra.org/

States Kennel Club
P.O. Box 389
Hattiesburg, MS 39403-0389
(601) 583-8345

Tatoo-A-Pet
6571 S.W. 20th Court
Ft. Lauderdale, FL 33317
(800) 828-8667
www.tattoo-a-pet.com

United Kennel Club
100 East Kilgore Rd.
Kalamazoo, MI 49001-5598
(616) 343-9020
www.ukcdogs.com

Westminster Kennel Club
P.O. Box 6163
Watertown, NY 13601
(800) 455-DOGS

Dog Publications/Videos

AKC Gazette and AKC Events
   Calendar
51 Madison Avenue
New York, NY 10010
Subscriptions: (919) 233-9767
www.akc.org/gazet.htm
www.akc.org/event.htm

AKC Hunting Test Herald
American Kennel Club
5580 Centerview Dr., Ste. 200
Raleigh, NC 27606-3309
(919) 233-9767

*The American Kennel Club Complete
   Dog Book*
Howell Book House, 1992

ARK, quarterly newsletter of the
   American Rottweiler Club
Marilyn Piusz
339 County Highway 106
Johnston, NY 12095

The Book of the Labrador Retriever,
   Anna Katherine Nicholas
TFH Publications, Inc., Ltd., 1983

*The Complete Idiot's Guide to Fun
   and Tricks with Your Dog,* Sarah
   Hodgson
Alpha Books, 1997

Direct Book Service
(800) 776-2665
www.dogandcatbooks.com/direct-
book

*Dr. Pitcairn's Complete Guide to
   Natural Health for Dogs and Cats,*
   Richard H. Pitcairn, DVM, Ph.D.,
   and Susan Hubble Pitcairn
Rodale Press, Inc., 1995

Dog Fancy
P.O. Box 6050
Mission Viejo, CA 92690
(949) 855-8822
www.dogfancy.com

Dog Lover's Guide to the Labrador Retriever (video)
Pet Visions, Inc.
1010 Calle Negocio
San Clemente, CA 92673

Dog Owner's Home Veterinary Handbook
Delbert Carlson, DVM, and James Giffin, DVM
Howell Book House, 1992

Dog Treats, Kim Campbell Thornton
Main Street Books, 1996

Dog World
500 N. Dearborn, Suite 1100
Chicago, IL 60610
(312) 396-0600
www.dogworldmag.com/

Dog Writers of America
173 Union Rd.
Coatesville, PA 19320
www.dwaa.org

Dogs and Kids, Parenting Tips, Bardi McLennan
Howell Book House, 1993

Dogs on the Web
Audrey Pavia and Betsy Siino
MIS: Press, 1997

The Final Farewell: Preparing and Mourning the Loss of Your Pet
Marty Tousley and Katherine Heuerman
Pals Publishing, 1997

For the Love of Labrador Retrievers, Robert Hutchinson
Browntrout, 1998

How to Raise a Puppy You Can Live With
Clarice Rutherford and David H. Neil, MRCVS
Alpine Publications, 1982

HRC Magazine
Hunting Retrieving Club, Inc.
100 E. Kilgore Rd.
Kalamazoo, MI 49002-5592

Just Labs, Steve Smith
Willow Creek Press 1995

The Lab Connection
National Labrador Retriever Club
105 Coles Dr.
Doylestown, PA 18901
(618) 235-8046

The Labrador Quarterly
4401 Zephyr St.
Wheat Ridge, CO 80033-2499

The Labrador Retriever, Bernard
    Zeissow
TFH Publications, Inc., Ltd., 1995

Labrador Retrievers
Fancy Publications
P.O. Box 6050
Mission Viejo, CA 92690-6050
(949) 855-8822

*Labrador Tales: A Celebration of
    America's Favorite Dog*
John Arringon and Walt Zientek
Azul Editions/LAB MED, Inc., 1998

*Loving and Losing a Pet: A Psycholo-
    gist and a Veterinarian Share
    Their Wisdom*
Michael Stern and Susan Cropper
Jason Aronson, 1998

NAHRA News
NAHRA
P.O. Box 1590
Stafford, VA 22555
(540) 286-0625

National Organic Directory
Community Alliance With Family
    Farmers
(800) 852-3832

*Old Dogs, Old Friends: Enjoying
    Your Older Dog*
Bonnie Wilcox and Chris Walkowitz
IDG Books Worldwide, 1991

101 Uses for a Lab, Dale Spartas
Willow Creek Press, 1998

Pet Care on a Budget, Virginia
    Parker Guidry
Howell Book House, 1998

*Pet Loss: A Thoughtful Guide for
    Adults and Children*
Herbert Nieburg, Arlene Fisher, and
    Martin Scot Kosins
HarperPerennial Library, 1996

*Preparing for the Loss of Your Pet:
    Saying Goodbye with Love,
    Dignity, and Peace of Mind*
Myrna M. Milani, DVM
Prima Publishing, 1998

The Retriever Journal
Wildwood Press
P.O. Box 968
Traverse City, MI 49685
(800) 333-7646

*Retriever Puppy Training: The Right
    Start for Hunting*
Clarice Rutherford and Barbara
    Brandstad
Alpine Publications, 1988

Retriever Training Tests, James B.
    Spencer
Prentice-Hall Press, 2nd edition,
    1997

Retriever Working Certificate Training
Clarice Rutherford, Barbara Brandstad, and Sandra Whicker
Alpine Publications, 1986

SIRIUS Puppy Training (video)
Ian Dunbar, PhD, MRCVS
James & Kenneth Publishers
2140 Shattuck Ave., #2406
Berkeley, CA 94704

Surviving Your Dog's Adolescence,
Carol Lea Benjamin
Howell Book House, 1993

Total Retriever Training (video)
Whistle Lake Productions
2635 Thornbrier Ct.
Lake Orion, MI 48360
(800) 848-5963

Two Dog Press
P.O. Box 307
Deer Isle, ME 04627
(888) 310-2DOG
www.twodogpress.com

The Versatile Labrador Retriever,
Nancy Martin
Doral Publishing, 1994

Fun, Grooming, Obedience, Training

American Dog Trainers Network
161 W. 4th Street
New York, NY 10014
(212) 727-7257
www.inch.com/~dogs/index.html

American Grooming Shop
Association
(719) 570-7788

American Herding Breed
Association
1548 Victoria Way
Pacifica, CA 94044
www.globalcenter.net/~joell/abba/main.htm

American Kennel Club (tracking,
agility, obedience, herding)
Performance Events Dept.
5580 Centerview Drive
Raleigh, NC 27606
(919) 854-0199
www.akc.org/

American Pet Dog Trainers
P.O. Box 385
Davis, CA 95617
(800) PET-DOGS

Animal Behavior Society
Susan Foster
Department of Biology
Clark University
950 Main Street
Worcester, MA 01610-1477

Association of Pet Dog Trainers
P.O. Box 385
Davis, CA 95617
(800) PET-DOGS
www.apdt.com/

Chesapeake Gift Co.
P.O. Box 705
Chesapeake City, MD 21915
(800) 266-5314
www.chesapeakerags.com

The Dog Agility Page
www.dogpatch.org/agility/

Intergroom
76 Carol Drive
Dedham, MA 02026
www.intergroom.com

Labradorables!
22647 Ventura Blvd., Ste. 183
Woodland Hills, CA 91364
(877) LUV-LABS
labradorables@earthlink.net

National Association of Dog Obedience Instructors
PMB #369
729 Grapevine Highway
Hurst, TX 76054-2085
www.nadoi.org/

National Dog Groomers Association
of America
P.O. Box 101
Clark, PA 16113
(724) 962-2711

North American Dog Agility Council
HCR 2 Box 277
St. Maries, ID 83861
www.nadac.com

North American Flyball Association
1400 W. Devon Ave, #512
Chicago, IL 60660
(309) 688-9840
www.muskie.fishnet.com/~flyball/fly-
ball.html

United States Dog Agility Association, Inc.
P.O. Box 850955
Richardson, TX 75085-0955
(972) 231-9700
www.usdaa.com/

United States Canine Combined
 Training Association
2755 Old Thompson Mill Road
Buford, GA 30519
(770) 932-8604
www.siriusweb.com/USCCTA/

Grief Hotlines

Chicago Veterinary Medical
 Association
(630) 603-3994

Cornell University
(607) 253-3932

Iowa State College of Veterinary
 Medicine
www.vm.iastate.edu/support/

Michigan State University
College of Veterinary Medicine
(517) 432-2696

Pet Loss Grief Support
www.petloss.com/

Tufts University (Massachusetts)
School of Veterinary Medicine
(508) 839-7966

University of California, Davis
(530) 752-4200

University of Florida at Gainesville
College of Veterinary Medicine
(352) 392-4700

Virginia-Maryland Regional College
 of Veterinary Medicine
(540) 231-8038

Washington State University
College of Veterinary Medicine
(509) 335-5704

Humane Organizations and Rescue Groups

American Rescue Dog Association
P.O. Box 151
Chester, NY 10918
(914) 469-4173
www.ardainc.org

American Humane Association
63 Inverness Drive E
Englewood, CO 80112-5117
(800) 227-4645
www.americanhumane.org

American Society for the Prevention
 of Cruelty to Animals (ASPCA)
424 East 92nd Street
New York, NY 10128-6804
(212) 876-7700
www.aspca.org

Animal Protection Institute of
America
P.O. Box 22505
Sacramento, CA 95822
(916) 731-5521

Humane Society of the United States
2100 L St. NW
Washington, DC 20037
(301) 258-3072, (202) 452-1100
www.hsus.org/

Massachusetts Society for the Prevention of Cruelty to Animals
350 South Huntington Avenue
Boston, MA 02130
(617) 522-7400
www.mspca.org/

SPAY/USA
14 Vanderventer Avenue
Port Washington, NY 11050
(516) 944-5025, (203) 377-1116 in
Connecticut
(800) 248-SPAY
www.spayusa.org/

Medical and Emergency Information

American Animal Hospital
Association
P.O. Box 150899
Denver, CO 80215-0899
(800) 252-2242
www.healthypet.com

American Holistic Veterinary Medicine Association
2214 Old Emmorton Road
Bel Air, MD 21015
(410) 569-2346
www.altvetmed.com

American Kennel Club Canine
Health Foundation
251 West Garfield Road, Suite 160
Aurora, OH 44202
(888) 682-9696

American Veterinary Medical
Association
1931 North Meacham Road,
Suite 100
Schaumburg, IL 60173-4360
(847) 925-8070
www.avma.org/

Canine Eye Registration Foundation
(CERF)
Veterinary Medical Data Program
South Campus Courts, Building C
Purdue University
West Lafayette, IN 47907
(765) 494-8179
www.vet.purdue.edu/~yshen/cerf.html

Centers for Disease Control and
Prevention
1600 Clifton Road NE
Atlanta, GA 30333
(404) 639-3311 (CDC Operator)
(800) 311-3435 (CDC Public
Inquiries)
www.cdc.gov

Delta Society
289 Perimeter Rd., E
Renton, WA 98055-1329
(800) 869-6898
www.petsforum.com/deltasociety/de-
fault.html

Foundation for Pet Provided
Therapy
P.O. Box 6308
Oceanside, CA 92058
(760) 630-4824

Institutute for Genetic Disease/Wind
Morgan
P.O. Box 222
Davis, CA 97617
(530) 756-6773
www.vetmed.ucdavis.edu/gdc/gdc.htm
www.working-retriever.com/library/
windmorg.shtml

Medical Management International,
Inc.
(503) 256-7299

National Animal Poison Control
Center
1717 S. Philo, Suite 36
Urbana, IL 61802
(888) 426-4435, $45 per case, with as
many follow-up calls as necessary
included. Have name, address,
phone number, dog's breed, age,
sex, and type of poison ingested,
if known, available
www.napcc.aspca.org

Orthopedic Foundation for Animals
(OFA)
2300 E. Nifong Blvd.
Columbia, MO 65201-3856.
(573) 442-0418
www.offa.org/

PennHip
c/o Synbiotics
11011 Via Frontera
San Diego, CA 92127
(800) 228-4305

Pet Assure, Inc.
(888) 789-7387

Pet First Aid: Cats and Dogs, by
    Bobbi Mammato, DVM
Mosby Year Book

Veterinary Pet Insurance
(800) 872-7387

Senior Dog Project
www.srdogs.com

*Skin Diseases of Dogs and Cats: A
    Guide for Pet Owners and Profes-
    sionals,* Dr. Steven A. Melman
Dermapet, Inc.
P.O. Box 59713
Potomac, MD 20859

U.S. Pharmacopeia
vaccine reactions: (800) 487-7776
customer service: (800) 227-8772
www.usp.org

Veterinary Medical Database/Canine
    Eye Registration Foundation
Department of Veterinary Clinical
    Science
School of Veterinary Medicine
Purdue University
West Lafayette, IN 47907
(765) 494-8179
www.vet.purdue.edu/~yshen/

Veterinary Pet Insurance (VPI)
4175 E. La Palma Ave., #100
Anaheim, CA 92807-1846
(714) 996-2311
(800) USA PETS, (877) PET
    HEALTH in Texas
www.petplan.net/home.htm

Nutrition and Natural Foods

California Natural, Natural Pet
    Products
P.O. Box 271
Santa Clara, CA 95052
(800) 532-7261
www.naturapet.com

Home Prepared Dog and Cat Diets,
    Donald R. Strombeck
Iowa State University Press
(515) 292-0140

Infectious Diseases of the Dog and Cat, Craig E. Greene, Editor
W B Saunders Company

PHD Products Inc.
P.O. Box 8313
White Plains, NY 10602
(800) 863-3403
www.phdproducts.net/

Sensible Choice, Pet Products Plus
5600 Mexico Road
St. Peters, MO 63376
(800) 592-6687
www.sensiblechoice.com/

Search and Rescue Dogs

National Association for Search and Rescue
4500 Southgate Place, Suite 100
Chantilly, VA 20151-1714
(703) 622-6283
www.nasar.org/

National Disaster Search Dog Foundation
323 East Matilija Avenue, #110-245
Ojai, CA 93023-2740
www.west.net/~rescue/

Service and Working Dogs

Canine Companions for Independence
P.O. Box 446
Santa Rosa, CA 95402-0446
(800) 572-2275
www.caninecompanions.org/

Delta Society National Service Dog Center
289 Perimeter Road East
Renton, WA 98055-1329
(800) 869-6898
www.petsforum.com/deltasociety/dsb 000.htm

Guiding Eyes for the Blind
611 Granite Springs Road
Yorktown Heights, NY 10598
www.guiding-eyes.org/

Labrador Retriever Club, Inc., Rescue Program
1320 County Rd. 272
Leander, TX 78641
(512) 259-3645
applyland@texas.net

The National Education for Assistance Dog Services, Inc.
P.O. Box 213
West Boylston, MA 01583
(508) 422-9064
www.chamber.worcester.ma.us/neads /INDEX.HTM

North American Working Dog
   Association
Southeast Kreisgruppe
P.O. Box 833
Brunswick, GA 31521

The Seeing Eye
P.O. Box 375
Morristown, NJ 07963-0375
(973) 539-4425
www.seeingeye.org/

Therapy Dogs Incorporated
2416 E. Fox Farm Road
Cheyenne, WY 82007
(877) 843-7364
www.therapydogs.com

Therapy Dogs International
6 Hilltop Road
Mendham, NJ 07945
(973) 252-9800
www.tdi-dog.org/

United Schutzhund Clubs of America
3704 Lemay Ferry Road
St. Louis, MO 63125

Appendix B:
Official Standard for the Labrador Retriever ____

General Appearance

The Labrador Retriever is a strongly built, medium-sized, short-coupled dog possessing a sound, athletic, well-balanced conformation that enables it to function as a retrieving gun dog; the substance and soundness to hunt waterfowl or upland game for long hours under difficult conditions; the character and quality to win in the show ring; and the temperament to be a family companion. Physical features and mental characteristics should denote a dog bred to perform as an efficient Retriever of game with a stable temperament suitable for a variety of pursuits beyond the hunting environment.

The most distinguishing characteristics of the Labrador Retriever are its short, dense, weather resistant coat; an "otter" tail; a clean-cut head with broad back skull and moderate stop; powerful jaws; and its "kind," friendly eyes, expressing character, intelligence and good temperament.

Above all, a Labrador Retriever must be well-balanced, enabling it to move in the show ring or work in the field with little or no effort. The typical Labrador possesses style and quality without over refinement, and substance without lumber or cloddiness. The Labrador is bred primarily as a working gun dog; structure and soundness are of great importance.

Size, Proportion and Substance

Size—The height at the withers for a dog is 22½ to 24½ inches; for a bitch it is 21½ to 23½ inches. Any variance greater than ½ inch above or below these heights is a disqualification. Approximate weight of dogs and bitches in working condition: dogs 65 to 80 pounds; bitches 55 to 70 pounds.

The minimum height ranges set forth in the paragraph above shall not apply to dogs or bitches under twelve months of age.

Proportion—Short-coupled; length from the point of the shoulder to the point of the rump is equal to or slightly longer than the distance from the withers to the ground. Distance from the elbow to the ground should be equal to one half of the height at the withers. The brisket should extend to the elbows, but not perceptibly deeper. The body must be of sufficient length to permit a straight, free and efficient stride; but the dog should never appear low and long or tall and leggy in outline. **Substance**—Substance and bone proportionate to the overall dog. Light, "weedy" individuals are definitely incorrect; equally objectionable are cloddy lumbering specimens. Labrador Retrievers shall be shown in working condition well-muscled and without excess fat.

Head

Skull—The skull should be wide; well-developed but without exaggeration. The skull and foreface should be on parallel planes and of approximately equal length. There should be a moderate stop—the brow slightly pronounced so that the skull is not absolutely in a straight line with the nose. The brow ridges aid in defining the stop. The head should be clean-cut and free from fleshy cheeks; the bony structure of the skull chiseled beneath the eye with no prominence in the cheek. The skull may show some median line; the occipital bone is not conspicuous in mature dogs. Lips should not be squared off or pendulous, but fall away in a curve toward the throat. A wedge-shape head, or a head long and narrow in muzzle and back skull is incorrect as are massive, cheeky heads. The jaws are powerful and free from snippiness—the muzzle neither long and narrow nor short and stubby. **Nose**—The nose should be wide and the nostrils well-developed. The nose should be black on black or yellow dogs, and brown on chocolates. Nose color fading to a lighter shade is not a fault. A thoroughly pink nose or one lacking in any pigment is a disqualification. **Teeth**—The teeth should be strong and regular with a scissors bite; the lower teeth just behind, but touching the inner side of the upper incisors. A level bite is acceptable, but not desirable. Undershot, overshot, or misaligned teeth are serious faults. Full dentition is preferred. Missing molars or pre-molars are serious faults. **Ears**—The ears should hang moderately close to the head, set rather far back, and somewhat low on the skull; slightly above eye level. Ears should not be large and heavy, but in proportion with the skull and reach to the inside of the eye when pulled forward. **Eyes**—Kind, friendly eyes imparting good temperament, intelligence and alertness are a hallmark of the breed. They should be of medium size, set well apart, and neither protruding nor deep set. Eye color should be brown in black and yellow Labradors, and brown or hazel in chocolates. Black, or yellow eyes give a harsh expression and are undesirable. Small eyes, set close together or round prominent eyes are not typical of the breed. Eye rims are black in black and yellow Labradors, and brown in chocolates. Eye rims without pigmentation is a disqualification.

Neck, Topline and Body

Neck—The neck should be of proper length to allow the dog to retrieve game easily. It should be muscular and free from throatiness. The neck should rise strongly from the shoulders with a moderate arch. A short, thick neck or a "ewe" neck is incorrect. **Topline**—The back is strong and the topline is level from the withers to the croup when standing or moving. However, the loin should show evidence of flexibility for athletic endeavor. **Body**—The Labrador should be short-coupled, with good spring of ribs tapering to a moderately wide chest. The Labrador should not be narrow chested, giving the appearance of hollowness between the front legs, nor should it have a wide spreading, bulldog-like front. Correct chest conformation will result in tapering between the front legs that allows unrestricted forelimb movement. Chest breadth that is either too wide or too narrow for efficient movement and stamina is incorrect. Slab-sided individuals are not typical of the breed; equally objectionable are rotund or barrel chested specimens. The underline is almost straight, with little or no tuck-up in mature animals. Loins should be short, wide and strong, extending to well-developed, powerful hindquarters. When viewed from the side, the Labrador Retriever shows a well-developed, but not exaggerated forechest. **Tail**—The tail is a distinguishing feature of the breed. It should be very thick at the base, gradually tapering toward the tip, of medium length, and extending no longer than to the hock. The tail should be free from feathering and clothed thickly all around with the Labrador's short, dense coat, thus having that peculiar rounded appearance that has been described as the "otter" tail. The tail should follow the topline in repose or when in motion. It may be carried gaily, but should not curl over the back. Extremely short tails or long thin tails are serious faults. The tail completes the balance of the Labrador by giving it a flowing line from the top of the head to the tip of the tail. Docking or otherwise altering the length or natural carriage of the tail is a disqualification.

Forequarters

Forequarters should be muscular, well-coordinated and balanced with the hindquarters. **Shoulders**—The shoulders are well laid-back, long and sloping, forming an angle with the upper arm of approximately 90 degrees that permits the dog to move his forelegs in an easy manner with strong forward reach. Ideally, the length of the shoulder blade should equal the length of the upper arm. Straight shoulder blades, short upper arms or heavily muscled or loaded shoulders, all restricting free movement, are incorrect. **Front Legs**—When viewed from the front, the legs should be straight with good strong bone. Too much bone is as undesirable as too little bone, and short legged, heavy boned individuals are not typical of the breed. Viewed from the side, the elbows should be directly under the withers, and the front legs should be perpendicular to the ground and well under the body. The elbows should be close to the ribs without looseness. Tied-in elbows or being "out at the elbows" interfere with free movement and are serious faults. Pasterns should be strong and short and should slope slightly from the perpendicular line of the leg. Feet are strong and compact, with well-arched toes and well-developed pads. Dew claws may be removed. Splayed feet, hare feet, knuckling over, or feet turning in or out are serious faults.

Hindquarters

The Labrador's hindquarters are broad, muscular and well-developed from the hip to the hock with well-turned stifles and strong short hocks. Viewed from the rear, the hind legs are straight and parallel. Viewed from the side, the angulation of the rear legs is in balance with the front. The hind legs are strongly boned, muscled with moderate angulation at the stifle, and powerful, clearly defined thighs. The stifle is strong and there is no slippage of the patellae while in motion or when standing. The hock joints are strong, well let down and do not slip or hyperextend while in motion or when standing. Angulation of both stifle and hock joint is such as to achieve the optimal balance of drive and traction. When standing the rear toes are only slightly behind the point of the rump. Overangulation produces a sloping topline not typical of the breed. Feet are strong and compact, with well-arched toes and well-developed pads. Cow-hocks, spread hocks, sickle hocks and overangulation are serious structural defects and are to be faulted.

Coat

The coat is a distinctive feature of the Labrador Retriever. It should be short, straight and very dense, giving a fairly hard feeling to the hand. The Labrador should have a soft, weather-resistant undercoat that provides protection from water, cold and all types of ground cover. A slight wave down the back is permissible. Woolly coats, soft silky coats, and sparse slick coats are not typical of the breed, and should be severely penalized.

Color

The Labrador Retriever coat colors are black, yellow and chocolate. Any other color or a combination of colors is a disqualification. A small white spot on the chest is permissible, but not desirable. White hairs from aging or scarring are not to be misinterpreted as brindling. **Black**—Blacks are all black. A black with brindle markings or a black with tan markings is a disqualification. **Yellow**—Yellows may range in color from fox-red to light cream, with variations in shading on the ears, back, and underparts of the dog. **Chocolate**—Chocolates can vary in shade from light to dark chocolate. Chocolate with brindle or tan markings is a disqualification.

Movement

Movement of the Labrador Retriever should be free and effortless. When watching a dog move toward oneself, there should be no sign of elbows out. Rather, the elbows should be held neatly to the body with the legs not too close together. Moving straight forward without pacing or weaving, the legs should form straight lines, with all parts moving in the same plane. Upon viewing the dog from the rear, one should have the impression that the hind legs move as nearly as possible in a parallel line with the front legs. The hocks should do their full share of the work, flexing well, giving the appearance of power and strength. When viewed from the side, the shoulders should move freely and effortlessly, and the foreleg should reach forward close to the ground with extension. A short, choppy movement or high knee action indicates a straight shoulder; paddling indicates long, weak pasterns; and a short, stilted rear gait indicates a straight rear assembly; all are serious faults. Movement faults interfering with performance including weaving; side-winding; crossing over; high knee action; paddling; and short, choppy movement, should be severely penalized.

Temperament

True Labrador Retriever temperament is as much a hallmark of the breed as the "otter" tail. The ideal disposition is one of a kindly, outgoing, tractable nature; eager to please and non-aggressive towards man or animal. The Labrador has much that appeals to people; his gentle ways, intelligence and adaptability make him an ideal dog. Aggressiveness towards humans or other animals, or any evidence of shyness in an adult, should be severely penalized.

DISQUALIFICATIONS

Any deviation from the height prescribed in the Standard.

A thoroughly pink nose or one lacking in any pigment.

Eye rims without pigment.

Docking or otherwise altering the length or natural carriage of the tail.

Any other color or a combination of colors other than black, yellow or chocolate as described in the Standard.

Approved February 12, 1994
Effective March 31, 1994
Copyright 1994, Labrador Retriever Club, Inc.

Index

Meet Your Lab Care Experts

Author   Virginia Parker Guidry is a long-time animal enthusiast, writer, and editor. Guidry graduated from Berea College in Berea, Kentucky, with a B.A. in English. Her editorial experience includes several staff positions on newspapers and magazines, including *Pet Health News* and *Horse Illustrated.* She is a contributing editor for *Dog Fancy* magazine. Guidry is a former professional small animal groomer and horse groom, and has worked as a veterinary assistant. Guidry is a member of Dog Writers Association of America, and writes regularly for many pet-related publications. Guidry lives in Southern California with her husband and son.

Trainer   Liz Palika has been teaching classes for dogs and their owners for over twenty years. Her goal is to help people understand why their dogs do what they do so that dogs and owners can live together successfully. Liz says, "If, in each training class, I can increase understanding and ease frustration so that the dog doesn't end up in the local shelter because the owner has given up, then I have accomplished my goal!" She is the author of 23 books and has won awards from both the Dog Writers Association of America and the ASPCA. Liz and her husband, Paul, share their home with three Australian Shepherds: Dax, Kes, and Riker.

Series Editor   Joanne Howl, D.V.M., is a graduate of the University of Tennessee College of Veterinary Medicine and has practiced animal medicine for over 10 years. She currently serves as president of the Maryland Veterinary Medical Association and secretary/treasurer of the American Academy on Veterinary Disaster Medicine, and her columns and articles have appeared in a variety of animal-related publications. Dr. Howl presently divides her time between family, small animal medicine, writing, and the company of her two dogs and six cats.